Report on the State of the European Union

G000091444

Also by Jean-Paul Fitoussi

ECONOMICS IN A CHANGING WORLD

Also by Fiorella Kostoris Padoa Schioppa

THE PRINCIPLE OF MUTUAL RECOGNITION IN THE EUROPEAN INTEGRATION
PROCESS (*editor*)

Report on the State of the European Union

Volume 1

Edited by

Jean-Paul Fitoussi

and

Fiorella Kostoris Padoa Schioppa

with contributions from

OFCE team:
Jérôme Creel
Éloi Laurent
Jacques Le Cacheux

ISAE team:
Efisio Espa
Luisa Sciandra
Marco Ventura
Roberto Basile
Sergio De Nardis
Cristina Brandimarte
Enrico D'Elia
Silvia Valli
Carlo Declich
Stefania Gabriele
Paola Tanda

First published 2005 by
PALGRAVE MACMILLAN
Houndmills, Basingstoke, Hampshire RG21 6XS and
175 Fifth Avenue, New York, N.Y. 10010
Companies and representatives throughout the world

PALGRAVE MACMILLAN is the global academic imprint of the Palgrave Macmillan division of St. Martin's Press, LLC and of Palgrave Macmillan Ltd. Macmillan® is a registered trademark in the United States, United Kingdom and other countries. Palgrave is a registered trademark in the European Union and other countries.

ISBN-13: 978–1–4039–1711–9 hardback
ISBN-10: 1–4039–1711–6 hardback
ISBN-13: 978–1–4039–1712–6 paperback
ISBN-10: 1–4039–1712–4 paperback

This book is printed on paper suitable for recycling and made from fully managed and sustained forest sources.

A catalogue record for this book is available from the British Library.

Library of Congress Cataloging-in-Publication Data
Fitoussi, Jean-Paul, 1942–
    Report on the state of the European Union / Jean-Paul Fitoussi and
    Fiorella Kostoris Padoa Schioppa.
        p.   cm.
    Includes bibliographical references and index.
    ISBN 1–4039–1711–6 (v. 1 : hardback) — ISBN 1–4039–1712–4 (v. 1 : pbk.)
    1. European Union.   I. Padoa-Schioppa, Fiorella, 1945–   II. Title.
JN30.F58 2005
940.56—dc22   2004057663

10   9   8   7   6   5   4   3   2   1
14   13   12   11   10   09   08   07   06   05

Printed and bound in Great Britain by
Antony Rowe Ltd, Chippenham and Eastbourne

Contents

List of Tables

List of Figures

List of Boxes

Preface: Is Europe Debatable?

Time has come for a permanent debate to take place on the political, economic and social state of the European Union (EU). 'Why now?' is the first question in the debate, and the easiest to answer: Europe is choosing its destiny before its inhabitants' eyes. Whether this choice is deliberate and deliberated enough is the complex issue we attempt to address throughout this volume.

Most certainly, the project of Constitutional Treaty – elaborated in the 2002–3 European Convention, unanimously acclaimed when presented in June 2003 and at the time of writing submitted for ratification – has included some improvements along the path to integration. But, to the puzzlement of many, it does not propose significant changes to the principles that reign over the economic and social governance of the EU (and the euro area); in fact, quite the contrary. Is nothing perfectible in the EU? Is accidental integration the only way forward for Europe?

To go further, we first have to detach ourselves from the sterile opposition between the 'unconditionally for' and the 'unconditionally against' Europe that, too often, has characterized our public space. Naïves and sceptics equally are partisans of immobility; we like to think of ourselves as methodical doubters. However, as we can both tell from long practice, there seem to be two obstacles standing in the way of a public, genuine and accurate European debate.

First, there is a long-enduring illusion in some countries – and a newly forged one in others – that European matters are foreign affairs. Even when the latter are perceived as being very important, their degree of interference with national concerns is supposed to be so low that it does not appear necessary for governments (and the media) to keep populations constantly informed of their advancement. Absolute illusion it is: our countries are de jure and de facto co-managed by national governments and European institutions; that is, truly federal European bodies (such as the European Commission, the European Central Bank (ECB), the European Courts of Justice, and so on) and other member states acting collectively through intergovernmental procedures (in the Council of the EU, the European Councils and so on).

This fact of life for the co-dependent countries of the EU finds its justification in the very nature of the process of integration that we have chosen: the will to live together and the ambition to build a common future. In this regard, it is necessary that national decisions, as long as they can harm and benefit partners, be submitted to the scrutiny of the European community.

Moreover, this devolution of powers was decided by governments and nations themselves when, equipped with their absolute sovereignty, they negotiated, signed and ratified the treaties that now form the European common law. In other words, European institutions normally act in conformity with the mandate they were given by their constituent member states. Things become abnormal when this co-management results in opacity, hypocrisy or arrogance. Opacity: when citizens simply do not know what European union means, and so little is done to improve their understanding. Hypocrisy: when governments blame Europe today for constraints they freely chose yesterday. Arrogance: when European institutions publicly chastise democratic governments while themselves lacking legitimacy.

The second obstacle is of more subtle nature. It derives from the 'criticism impossibility theorem' regarding European institutions and policies. It goes roughly like this: if a person criticizes the European government or its actions, he or she would be considered an irremediably virulent opponent of the very idea of Europe and thus be labelled 'un-European'. Not only that, but he or she would be accused of endangering Europe by this criticism.

Such an argument can be drawn from two alternative sets of propositions. The first comprises the belief that European rules are the best imaginable, and that they constitute a necessary bound to democracy's erratic outcomes. Defiance against democracy is a constant feature of the vast literature aimed at justifying the 'reason' behind European rules. But given their alleged inherent moral weakness, does it seem impossible that national governments negotiate flawed rules or wrongly enact them? After all, there is no such thing as a good universal rule. Moreover, whatever the intelligence that designed them, it is always possible that a good contingent rule can be over-determined by the specific context in which it was forged. The whole European institutional architecture might well itself one day become irrelevant, not only because of new enlargements, but because of the geopolitical, economic and social dynamic that the birth of the single currency has triggered.

The second set of arguments is even more paralyzing: 'You could be right (and an acceptable European), but the European integration is weak and your criticism is giving free material to the anti-European crowd. For the sake of avoiding a small intellectual inconvenience, you are jeopardizing what took so many years to achieve.' According to this view, the single currency itself would be in danger if rules, that the very persons in charge of preserving criticized as 'stupid', were not safeguarded from public debate. Alas, this line of reasoning frequently reaches its goal, while governments accept the perils of bad compromises for the future in the name of the illusory conservation of the past. Despite appearances, Europe is a continent where one hardly dares to say 'no'.

The time has thus come to open a lucid debate on the ways and means of making Europe better, and deliver democracy and sustainable growth; that is, progress for its population. The resilience of the opposition to this suggestion is becoming a concern. According to Popper (1963) a scientific theory cannot be accepted unless submitted to falsification. An analogous principle rules the political debate: an institutional regime is only democratic when it is subject to reasoned criticism.

It is, then, to be expected that 'Democracy and legitimacy' are the first European issues to be addressed by us (Part I), followed by 'Convergence and cohesion' (Part II), 'Macroeconomic policies' (Part III) and, finally, 'Social integration' (Part IV). The contributions assembled here are the highlights of the *Rapport sur l'état de l'Union européenne*, published by the Observatoire Français des Conjonctures Économiques (OFCE, Paris) since 1999, and of the 2001 and 2002 editions of the *Report on the State of the European Union* published by the Istituto di studi e analisi economica (ISAE, Rome).

On each of the topics in this volume, OFCE and ISAE are, at the same time, joining comparative advantages in European studies and confronting conflicting views on European policies, so that each reader can better choose – and possibly invent – the Europe s/he wants and believes in as a citizen.

Our shared belief is simple but demanding: if Europe is to be trusted, then Europe is to be doubted.

JEAN-PAUL FITOUSSI
FIORELLA KOSTORIS PADOA SCHIOPPA

Part I
Democracy and Legitimacy

1
Democratic Legitimacy and Political Representation in the EU Institutions

The integration of the European Union (EU) has been an ever-changing process of institutional reform. The summit agendas of the heads of state and governments are characterized by discussions and debates between member states on treaties, conventions, intergovernmental conferences and, more specifically, on Union rules, on changes in the modus operandi of the supranational bodies of Brussels and Strasbourg and on enlargements to include new members. Moreover, the planning of institutional change has to be carried out alongside the EU's increasing day-to-day activity.

The proceedings of the European Convention – begun on 1 March 2002 – have offered the chance to reconsider the Union's mission, its structure, its rules and its relationship with the member states. Many questions of great importance for the future of the EU were set aside or removed because of the resistance, crossed vetoes and fears of some member states. But any attempt to postpone solutions to problems such as the qualified majority vote, the need for a common European foreign policy, relations between the European Parliament and other European institutions, and the reviewing of the principle of subsidiarity has been overcome by EU enlargement towards Central and Eastern European countries (CEECs), and not only towards them. The enlargement of the boundaries and of the composition of the European Union brings about – and indeed worsens – a whole series of problems that now need solutions.

As is well known, the Declaration on the Future of the Union – annexed to the Treaty of Nice of February 2001 – contained an invitation to a 'more thorough and ample debate on the future development of the European Union'. After a large discussion in the main institutional bodies of the member states in December 2001, under the Belgian presidency, the

3

Laeken European Council approved a second Declaration on the Future of the European Union, where the EU decided to hold a Convention on the Future of Europe. That Convention – which paved the way to a new Intergovernmental Conference (IC) and the subsequent approval of a project of a treaty establishing a constitution for Europe – contributed, to an in-depth reflection (open to the contribution of the civil society) on four main subjects: namely, the competence division between the European Union and member states; the simplification of the Union's policy tools; the problems of democracy, transparency and effectiveness in the EU; and the simplification and possible reorganization of the existing Treaties (taking into account the Charter of Fundamental Rights approved in Nice).

In synthesis – apart from whether a European Union constitution will be finally adopted – the Convention, led by Valéry Giscard d'Estaing, Giuliano Amato and Jean Luc Dehaene – being called to define competences, decision-making arrangements, and the Parliament's powers in relation to national parliaments – has had the task of fully rewriting the contract defining the relationship between European citizens and the Union in such a way that even the citizens of Warsaw, Prague and Budapest will see themselves mirrored in the Union.

The redefinition of the structure of the European Union will inevitably have an impact on a subject which, in recent years, has been drawing the attention of both member states' representatives and European policy-makers – as well as of Community institutions themselves – and has been given great coverage in the policy-related literature: namely, democratic legitimacy and citizens' political representation in Community institutions. The matter has often been referred to as a 'democratic deficit', to highlight the gap of legitimacy and representation existing between EU functioning and the citizens' opinions and rights.

The analysis of these questions is the main subject of this chapter. A definition of the concepts of democratic legitimacy and political representation within the context of the EU is followed by an analysis of the two main 'circuits' linking European citizens to Community institutions in an attempt to verify the real degree of legitimacy of those institutions. Next, on the basis of a series of elaborations of data drawn by the EU Commission surveys, the chapter also describes European citizens' approaches to the integration process as a whole, and to the actions of the Community institutions in particular. The examination of the complex problems of competence division between the European Union and the member states underpins the concluding remarks on possible reforms of the Union's decision-making mechanisms.

Democratic legitimacy and citizens' political representation

Within the European Union, democratic legitimacy and political representation are defined on the basis of a number of criteria present in the recent literature (Thomassen and Schmitt, 1999). In particular, the Community institutions' legitimacy refers to the relationship between European citizens (the demos) on the one hand, and the tasks of supranational bodies and their decision-making and institutional schemes on the other. Thus legitimacy means the existence and visibility of a permanent mandate given by European citizens to the institutions entrusted with those particular tasks.

The concept of political representation within the European Union is perhaps less complex, as it is closely linked to the fundaments of any representative democracy. It embraces that 'political process by which the making of government policy is related to the wants, needs and demands of the public' (Thomassen and Schmitt, 1999, p. 4). It is all too clear that the ideas of legitimacy and representation are strictly connected. Indeed, it is difficult to think that the Community institutions could be considered politically representative if there were no mechanisms guaranteeing their legitimacy. And legitimacy risks remaining in limbo if the actions of members of the European Parliament and of the heads of state and government do not meet the needs of the European citizens.

These considerations immediately point out the complexity of the problems at stake, which are deeply rooted in the history of Western policy. The first problem concerns the European demos: does it in fact exist? Is there anything today that might be defined as the 'people' of Europe? Or is it only the sum of different national identities, each free to define his/her own legitimacy relationship with Brussels or Strasbourg? Or, will such people only exist – as indeed will supranational Community institutions – if the European elites – beginning with those responsible for the European Convention – are able to offer a 'European citizenship' implying rights and duties for all EU citizens?

But even setting aside that important question, or assuming that the European demos does exist – as a contemporary economist would do – what are the confidence- and transparency-based relationships between a European citizen living in London or in Athens and the de facto competences of the European Union? And between these citizens and the legislative role of the Union and, in particular, of the Commission? This problem is at the heart of the 'democratic deficit' and is the core of the draft reform that the Convention is called upon to prepare.

As mentioned before, the existence of a problem of legitimacy for EU institutions and of a problem of quality for the relationships between European citizens and the Community institutions has been known for a long time. For example, in 1996, the Club di Firenze wrote that, in the light of the then-insufficient powers of the European Parliament, 'integration implies a general expropriation of the legislative power, while the Community legislation, brought about by the co-operation between national administrations and the European one, seems deprived of the legitimacy which usually characterises the people's representatives' (Club di Firenze, 1996, pp. 66–7).

In spite of the changes introduced in the Strasbourg Assembly's competence, it is worth noticing that these severe remarks about the Community's democratic deficit have not been amended over the years, and indeed events such as the French and Dutch elections of Spring 2002 again raised the question of the need for a better harmonization between European public opinion and EU policies.[1]

The European Commission itself does not deny the problem. In its Communication to the Convention (European Commission, 2002a, pp. 20–5 in particular), apart from a 'lack of clarity' (connected to the complexity of the procedures and the number of instruments) and to a 'lack of effectiveness' (linked to the time-consuming decision-making arrangements), the Commission also reports a 'lack of responsibility' (whenever 'the decision-making process is obscured by complexity) *when those whom the citizens can sanction are not always those who take the decisions or are reluctant to shoulder their share of responsibility before the people who voted them in, democracy is ill-served'* [the italics are the author's] and a 'lack of proximity' (because the principle of subsidiarity is not always respected).

A possible intervention on the mechanisms regulating the relationship between citizens and the European Union is increasingly being urged, along with a transfer of competence from national states to supranational bodies. Admittedly, it is a shift of power that, particularly in the early phases of the Community project, takes place with the explicit consensus of the member states and in a context where the criterion of the unanimity vote within the Council guarantees the full involvement of all countries. Indeed, as time goes by, the heads of state and government, fully legitimated by their electors – and rightly so – take decisions that gradually shift the policy-making centre from their countrys' capitals to Brussels, Strasbourg and Frankfurt.

The European Union stemming from this gradual – though very disordered and rich with *ad hoc* solutions – shifting of power from national governments to the Community-level government is a strange, unprecedented and unparalleled 'creature'. It is a sort of federal organization, the first step – according to some European leaders – towards a 'federation of states' or even an out and out, though not well specified, 'political union' (European Commission, 2002a). However, it should consist of a federal system characterized by a summit (corresponding to the 'central' administrations of federal states) with a very strong legislative responsibility on a growing number of subjects: legislative functions that have taken up the importance of binding 'primary laws' – sometimes also on merely regulatory details – for member states. And, indeed, it is a very limited summit in terms of both human resources (about 20,000 permanent staff) and in terms of financial allocations (the EU budget accounts for even less than the official 1.27 per cent of the Community overall GDP, which is a small percentage compared to the average 40 per cent usually allocated to central administrations in federal systems).

It is still a federation in embryo, where the enormous transfer of legislative responsibilities and government occurring over a forty-year period has upset the balance of power between the European Union and the member states. Following the principle of subsidiarity, the whole system of administrative and managing functions remains in the hands of national administrations, which is an anomaly if one thinks that, in federal states, the 'core' of the system has the main management and operational responsibilities.

In synthesis, EU decisions concern European citizens as a whole over a growing number of subjects and thus a direct link between EU choices and the people of Europe is emerging. Therefore, as is usual when refering to single member states, the relationships between citizens of the EU and European common institutions need to be considered. The most telling example in this respect is provided by taxation policies. If the connection between *taxation* and *representation* is interpreted in such a way that fiscal matters may only be left to a particular government level if there is an adequate representation of tax-payers, then the *upward devolution* of fiscal policies may only be attained if European tax-payers gain more room for controlling the specific choices on taxation matters taken by European institutions.

The relationship between citizens and European institutions

In the institutional framework of the European Union, there are two kinds of 'circuit' connecting citizens to EU policies. The first creates a link between citizens of a specific member state, their own head of government or state, and the European Council (formed by the institutional leaders of the member states). In the dynamics of the so-called 'intergovernmental method', the legitimacy of the decisions taken by the European Union through the Council is directly proportional to the prime minister's degree of representation of his/her citizens. As the Council has been acting for decades as an 'upper chamber of member states' or, if you like, as a sort of 'chamber of the regions' – based on the unanimity vote – it is difficult to state that EU policy choices have no 'democratic coverage'.

However, it is sometimes maintained that European prime ministers and heads of state – who are legitimated by a popular vote – are often not legitimated to tackle questions concerning Union policies, because in national elections European subjects are often given little coverage and thus the electorate does not give its representatives a mandate to deal with those matters. This consideration is partly weak and partly bizarre. It is weak because while it might have been justified when the EU had little power – and that limited mainly to certain specific areas (agricultural policy, customs and so on) – but at the time of writing, with the gradual increase in the European Union's power and competence, stating that European matters are not represented in national electoral campaigns and in European citizens' choices sounds strange. And it is bizarre, because, if the idea that European questions are less important holds true, this would apply inevitably to all international questions, hence the heads of state and government would be legitimated to take up no stand whatever at international level; but fortunately this is not the case.

Quite the reverse in fact: a much more delicate question related to the citizens–prime ministers–European Council connection concerns the greater use of a qualified majority in EU decisions as well as the proposal whereby the qualified majority formula[2] in the EU-30 will (perhaps inevitably) be adopted more frequently. Undoubtedly, the possibility that a country opposing a specific Union decision might be compelled to accept and introduce it poses important problems of legitimacy and 'quality' of representation. In this case, the paradox is that the problem of a loss of confidence in the relationship between citizens and Community institutions emerges in that form because the Union is no real federal state (and is not likely to become one in the immediate future) and remains an ill-defined group of national states. Only if a formally-recognized federal formula is adopted, the problem of being a minority in a given area of the Union would have the same importance that the opposing votes of, say, one of the two Wisconsin representatives in the Senate of the USA have today.

Thus, the problem exists and it is quite relevant: a solution is only possible with a new balance of power within the European Union, which we shall discuss later.

The second circuit recalls the one that usually exists in parliamentary democracies: namely, the close relationship between citizens and their directly elected representatives in the European Parliament. Hence, the degree of legitimacy of the EU institutions depends largely on the real power that Members of Parliament have in terms of legislative power and of control over other European institutions, and over the European Commission in particular.

In this case, the criticism to the legitimacy of EU policies stems from the awareness that the European Parliament's powers are different from those of national Parliaments. Indeed, the legislative power of the European Parliament – controlled by the Council and the Commission with its 'exclusive right of initiative' – and its relationship with the national governments are limited by a framework within which the Commission's role as intergovernmental mediator and its independence leave little room for the European Parliament.

However, this approach seems to have been overcome, at least partially, by the joint action of a series of decisions taken by the Union in-recent years. First, the European Parliament's legislative power was enlarged by the co-decision power introduced by the Treaty of Maastricht and enhanced by the Treaty of Amsterdam. In spite of its complicated enforcement procedures, the 'co-decision procedure' enables the Parliament to oppose a given rule. Also, by setting up a joint Committee with the Council, it is directly involved in the legislative procedure of the European Union rules and regulations. Admittedly, after the approval of the Treaty of Amsterdam, the matters involved in the co-decision procedure are numerous and important, ranging from consumer protection to the internal market, and from the environment to social policy. Second, the influence that the Strasbourg Parliament can exert on the setting-up procedure and on the actions of the European Commission has definitely grown. At present, on the basis of amendments introduced by the Treaty of Maastricht and by the Treaty of Amsterdam, the European Parliament is called on to approve the election of the Commission's president and members. And these are not mere formalities, if it is true – as indeed it is – that it was the Parliament that compelled the Santer Commission to resign in March 1999, after an *ad hoc* Parliamentary Committee had been set up to verify possible irregularities in the Commission's work.

The 'democratic nature' of the relationship between European citizens and European Parliament has thus improved considerably and, in our opinion, the present situation by no means mirrors the words (which we endorsed at the time) of the Club di Firenze (1996, p. 65) that 'in the public opinion, the Union is a technocratic closed system not responding to citizens' needs'.

Is it possible to further improve this situation so as to strengthen the democratic legitimacy of European institutions and, in particular, of the European Parliament? Some steps may be taken, as we shall see in what follows, but we should remember that it is not easy to have supranational EU policies alongside a better safeguard of national interests and more democratic control.[3]

However, before turning to institutional policy indications, it is worth looking at the problem of the 'quality' of the citizens' political representation in greater depth. And, indeed, the analysis should be enriched by a more thorough analysis of European citizens' opinions.

Citizens and Europe

European citizens and EU membership

The surveys carried out regularly by the EU through the 'Eurobarometer'[4] (European Commission, various years) enables us to observe closely the attitudes of European citizens, sub-divided by member state, towards the EU.

The synthesized indicators, such as those presented in this chapter (see Figure 1.1 and Table 1.1) show the degree of support for EU membership. Generally speaking, they show that public opinion continues to back the European integration process. Small wonder that the data mirror the different phases and difficulties experienced by the Union since the 1980s. Thus a rise in the overall favourable opinions experienced in the late 1980s – coinciding with the 'take off' of the European Single Act – is offset by a considerable reduction in backing for the EU when the Treaty of Maastricht was approved and implemented. In those years – as documented by the elaborations of the European Representation Study (Thomassen and Schmitt, 1999, pp. 192–5) – the announcement that national currencies would give way to a single currency after a few years caused negative reactions in public opinion.

With the dispelling of the fears caused by the loss of sovereignty, and with the emergence of the advantages deriving from the changeover, favourable opinions on EU membership have been rising again since the latest Autumn survey (*Eurobarometer* 56, 2002, See European

Figure 1.1 Support for EU membership, 1981–2001 (EU average, percentage of favourable opinions)
Source: European Commission, various years.

Commission, various years), reaching levels not far from those registered in the mid-1980s.

Similarly, the backing of people for the European Union differs from country to country. In particular, since 1997, it is interesting to note that there is a large group of countries (mainly the Scandinavian countries, but also the United Kingdom and Germany), where the percentage of people supporting EU accession is constantly below the European average, while a similarly large group of member states (the Southern European countries, Luxembourg, the Netherlands and Ireland) shows a majority of favourable opinions for the whole period under examination.

Furthermore, two important elements are to be considered for an in-depth data examination. First, there are no strong links between the trend towards EU membership support and the cyclical evolution of European economies. ISAE estimates show a weak correlation in each member state between the percentage of favourable opinions and GDP, considered in both its overall dynamics and as per capita GDP. A slightly more significant correlation is noticed when comparing EU membership support and national unemployment trends. Hence the 'Eurobarometer' (European Commission, various years) surveys show the public opinions of single member states irrespective of either

Table 1.1 Support for EU membership, 1996–2001 (balance of favourable opinions)

	Spring 1996	Spring 1997	Autumn 1997	Spring 1998	Autumn 1998	Spring 1999	Autumn 1999	Spring 2000	Autumn 2000	Spring 2001	Autumn 2001
Belgium	30	22	33	24	38	39	48	52	55	46	50
Denmark	13	25	34	31	36	28	33	29	29	27	47
Germany	23	21	28	23	37	33	35	26	34	34	44
Greece	46	53	50	52	58	43	52	53	53	47	61
Spain	40	39	47	44	56	51	60	61	58	50	50
France	27	34	37	34	40	33	32	35	33	37	37
Ireland	71	77	76	80	75	75	79	69	71	68	76
Italy	60	54	64	63	63	57	54	51	49	50	59
Luxembourg	66	71	65	61	71	74	78	69	75	69	78
Netherlands	69	66	72	67	69	68	67	67	64	54	58
Austria	6	3	17	30	19	13	24	8	14	13	28
Portugal	44	46	54	50	49	55	64	59	55	49	55
Finland	16	14	11	14	24	26	24	18	17	13	14
Sweden	-18	-14	-6	-15	-1	1	7	-4	1	-4	14
United Kingdom	8	10	22	13	15	8	5	1	5	5	11
EU-15 Average	33	35	40	38	43	40	44	40	41	37	45

Source: European Commission, various years.

favourable or unfavourable economic trends. Thus they seem to provide detailed and consistent information on the attitude of European citizens towards the European Union over time.

The latter element concerns one of the subject of the survey, namely the EU, with the characteristics related to the period of time when the survey was carried out. Indeed, over time, the respondents' replies refer to continuously changing political and institutional systems of supranational competence. The rise in favourable opinions registered in 2001 mirrors favourable assessments on an EU system that was much more mature than the one emerging ten years before. Thus data show that the ongoing integration process would not lead to a loss of support for European Union membership.

European citizens and the perception of benefits deriving from integration

Another factor worth considering while weighing European public opinion concerns the perception of benefits deriving from EU membership (see Figures 1.2, 1.3 and 1.4). Following on from previous analyses

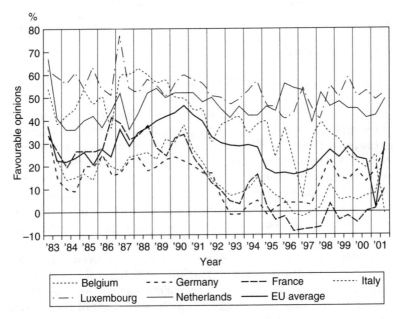

Figure 1.2 Perception of EU membership benefits of the first member states (percentage of favourable opinions)
Source: European Commission, various years.

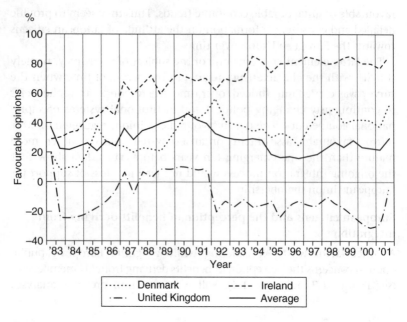

Figure 1.3 Perception of EU membership benefits, Denmark, Ireland, UK (percentage of favourable opinions)
Source: European Commission, various years.

(Marsh, 1999), data on the fifteen member states are broken down by year of accession.

The trend of EU average figures substantially follows the time evolution of the indicator of EU membership support, with a gradual improvement in the perception of EU entry benefits in the 1980s and a considerable fall in the 1990s, up to the recovery of the period most recent for which data is available. Thus one might say that support for EU membership depends mainly on the awareness of the benefits drawn from such membership.

By examining the first six countries that signed the Treaty of Rome, it is worth noting that the trends of different member states were extraordinarily similar, with the perception of benefits remaining unchanged from country to country. A more erratic trend is recorded for Italy: in particular, we note that the 1986 trend shows different behaviour from the averages of the other European countries, alongside a negative assessment in 1996 that is probably a result of the difficult economic and financial situation at the time.

A second group of countries (Denmark, Ireland and the United Kingdom, which joined the Community in January 1973) shows trends close to the European average, though with very heterogeneous absolute values.

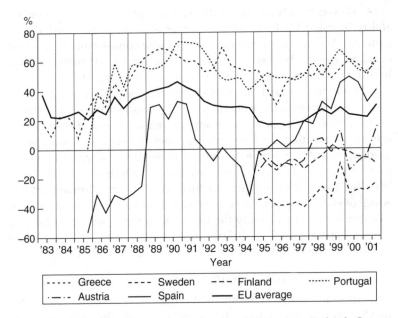

Figure 1.4 Perception of EU membership benefits, Austria, Finland, Greece, Portugal, Spain, Sweden (percentage of favourable opinions)
Source: European Commission, various years.

It is worth noting that the Irish 'take off' – linked to advantageous fiscal incentives for both national and foreign firms, but also to the efficient use of structural funds – mirrors the awareness of the strong benefits deriving from EU membership. These data regarding the UK explain better than any other remarks the careful approach of the British government in establishing closer links with Brussels, also in monetary terms.

The results of the third group of countries leaves room for discussion.[5] The distinction between Southern countries, on the one hand, and Northern countries (plus Austria), on the other, is self-evident: the former countries were strongly convinced of the benefits deriving from EU accession, while the latter group was orientated negatively towards the Community project. It is worth discussing two outstanding cases – first Spain, where citizens moved from a critical perception of EU membership, even in the late 1980s (that is, upon accession) to a very positive (more than the average) approach to the European Union. In this case, the role played by the idea of a Union sensitive to regional development and cohesion problems is of the utmost importance, even though – as happened with Ireland – the 'merit' of the better perception of the EU was mainly a result of the national government's outstanding ability in using EU funds in the best possible way. The second case concerns Austria, where pro-EU opinions rose considerably in a period characterized by the speedy growth of a clearly anti-EU party, perhaps to offset the positions expressed by nationalist movements.

An in-depth examination of data conveys three major messages. First, countries characterized traditionally by an inefficient public administration welcome with hope and faith any supranational form of government. It is a generalization – diffused among policy-makers as well as in public opinion – of the principle whereby it is better to 'tie one's hands' at Community level. Second, citizens usually appreciate immediately what the Union does for them (particularly in terms of infrastructure), which often reverses their earlier negative approaches. Third, there are some member states – particularly the United Kingdom – where inculcating a pro-Europe approach is difficult, but in other cases – in Austria, for example – hostility quickly changed into a positive relationship.

European citizens and institutions

Another source of useful information is the degree of confidence shown by citizens of the various member states towards the main European institutions. The time trend of these indicators shows significant surprises.

The European Parliament is at the top of the citizens' ranking – and it is no coincidence, both because citizens have been called to vote directly for it since 1979, and because there has been an increase in information about the parliament – closely followed by the Court of Justice, the European Commission and the European Central Bank, as well as – some what more distantly – the Council of Ministers of the European Union (see Figure 1.5). This positive attitude towards the European Parliament has been improving over time (see Figure 1.6). This confidence is widespread in all member states, particularly in Luxembourg, Italy and Ireland (see Figure 1.7). Even the generally sceptical United Kingdom indicates a positive attitude in British public opinion. It is even more significant that the consensus towards the European Parliament exceeds that in favour of national Parliaments (see Table 1.2).

The results deriving from the comparison between the EU priority objectives perceived by citizens and those of the members of the European Parliament (MEPs) are more controversial. Should those perceptions be similar, this would signal a good degree of representation of the interests and opinions of the people of Europe on the part of the European Parliament.

Comparing the data of the 'Eurobarometer' survey, on the one hand, and those surveyed by the European Members of Parliament Study

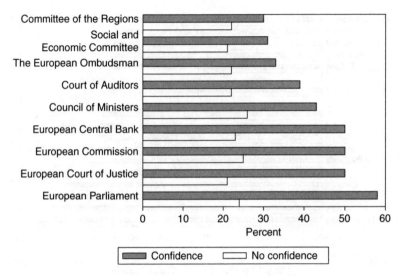

Figure 1.5 Trust in European institutions and bodies (percentage of favourable opinions)
Source: 'Eurobarometer' 56 (European Commission 2002).

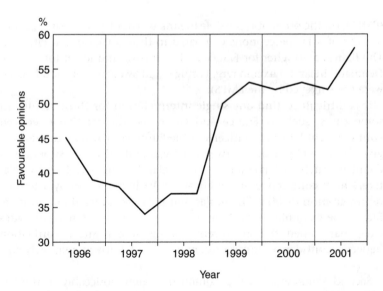

Figure 1.6 Trust in the European Parliament (percentage of favourable opinions)
Source: European Commission, various years.

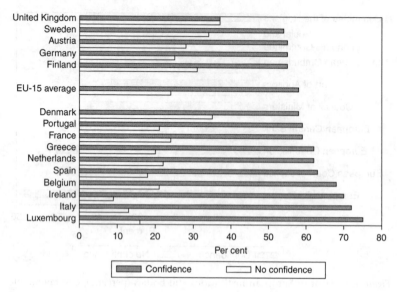

Figure 1.7 Trust of EU countries in the European Parliament (percentage of favourable opinions)
Source: 'Eurobarometer' 56 (European Commission 2002).

(EMPS), on the other, it is possible to rank by country the degree of conformity of MPs' perceptions compared to those of European citizens.[6] The figures are higher for France and Germany, and lower for Austria, Denmark, Ireland, Luxembourg, Portugal and Sweden (Italy and Finland were not surveyed by the EMPS).

It is difficult to find one single interpretation for those results. In some cases, such as France and Germany, the relatively reduced confidence of European citizens in the European Parliament seems to give rise to a closer link between citizens and MPs. The situation of countries such as Luxembourg and Ireland – characterized by relatively high confidence in the European Parliament and by a limited representation of MPs – is similar, but positive rather than negative. But, some examples, mainly Sweden and Austria – that is, of countries that joined the EU recently – signal a positive correlation between confidence and representation, but both at relatively low levels.

Second, confidence in the Commission grew noticeably in the late 1990s, and decreased only in 2001.

Table 1.2 Trust in Parliaments (percentage of favourable opinions)

	Spring 1996			Autumn 2001		
	European Parliament (%)	National Parliament (%)	Difference (%)	European Parliament (%)	National Parliament (%)	Difference (%)
Belgium	47	42	5	68	55	13
Denmark	39	62	−23	58	73	−15
Germany	24	39	−15	55	52	3
Greece	53	56	−3	62	63	−1
Spain	51	45	6	63	56	7
France	51	46	5	59	47	12
Ireland	50	53	−3	70	50	20
Italy	46	29	17	72	43	29
Luxembourg	55	67	−12	75	72	3
Netherlands	55	68	−13	62	67	−5
Austria	29	48	−19	55	54	1
Portugal	36	48	−12	59	55	4
Finland	38	55	−17	55	58	−3
Sweden	26	47	−21	54	65	−11
United Kingdom	29	37	−8	37	47	−10
EU-15 average	39	42	−3	58	51	7

Sources: 'Eurobarometer', 45, Spring 1996; 'Eurobarometer' 56, Autumn 2001 (European Commission, various years).

As happened with the European Parliament, it is also worth noting the strong rise of consensus, in each member state, towards the EU Commission (Table 1.3).

European citizens and their perception of priorities

A very interesting measurement concerns the 'scale' of EU priority objectives on the basis of citizens' evaluations. Figure 1.8 shows the percentage of favourable opinions expressed by European citizens on the priority ranking of the Community objectives.

Data must not be interpreted as the public opinion expression on whether the supranational dimension is more suitable than the national one for tackling some problems (on this point, see next paragraph). At the same time, the survey may be interpreted as a sort of *nulla osta*, namely an approval of the EU dealing with unemployment and the fight against crime, which are typically national questions. Indeed, the

Table 1.3 Trust in EU and in national institutions, 1996 and 2001 (percentage of favourable opinions)

	Spring 1996				Autumn 2001			
	European Commission (%)	Council of Ministers (%)	National Government (%)	Difference[a] (%)	European Commission (%)	Council of Ministers (%)	National Government (%)	Difference[a] (%)
Belgium	48	41	40	4.5	61	54	51	6.5
Denmark	39	38	56	−17.5	52	49	63	−12.5
Germany	21	21	37	−16	42	37	47	−7.5
Greece	50	49	51	−1.5	54	53	50	3.5
Spain	50	46	38	10	59	55	55	2
France	50	45	46	1.5	54	46	43	7
Ireland	50	46	55	−7	64	65	49	15.5
Italy	43	40	27	14.5	62	52	41	16
Luxembourg	58	55	73	−16.5	67	65	73	−7
Netherlands	58	54	68	−12	59	53	70	−14
Austria	30	28	49	−20	48	43	47	−1.5
Portugal	34	36	50	−15	58	53	52	3.5
Finland	40	35	46	−8.5	52	45	60	−11.5
Sweden	28	28	40	−12	45	48	56	−9.5
United Kingdom	28	26	33	−6	35	20	43	−15.5
EU-15 average	38	35	39	−2.5	50	43	48	−1.5

(a) Difference between the average of confidence in European Commission and Council of Ministers and confidence in National Government.
Source: 'Eurobarometer' – as Table 1.2.

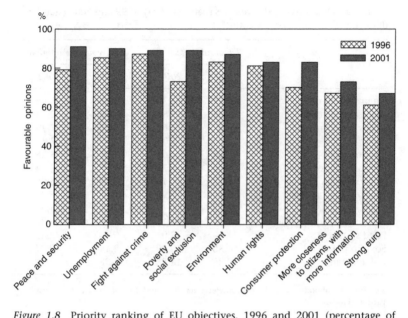

Figure 1.8 Priority ranking of EU objectives, 1996 and 2001 (percentage of favourable opinions of European citizens)
Source: 'Eurobarometer' 56 (European Commission, 2002).

ranking did not change between 1996 and 2001. However, a rise may be seen supporting the idea that the EU should tackle unemployment and, in particular, poverty and social exclusion. Furthermore, the higher sensitivity to topics of consumer protection (to this end, the BSE mad cow disease – question certainly played a role) and peace and security (in this case too an unprecedented and dramatic event such as the terrorist attacks on the USA helps to explain the reverse of this trend) should not be surprising.

If one observes from national data the degree of dispersion of opinions ('Eurobarometer' 51, 2000; see European Commission, various dates), then unemployment, peace and security, drugs and crime, and poverty seem to be the items fairly evenly distributed across countries, while enlargement and the euro show the widest differences from country to country (see Table 1.4). Such measurement is, however, important to avoid conclusions based on the mere observation of EU average values.

Indeed, a further element is to be outlined. As shown by Figure 1.8, the percentages of replies gathered in 1996 are smaller than those of 2001, a clear sign that the share of the so-called 'don't knows' had decreased, which seems to show a growth in citizens' awareness of the EU's problems.

Table 1.4 Opinions on EU priorities (national data), 1999 and 2001 (standard deviation of percentages by country)

	Favourable opinions		Unfavourable opinions	
	1999	2001	1999	2001
Unemployment	3.59	4.30	3.32	3.66
Peace and security	3.22	3.51	1.62	2.13
Drugs and crime	3.75	3.63	2.01	2.49
Poverty	3.77	4.03	2.59	2.80
Environment	5.28	4.61	3.64	3.28
Human rights	5.36	6.75	3.08	3.94
Consumer protection	5.13	6.16	4.49	5.05
Closeness to citizens	6.76	7.95	3.69	5.35
Euro	12.77	16.72	10.77	14.90
Reform of EU institutions	8.44	10.16	7.76	9.30
Food security	–	5.03	–	3.642
Foreign policy	8.36	10.49	8.14	10.27
Enlargement	10.85	14.88	11.98	14.90

Source: ISAE elaborations on 'Eurobarometer' data, 1999 and 2001 (European Commission, various dates).

Competence division between the European Union and member states

The problem of competence division between the Union and the member states is one of the most complicated issues the Convention faces. It is difficult to propose clear and unique criteria for competence division between different levels of government in a fully federal state. It is even more so in such a continuously changing political system as that in Europe, though the EU seems gradually to be approaching a federal-like system.

In defining the guidelines on competence division, the political literature (for example, De Winter and Swyngedouw, 1999; Sinnott, 1995) tends mainly to highlight institutional reasons, such as the prevalence of a government level on others in the competence partition (one can think of some judgments of the European Court of Justice which played a fundamental role in the process aimed at finding supranational solutions to some problems), or 'legal' reasons, whenever public opinion or certain lobbies are urging the establishment of a particular structure of institutional powers (think of Italy, for example, where a trend in favour of decentralization contributed to the introduction of constitutional amendments close to a federalist approach).

The recent economic literature (Alesina *et al.*, 2001) states that the 'policies where economies of scale and/or externalities are predominant should be allocated at the Union level, or even at the world level. Instead, policy areas where heterogeneity of preferences are high relative to externalities should be allocated to a national or sub national level'.

On the basis of these considerations, a very explicit criticism was made about the competence division of the European Union, as there is an excess of competence at European level which has no economic grounds, while there is a lack of competence at European level in areas such as foreign policy, where the presence of externalities would justify a common European stand.

Although in some of those criticisms (Alesina *et al.*, 2001; Tabellini, 2002) the evaluation of the degree of EU involvement is too mechanical, they highlight the lack of transparency of European sources in identifying the right competence distribution between the European Union and member states.

It is interesting to analyse the European citizens' evaluations in this case too (see Table 1.5). The results seem to confirm a very careful perception of public opinion on the competence division between the

Table 1.5 Competence division between the EU and member states (percentage of opinions expressed)

	Autumn 1996			Autumn 2001		
	EU	Member states	Difference	EU	Member states	Difference
Professional training	37	59	−22	36	61	−25
Health care and welfare	34	62	−28	37	59	−22
Media	41	52	−11	38	56	−18
Cultural policy	38	56	−18	44	49	−5
Defence	51	44	7	51	45	6
Fight against unemployment	53	43	10	53	44	9
Agricultural policy	44	49	−5	54	40	14
Environment	65	32	33	64	33	31
Aid to areas in economic difficulty	63	32	31	63	32	31
Monetary affairs	54	40	14	65	31	34
Scientific research and technology	70	25	45	68	27	41
Foreign policy	69	23	46	71	22	49

Sources: ISAE elaborations on 'Eurobarometer' 46 data, 1996 and 'Eurobarometer' 56, 2001 (European Commission, various dates).

European Union and member states. Citizens clearly prefer that the European Union deals with foreign policy, human rights, scientific research, fighting poverty, aids to areas in economic difficulty, monetary affairs and the environment. It is a surprising result, if one thinks that, in practice, only monetary policy is unequivocally part of supranational competencies. The most important indication concerns 'foreign policy human rights', where there is a strong perception that national interests are better defended through a strongly co-ordinated – even centralized – intervention.

Conversely, the replies concerning the media, cultural policy, professional training, health care and welfare – which the European citizens prefer to belong to national competencies – are in keeping with the present EU role. Indeed, the distinction between welfare and the fight against poverty and social exclusion is by no means clear, and the latter is considered to be more effective if tackled at European level. The reply on the agricultural policy is indeed ambiguous: agricultural policy has been an essential part of EU policies since the late 1950s, but a considerable proportion of citizens – though a smaller number than those who consider it should be a European competence – feel that it should be a national competence (indeed, the cost and low effectiveness of the Common Agricultural Policy (CAP) plays a role in this generally critical evaluation).

European citizens and the future of the European Union

The 'Eurobarometer' surveys on the 'desired velocity' of European integration provide comforting indications about the consensus of European public opinion regarding the Community project. These data are compared with the perception of the 'present velocity' of the unification process in Figure 1.9. In the European citizens' evaluation, this is always below the desired velocity of integration. It is worth noticing that the 'desired velocity' has long remained stable, which shows a consolidation of the European perception and of the public opinion on the desired 'degree' of European involvement. At the same time, over the years, European citizens' opinion is that the dynamics of unification is becoming more rapid, which is reducing the gap between the desired and the actual velocities.

It is worth underlining that the desired velocity reaches very high values for countries, such as Greece and Portugal, characterized by a relatively small per capita GDP, and that member states with a much larger per capita GDP prefer a less intense integration process. It is, however, impossible to generalize about the relationship between development and a desire for integration, as countries with a high per capita GDP – such as Luxembourg

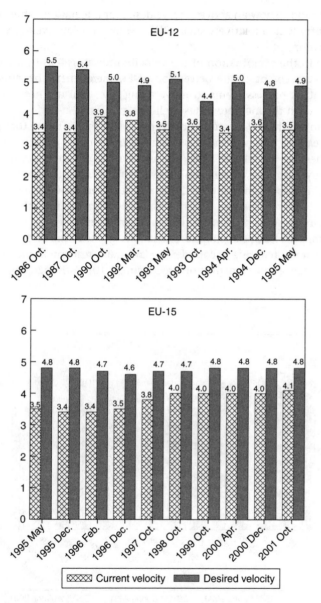

Figure 1.9 The 'Euro-dynamometer': current and desired velocity of European integration[1] (trend on a scale from 1 to 7)
Note: (1) From 1 = static to 7 = fast.
Source: Eurobarometer, 56, 2002.

and Ireland – show an above-average desire for integration, while Spain – a country with a relatively small GDP – shows a below-average wish for integration.

Also in the examination of the velocity indicators – as in the case of the measurement of the perception of EU membership benefits – the integration process seems to move along lines that are not correlated closely with the member states' well-being.

All in all, these data are out of keeping with those stating that part of European public opinion is not aware of the benefits deriving from EU membership. To tell the truth, the two statements are a contradiction, as many European citizens are so aware of the benefits stemming from the EU membership that they desire a closer integration, which does not mean, however, that it is not necessary to weigh carefully the tensions emerging in some sections of the European population.

Within the European citizens' evaluations on the future of the European Union, it is interesting to consider the favourable reaction to the hypothesis of a European Constitution (see Figure 1.10). Although one should

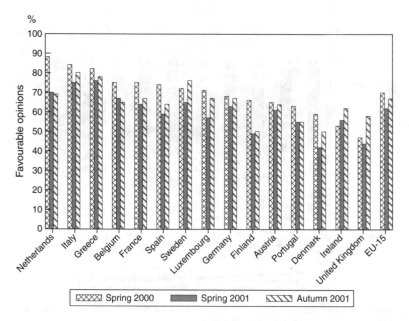

Figure 1.10   Opinions in favour of the Constitution (percentage of favourable opinions)
Source: Eurobarometer, various years.

be aware that the question posed to respondents was rather vague, there was a majority consensus regarding a European Constitution shared by all member states.

More legitimacy for European institutions: some early remarks

This chapter has tried to show to what extent it is necessary to redefine the Community decision-making mechanisms, both in view of its effectiveness and to solve problems of legitimacy. Given the decision to move towards the EU enlargement, it is even more urgent to make the right choices, thus avoiding an integration slowdown and enabling a 'gradual' absorption of the twelve new member states within the Union structure, guaranteeing at the same time a democratic control of citizens over European policies.

Indeed, the integration process has reached such a degree that the European Union's powers are bound to be strengthened, in both quantitative (number of areas covered by the Commission) and qualitative terms (the EU's prevailing role in making rules and regulations). The Convention has had to face the question of competence division in a very balanced way to enable a reduction in the ambiguity of indications on this subject contained in the Treaties. In our opinion, it would be necessary to consider that, apart from the traditional *acquis communautaire*, there is another, more practical, *acquis* consisting of practices and a gradual and inevitable involvement of a supranational governing body.

The gradual transfer of sovereignty poses the problem of the amount of democratic control that citizens exert over the policies proposed or introduced at various government levels. For example, the introduction of important elements of fiscal policy at the European level should be linked to a change in the degree of control that European citizens have over Community institutions.

Furthermore, some improvements may be obtained in the degree of legitimacy of the institutions of the European Union. In particular, mention was made of the possibility that the present forms of collaboration between the European Parliament and national Parliaments could be strengthened, involving national Parliaments more directly in the delicate 'growing phase' of Community policies.

The full adoption of co-decision procedures, the growing role of the European Parliament in the Commission's action, the increasing involvement of national Parliaments in the Union's decision-making process, and the higher degree of political representation that prime ministers will have as the role of European-level decisions increases in public opinion are all factors that will enhance the Community institutions' legitimacy and accountability. Indeed, these steps forward seem able to guarantee the role of the European Commission in pushing forward with the European integration process.

However, there is a second group of initiatives that can contribute similarly to solving the problem of legitimacy; namely, the implementation of principles and instruments which, by their nature, seem able to guarantee that the integration process will go on, even though national interests are to be safeguarded and the delicate equilibrium between the legitimacy of national institutions and of EU institutions is to be maintained.

Considerations of that kind are mainly linked to the principle of mutual recognition. As analysed in-depth in the first ISAE Report on the State of the European Union (Padoa Schioppa, 2001), this principle marks an important step forward in the path towards co-operation and mutual acceptance of the differences existing between member states in many noncoordinated areas of Community life (from welfare to the banking sector). The potentialities of mutual recognition as an instrument to prompt 'non-forced' integration must be further exploited.

The second group of more flexible institutional instruments concerns the strengthened co-operation method. This method enables groups of member states to cluster around specific initiatives requiring an integrated approach, while leaving at the same time, for countries not joining the agreement, the possibility of joining it in the future. This should safeguard both the braver initiatives aimed at facing new matters at the European level – though with rules in keeping with the Treaties and the *acquis communautaire* – and the possibility that one or more member states adapt to the decisions taken by other EU members. The strengthened co-operation method seems particularly effective in view of the EU enlargement to twenty-seven member states.

The third group of 'flexible' initiatives lies in the 'open co-ordination method' that has already been adopted. Its procedures enable a gradual adaptation, and thus a better safeguard of national interests in some areas. Unlike the situation in 'strengthened co-operations', the open co-ordination method excludes no member state from collaboration mechanisms. However, as in the principle of 'mutual recognition', it introduces flexible convergence based on the voluntary acceptance of some policy choices on the part of some countries rather than a rigid insistence on adaptation to common rules.

Democratic legitimacy and the Treaty establishing a Constitution for Europe

This chapter was completed in its original Italian version in October 2002. Since then, two main events have produced obvious repercussions on the problems of political legitimacy and representation within the European Union: the approval by the Council of Ministers in June 2004 and the signature at the end of October 2004 by EU member states of the Treaty establishing a Constitution for Europe and the enlargement of EU membership to ten new countries in May 2004. None of the main conclusions of the chapter seems to be especially affected by these events.

As far as EU institutions are concerned, their overall accountability and democratic legitimacy seem to have been strengthened by the Treaty establishing a Constitution for Europe. In particular, the powers of the European Parliament have been increased by the new Constitution and the Parliament will have in coming years a higher profile in the decision-making process which leads to the appointment of the European Commission. Especially relevant, in this respect, is the provision (art. I-20 of the Treaty) that '[the Parliament] shall elect the President of the Commission'. As argued above, the Strasbourg assembly had already acquired a strong role in the Commission appointment procedure; it was emphasized how the Parliament accelerated in 1999 the fall of the Commission led by Jacques Santer and it can now be added how severe the European Parliament was in evaluating the first composition of the Commission led by the new President José Manuel Barroso. In other words, given the stronger role of the European Parliament, the Constitution reinforces the legitimacy of the Commission and it will therefore become very difficult to criticize the EU because of a democratic deficit in the Commission functioning.

Within this context, the new Treaty has often been negatively evaluated because of the persistence on such matters as foreign and fiscal policies of the unanimity rule. As always, in discussing the question of enlarging the scope of the qualified majority vote, a clear trade-off emerges between reasons for the efficacy of EU policies and reasons invoking a more democratic character of the overall EU decision-making process. In short, a decision taken by a majority of member states inevitably forces other states (and thus other citizens) to comply with it.

The solution to this dilemma is not an easy one and, understandably, the new Constitution does not make a clear choice. In fact, on the one hand the text approved in Brussels in June 2004 increases the number of subjects on which a decision taken with a qualified majority vote is possible, while on the other hand, it keeps the unanimity rule on the most delicate areas such as foreign and fiscal policies.

In this chapter we stressed the need for a more transparent division of competences between the EU and its member states. The new Treaty makes an attempt to clarify the distribution of policies between different levels of government; this attempt has only been partially successful. Indeed, we still have a complicated classification of categories of competences including 'areas of exclusive competence' (art. I-13), 'areas of shared competence' (art. I-14), areas where 'the Union shall have competence to carry out activities, in particular to define and implement programmes' (art. I-14, c. 3), areas where 'the Union shall have competence to carry out activities and conduct a common policy' (art. I-14, c. 4), 'areas of supporting, coordinating or complementary action' (art. I-17), areas in which the Union has the task of coordinating policies, and specific areas like foreign and security policies with even more peculiar arrangements.

Maybe inevitably, the division of competences in the new Constitutional Treaty still mirrors the *sui generis* character of the EU institutional construction where the process of progressive devolution of several areas from the national towards the supranational level, far from being a linear and a coherent one, is heavily characterized by difficulties, resistances, lack of clear priorities, delays and differences among member states, and so forth.

Finally, with regard to the opinions of European citizens towards EU institutions and policies, no relevant changes seem to have occurred recently. The need for a European Constitution, in particular, is still felt by the vast majority of the European public, despite differences among member states. Nonetheless, more recent data reveals the decrease, albeit limited, of perceived advantages of EU membership and of the confidence in EU institutions.

2
Overruled Europa: Market versus Democracy in the EU

On the eve of the introduction of the euro in 1999, Jean-Paul Fitoussi stated that he was deeply worried by the deafening silence surrounding the advent of the single currency: 'the economic policies of the forth-coming years, namely the post-euro period, are presently being given shape. This may seem like stating the obvious, and yet the happening of such important events has aroused neither debate nor questioning'.[1] He then added: 'the focus ought to be on the choice of a model for our society, as this is the European peoples' only real concern'.

The European situation has since witnessed some drastic changes that can be assessed from several standpoints. First, at the economic level, growth has fallen back, the euro has switched from being a protector to an attacker, monetary stability has given way to deflationary threats, and mass unemployment is again readily overshooting the most pessimistic forecasts. At the political level, the European Union (EU) enlargement process, with ten new members by 2004, was duly initiated at the Copenhagen summit of 11–13 December 2002. Finally, at the inter-national level, the attacks of September 11, symptoms of the globalisation of goods, capital and terror, have fragmented the world. The EU *Nautilus* nevertheless remains *immobilis in mobili*. Worse still, its autopilot is the sole master on board, and that is what is keeping the ship at anchor.

It is also true that the EU started work on a constitution in March 2002. By entrusting the 'Convention on the future of the EU' with a wide-ranging mandate given by the Laeken Declaration of 15 December 2001, the European Council expressed its firm commitment to a 'more democratic, more transparent and more efficient' Union. It recom-mended that 'three basic challenges [be] resolved' before the objective could be met: 'How to bring citizens ... closer to the European design and the European institutions, how to organise politics and the European political area in an enlarged Union and how to develop the Union into a stabilising factor and a model in the new, multi-polar world'.[2] If what resulted from the draft constitution is any indication, none of the three questions – which really come down to only one – have been addressed: although EU enlargement is imminent, silence weighs even more heavily upon the future of European democracy than it did in 1999. After failing to convert the future, will the EU now be forever reduced to averting it?

This inertia is neither fortuitous nor accidental, since it is 'liberalism at face value', the scenario implying that politics is to be done away with, which has prevailed over the other three proposals contemplated four years ago. Structurally, the European Union can neither face up to the vagaries of time nor command its own destiny, because it gave up on choice, and decided instead that the rules already established should be held sacred.[3] Against this background, the expectations raised by the work of the European Convention and by the process of enlargement to include countries of Central Europe can be appraised along two lines. The first concerns the unstable opposition to change whereby sticking to the rules will lead to a weakened and multi-level 'exit Europe'. The second element involves political leverage, or 'voice',[4] as democracy is the true stability pact that Europe needs in order to benefit from the growth promised by globalization. The paradox is apparent: 'deregulating' Europe should put it back on track.

Introduction: the euro, our currency, our problems

There has been no abatement in European concern over the course of the three stages undergone by the euro since its introduction (see Figure 2.1). Europe became worried when the euro started to drop. Europe was worried again when the euro enjoyed relative stability, and Europe is still worrying now because the euro is picking up again. The problem therefore is Europe, not the euro.

Contrary to the expectations of greater EU-generated growth and better protection from external shocks raised by the introduction of the single currency, the euro now appears to have contributed to the Union's vulnerability. So whence the paradox? In the early 1970s, US Treasury Secretary John B. Connally said, rather provokingly, and yet probably fairly: 'the dollar is our currency, but it is your problem'. The euro has indeed become our currency, so it also mirrors our problems and reflects the economic instability generated by Europe's political dithering. It is therefore no surprise that a doctrinaire model should

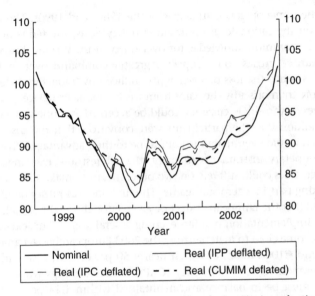

Figure 2.1 The euro's effective exchange rate trends since its introduction
Source: ECB, *Monthly Bulletin,* June 2003.

develop into empty abstractions that make the situation increasingly unsustainable.

The following warning was attached to the list of the 'sociopolitical' models singled out in 1999: 'even though only one of the selected models will eventually hold sway over political decision making, it may well be that reality will not entirely conform to any of them but rather proceed from the complex blending of some of their separate elements. Out of the four possible plans for the future, the one that was eventually implemented actually results from the combination of a watered down version of three of them' (Fitoussi, 1999).

Three futures for one present

1. Economic federalism pared down to the monetary rump

'The federalist model' was the first model for the future to be considered in 1999. The choice was based on the optimistic assumption that, thanks to the reborn collective logic generated by the single currency, European governments would not miss out on the opportunity to face up to their responsibilities in global regulation. The idea was far from quixotic, as it was premised on the expectation that the euro would prompt a breakaway from the noncooperative strategies of the 1980s and 1990s. The gamble rested on the rationale of optimum currency areas, the terms of which had been common knowledge for over thirty years. Within this context, European countries could expect a greater command over their own destinies, since the loss of sovereignty induced by 'monetary federalism' was more than offset by the gains from weaker market tutelage.

However, the single currency could be accepted as a one-way bet only on condition that the participants were convinced that the cost–benefit equation would eventually turn out to be to their advantage. Divested of their monetary instruments (namely, the interest and exchange rates), member states could still rely on two other means to make sure they were not taking part in a zero-sum game. The first one was rather daring, as it required that the European budget be given enough weight to make room for the implementation of a far-reaching federal policy. This expectation did not come close to materializing: the 2003 European budget amounted to around €100 billion, of which nearly 50 per cent was earmarked for the Common Agricultural Policy (CAP). To make things worse, the EU budget must be in balance and maintained within 1.24 per cent of all members' gross national income, which is much too low a ceiling for the automatic stabilizers to have any impact or cushion economic shocks.

Co-ordination of discretionary economic policy proved to be an equally disappointing alternative. Two EU bodies were in fact set up to take charge of economic co-ordination. Members were first to co-ordinate their economic policies in Ecofin, a council made up of economic and finance ministers. Countries whose economic policy this Council deemed to be reckless might be sent an early warning. The Maastricht Treaty (1992) also introduced an Economic and Financial Committee, later to be renamed the Euro Council, and finally the Eurogroup. The Eurogroup was assigned the following objectives: to encourage the exchange of information relating to the economic and political developments that were likely to have a cross-border impact; to monitor closely the changes in the member states' macroeconomic and fiscal policies; and to clarify the nationally-run labour market programmes. Furthermore, some decisions concerning Denmark and the United Kingdom about ERM 2 might also be discussed in preparation for G7 summits. Hence the Eurogroup helps to outline the economic policy measures that will eventually be adopted officially by the Ecofin Council.

It is obvious that such informal harmonization is far removed from the economic government many had originally called for. This was probably the most fundamental gamble taken in 1999, and yet it was subsequently lost. Success would have required all member states to decide on

Table 2.1 Balassa's[5] typology and European economic integration

Integration steps according to Balassa's typology	Implementation and type of economic policy required	Completion and validity in the euro zone as of 2005
Free-trade area	Revocation of all customs duties and quotas	Achieved (between 1961 and 1968)
Customs union	Common external tariff	Achieved (in 1968)
	Common trade policy	Enforced
Common market	Free movement of goods	Achieved since 1993
	Free movement of capital	Achieved since 1993
	Free movement of services	**Incomplete**
	Free movement of labour	**Incomplete**
	Free competition policy	Enforced
Economic union	Economic integration	**Incomplete**
	Economic policy coordination	**Partly achieved**
	Structural adjustment	**Partly achieved**
Economic and monetary union	Economic and financial union	**Incomplete**
	Unification of monetary policy and single currency	Achieved in 1999
	Unification of taxation policy	**Incomplete**
	Unification of fiscal policy	**Incomplete**

Source: Adapted from Balassa (1961).

a common political destiny. Never redressed, the initial institutional imbalance between an independent Central Bank and a plethora of other fiscal authorities under the yoke of the Stability Pact has become even more precarious. Even worse, it is the whole European economic integration process that currently appears to be deficient, if not inconsistent (see Table 2.1).

2. 'Social Europe': from separation to instrumentation

Before the introduction of the single currency, 'the separation model' was regarded as the second way to Europe's future. It was expected that the economic and social spheres would come to be considered as distinct entities, and that, since the national states remained in charge of social policy, social issues should be considered as being detached from Europe as a whole.

This had been Europe's traditional philosophy since the Treaty of Rome (1957), which instituted a twofold separation based on both institutional and rational grounds. On the one hand, the Treaty acknowledged that member states retained some form of social sovereignty because economic integration was the most pressing priority. Yet it implied, on the other hand, that Europe's social policies were only a by-product of Europe's economic objectives.

The 'new social Europe' that has emerged gradually since 1997 attempts to move away significantly from the separation model by 'reconciling' both economic and social policy. Thanks to its 'European employment strategy' and its 'open method of co-ordination', it vows to restore institutional harmony between national and community authorities. The 'employability' objective and the 'social protection as a productive factor' dogma have become the foundation of a new economic policy in which social policy maximization will take up the challenge of economic competitiveness.[6]

In the wake of the Luxembourg summit of 20–21 November 1997, the Lisbon summit of 23–24 March 2000 set a new strategic objective for the Union, 'to become the most competitive and dynamic knowledge-based economy in the world by modernising the European social model and building an active welfare state' (European Council, 2000a). Employability and social activation policies lie at the heart of this new scheme.

This founding instrument may denote a transmutation of Social Europe from some residue into an appendix. Its conclusions seem to point to a European preference for structural reform over macroeconomic policy. Yet the passage from the separation to the instrumentation model involves little change. The perception has become more subtle but remains untainted: however valid an argument in the past, the malfunctioning of the economy can no longer be blamed for unemployment, as the fault now lies in part with the workers' ill-adapted skills.

3.   The hazardous comeback of the nation-state

Akin to the unconscious, the nation-state never goes away, but simply keeps changing places. The third model envisaged the 'resurgence of national sovereignty'. In 1999, this meant re-establishing the authority of the nation-state – which was thought to be able to regain some room for manoeuvre – as well as resurrecting political power so the all-too pervasive market forces could be confronted.

Backlashes did occur on these two fronts, but they translated into the alarming rise of both far right and far left political parties in Europe, felt most spectacularly in Austria, Italy, the Netherlands and France. As became clear from the French elections, this upsurge was fuelled equally by European integration and globalization. At stake here is undoubtedly the European malaise in face of globalization: the EU seems to be perceived by many citizens as more like a Trojan Horse than a shield.

'Liberalism at face value', the fourth model in the series, is currently dominant but it will not succeed in calming down present anxieties because, instead of changing course, the European Union has persisted in expanding its empire with 'the Rule' as its emperor.

The game of the rule and the benevolent despot[7]

'If it were to opt for a neo-liberal model of society, as is eventually most likely to happen, the European project would then become more positively justified' (Fitoussi, 1999). In fact, this is the prediction that finally materialized, beyond all (mis)apprehension.

'That which is well conceived is easily worded', as Boileau's dictum goes: torn between market and democracy, Europe's institutional architecture is biased towards the market. In the name of efficiency, the resulting 'democratic deficit' (a political concern in an economic concept) is supposed to be taken for granted by all, both at the European level and at that of the member states. However, to become binding, the relationship requires the prerequisite of the acknowledgement of a very specific economic doctrine that has remained controversial since its inception in the eighteenth century. Most importantly, the system is underpinned by a strict hierarchy between economic and political values which prescribes that economic freedom should take precedence over political freedom. Such a construction is undoubtedly most debatable. 'Sweet trade' alone has never managed either to keep social unrest in check or to pervade the whole political sphere.

At the operational level, the EU 'economic government' comprises three members: a Secretary of State for Fiscal Surveillance, a Minister of State for Competition, and a Chancellor of the Euro. The three members of the European government do not enjoy equal status. The Secretary of State for Fiscal Surveillance does not make any effective decisions as s/he only holds investigative powers. It (the Commission) 'will exercise its right of initiative under the Treaty in a manner that facilitates the strict, timely and effective functioning of the Stability and Growth Pact'.[8] However, the Secretary of State does exert a powerful influence because his/her investigation files and recommendations are made public even before the decision-making authority (read the European Council) has dealt with the case. The Minister of State for Competition (the other body of the Commission) wields both legislative and judicial power. In some circumstances – most extraordinary ones, it must be said – the European Parliament can force these two economic government members to resign. The Chancellor of the Euro (read the European Central Bank – ECB) holds extensive powers within the framework imparted to him/her by the Treaties, the limits of which are left to the Chancellor's own interpretation. In no legal sense can the Chancellor be dismissed or held accountable before any political authority whatever. No head of government co-ordinates the briefs of the Secretary of State, or that of the two other members of the 'economic government'. From a global standpoint, this architecture recalls the federation system. But the word 'federation' is in fact hardly ever used, because the Union's economic government is ruled by merely juxtaposed independent governments rather than by a common political decision-making authority. As for competition policy – which aims at removing obstacles to competition through structural reform – it will not be discussed here because it is not usually thought of as being instrumental in macro-economic policy.

Monetary policy was handed over to an independent body – the industrial world's only institution that does not have to answer to democracy for its actions (although it can in fact do so) – and the member states' fiscal powers were carefully capped by a set of rules. Europe's economic constitution has no provision for ECB accountability to any political assembly. In theory, ordinary procedure – whatever the minutiae – would demand that the Central Bank be made accountable to an authority that has the power to modify the Bank's statutes, even though the whole process is subject to a strict legal framework. This is the rule for central banks all over the world, so one wonders why Europe's does not fall under the 'common law'. Although national Parliaments make use of this power only exceptionally, it does not mean that the procedure is totally useless. The mere possibility of legal action is incentive enough for central banks to internalize the representative assemblies' concerns and make information more forthcoming.

This 'democratic deficit' is all the more worrying as it could, in theory, cause a major crisis since it inverts the traditional hierarchy of powers by ranking governmental power under that of an independent agency. The problem would be less serious had the ECB not formed a precise opinion as to what constitutes the right general economic policy for Europe. This dogma is mentioned constantly in the Bank's publications and in its leaders' speeches: it is first argued that the state should take a lesser role in the economy by cutting public spending, and then that the labour market should be made more flexible and more attractive by trimming the over-generous social protection systems. As the ECB chose to keep interest rates at too high a level, it then has the power to sanction the states that do not implement the policy it advocates. This power is considerable, yet it only works one direction, as the ECB may sanction the Union's governments, but national governments cannot sanction the ECB. Even though European Councils may disagree with the ECB on what the right monetary policy should be, there is no way they can impose their views. By contrast, the ECB has the power to increase the economic and social costs to be paid by the governments that decide not to adhere to its policy.

Fiscal and monetary rules complement each other perfectly. Like monetary rules, fiscal rules have had every virtue attributed to them: they are supposed to lend 'credibility' to fiscal policy, clear the governments suspected of running a loose policy, and thus hold inflationary pressure in check. If monetary and fiscal authorities established better communication, they would find it easier to make decisions on the co-ordination of the policy mix. As a result, disagreement over the level at which to set the economic equilibrium could be avoided, and interest rates and fiscal deficits would not need to be both simultaneously and needlessly high.

The Stability Pact was the rule chosen for Europe. Not only does it include a sanction procedure for 'excessive' deficits – namely over 3 per cent of GDP – but it also forces governments to commit themselves to reaching 'the medium-term objective of a budgetary position close to balance or in surplus'. The rule rests on shaky ground[9] and therefore carries no 'credibility' at all.

Taken literally, the European rule offers no other option but a tight fiscal policy for all euro zone countries until 2005, even though, and especially if, growth happens to undershoot its potential level. In the present circumstances, it incites most European countries to run pro-cyclical fiscal policies, namely a tightening of policy in times of recession. As an example, France, Germany and Italy at the time of writing do not have sufficient room for manoeuvre to let automatic stabilizers operate fully, partly because of the weight of their national debt burden. As they are included in the total public spending balance account, debt charges limit the scope left for fiscal policy to respond to external shocks, however transient. Is it conceivable that all the countries concerned should then be forced to run tight fiscal policies only because they must ensure compliance with the Stability Pact? No sound – let alone 'credible' – fiscal policy can be based on such a principle.

After deciding to hand over monetary and exchange policy to the ECB, EU governments have become part of the euro zone, an economic area in which they are left with no other adjustment tool but the fiscal instrument. Should strict observance of the Stability Pact then mean they cannot even feel free to use this last instrument as they wish, and even worse, that they have no alternative but to take up the proffered dagger and turn it on themselves?

The upshot is that EU governments have been forced to become experts in mumbo jumbo. They are now proficient in the art of over-rating growth forecasts and have learnt how to massage public finance accounts, while the Commission and the ECB calmly sit by, casting a critical eye over them. The current procedure is an open invitation to prevarication. Governments have to do their homework, and every year must hand in progress reports called 'stability pro-grammes'. As noted above, a resolution of the European Council in fact provides that 'the Commission will exercise its right of initiative under the Treaty in a manner that facilitates the strict, timely and effective functioning of the Stability and Growth Pact'. So the Commis-sion serves in some way as the elected governments' official watchdog on fiscal orthodoxy. It therefore has full responsibility for drafting the early warnings to be sent to the countries that choose to veer away from the 'canon' of European law: overall public deficits must remain under 3 per cent of GDP, with the medium-term objective of a balanced, or even better, surplus budget. The procedure produces political repercussions as the Commission can send public warnings and consequently, as often happens with ordinary legal cases, the media tend to pass a 'guilty until proven innocent' verdict. Besides, the eventual clearing of the accused by other member states at an Ecofin Council may fail to convince the public, because the late decision may be felt to be a political abdication of the responsibility to fulfil the previously consecrated fiscal obligations. Ultimately, it is the Council that stands accused of weakening the credibility of fiscal policy, whereas the fault should lie with the unsustainable Rule, as was officially acknowledged by the president of the EU Commission in October 2002 in an edifying speech on the overall functioning of the European Union (see Box 2.1).

All in all, and in a fairly decent echo of Romano Prodi's speech, it can be said that it is most difficult to distinguish Europe's 'economic government' from that of an enlightened despot who is sheltered from the pressure of the great unwashed but is nevertheless striving to achieve the common good by inflicting the most rigorous stream of neo-liberalism on all his subjects, because this is what is believed to be the ultimate in terms of economic efficiency. Ever since Condorcet, and Kenneth J. Arrow[10] more recently, it has been accepted that majority

Box 2.1 The Stability and Growth Pact seen through
Romano Prodi's eyes

The Stability and Growth Pact has been the cornerstone for
promoting and managing the culture of stability so successfully
introduced with the Maastricht criteria.

Nevertheless, awareness of the extraordinary things the Pact has
already brought about and will continue to bring about in the future
should not blind us to the limitations of the institutional framework
in which we have to apply it. Still less does it mean enforcing the
Pact inflexibly and dogmatically, regardless of changing circumstances.
That is what I called – and still call – 'stupid'.

I do not think that it is the role of the Commission or of myself
as President of the Commission to apply rules in that way. Neither
the Commission nor myself have been appointed to enforce rules
blindly, ignoring their limitations. The European citizens have a
right to be informed, and we have a duty to tell them what we
think is right, what we think works, and what, on the other hand,
we think could and should be improved.

Politicians like yourselves, economists, bankers and businessmen,
with whom I have discussed this matter a thousand times, have
been saying for months and continue to say in private and in their
everyday conversations the same things that I said openly and
frankly in the interests of our institutions' credibility. It is therefore
time that we started to say in public what we say amongst ourselves
in private.

The public mistrusts us and our institutions not least because
they suspect that only minor matters are aired in public and that
the truly important decisions are taken behind closed doors.

Source: Romano Prodi, 'The Stability and Growth Pact', Speech to
the European Parliament, 21 October 2002.

voting can produce inconsistent results, hence the conclusion that
democracy may not be the system that best represents public interest. It
is even believed to lead to weak governments, utterly helpless against
the popular demand for more redistribution. Absolute dictatorship is in
no way a better system as it rarely tolerates economic freedom. This is
why some eminent economists, such as Robert Barro,[11] have dreamed of
the coming of the benevolent dictator in whose reign collective choice

would become rational, and extensive economic freedom lavishly granted but political liberty severely restricted. In a way, the European authorities are about to make this dream come true. Because it is defined by a set of economic freedoms such as price stability, a balanced budget or free competition, the EU preference function would allow for a consistent approach to public interest and could therefore afford to remain constant whatever the vagaries of democracy. In other words, the dreamt-up despot is probably already alive and well, since a certain number of decisions are being made at present outside democracy's frame of reference. Yet, much enlightened, he must be this despot who will abide by the rules of a pre-existent economic doctrine.

Alternatively, it can also be argued that the market consists of only individuals and free electrons, and that optimal resource allocation is bound to suffer from the introduction of anything more collective. Pierre Rosanvallon wrote that

> besides, the Theory of Exchange...offers a simultaneous and consistent solution to the twofold problem posed by Institutions and social regulation: human relationships are ruled by need and interest. This representation of society as a market came fully into bloom with the Scottish School in the 18th century, and most particularly with Adam Smith. Essentially, the idea suggests that politics should be cast aside irrevocably. Society must no longer be governed by politics, the law or conflicts, but by the market...Viewed from this angle, Adam Smith is not to be regarded primarily as the founding father of political economy, but rather as the theorist who advocated the decline of politics.[12]

These considerations may indeed look overblown when compared to the relentless efforts that have been expanded over the building of Europe. Yet, in the absence of a coherent political project, Europe is looking like a sovereignty-free vacuum where the Rule has become the ruler of a government that should instead be led by freedom of choice. Dogmatism has never been the right method for achieving the ultimate goals for which all societies rightfully long, and among which full employment naturally ranks first. Europe's poor performances in the 1990s – soft growth and mass unemployment, among other problems – should at least have aroused some suspicion.

So what can be said about the future of the EU-turned Empire of the Rule in the light of the work done by the 'Convention on the Future of Europe'? Careful reading of the draft constitution presented in June

2003 to the EU Council gives an illuminating insight into what the future may hold. What can we learn? First, the "regulatory state" has become enshrined. Not only have the Stability Pact and the ECB's statutes remained entirely untouched, but they have now been written into the stone of the European fundamental law which grants unhoped-for permanent status to the theory on which they were originally based.[13] In sum, the Convention aims at merging all the former Treaties' dispositions into one constitution for the European Union, thereby causing Europe's non-economic government to become frozen in its present form. To this effect, the project subjects economic policy to restrictive co-ordination, as is expressly formulated in article III-69 which consequently deserves to be quoted in its entirety:

> 1. For the purposes set out in Article I-3, the activities of the Member States and the Union shall include, as provided in the Constitution, the adoption of an economic policy which is based on the close coordination of Member States' economic policies, on the internal market and on the definition of common objectives, and conducted in accordance with the principle of an open market economy with free competition.
> 2. Concurrently with the foregoing, and as provided in the Constitution, and in accordance with the procedures set out therein, these activities shall include a single currency, the euro, and the definition and conduct of a single monetary policy and exchange rate policy, the primary objective of both of which shall be to maintain price stability and, without prejudice to this objective, to support the general economic policies in the Union, in accordance with the principle of an open market economy with free competition.
> 3. These activities of the Member States and the Union shall entail compliance with the following guiding principles: stable prices, sound public finances and monetary conditions and a stable balance of payments.

The dichotomy between fiscal and monetary powers is clearly underlined by the choice of the adverb 'concurrently' – which de facto rules out any virtuous policy mix – and is further accompanied by a still more arresting revelation: the adoption in paragraph 3 of an accounting triangle of intermediary objectives replacing the magic square of final objectives of economic policy. Employment is therefore relegated to the rank of 'policies in other specific areas' and dealt with in article III-97. Thus the Convention can be said to have advanced on many points, with the notable exception of economic governance,[14] which only ranked as one of the fundamental tasks originally assigned to it. The exception merely confirms the rule and thus becomes an admission of helplessness. Is the power of the regulatory state really offset, as one was told when the draft was presented, by the rise of a democratic state buttressed by a Council made more stable and a Commission more legitimate? This is not very obvious.

The Convention on the future of Europe had rightfully set itself the ambitious objective of building for the European Union the democratic legitimacy it was lacking (see below). The institutional triangle that underpins the EU political system, as we all know, is based on power sharing and separation of legitimacies. The legislative and executive powers are held in pairs by the Council, the Commission and Parliament, while each of these institutions taken individually upholds, respectively, the interests of the states, the Union and Europe's citizens. The draft Constitution remains faithful to the European liberalism's doctrine when it plans to set the different legitimacies in competition with each other, but it increases power confusion when it hands over more co-decision and control to the European Parliament. In strict conformity with the Franco-German proposal to the Convention, it considers making the presidency of the European Council more permanent by providing it with a long-standing president, and makes provision for the Commission's president to be elected by the European Parliament. Whereas it is fairly easy to see why these changes will put the 'institutional triangle' and the Community's method off balance, it is more difficult to discover what is supposed to replace them. In the future European Constitution, no checks and balances will arise from the limits set to the different legitimacies, because they will all tread on each other's toes and elbow one another aside. The odds are that the new institutional regime will require the appointment of an arbitration board of governmental power, a Directorate for Legitimate Competition – a task that may well fall to the Court of Justice of the European Communities (CJEC). Some will object, however, that it will be up to the men (and one hopes, the women too) holding these public offices on where to place the goalposts, at which the delegates merely hinted. But one would have thought protecting individuals from such risks was the most basic point in having a Constitution at all.

The major attraction of this political architecture is probably more political than architectural, as it could be viewed as the skilful reconciliation of two opposed interpretations. If the Commission is to become the seat of supranational power, then the future enhanced legitimacy derived from the president of the Commission's election by a qualified majority cannot but enthuse the supporters of federal integration. On the other hand, if the Council is to become the centre for intergovernmental power, then the ambitious provision of a more permanent presidency will reassure those who fear that the voice of national sovereignty may become muted within the Union.

Can such a compromise make up a satisfactory solution? It depends. The answer will be positive for those who think a Constitution is only a long list of legal rules, but it will be negative for those who believe a Constitution must also include democratic vision and many varieties of political decision. In other words – and while the issue was swept away by all the twists and turns that yearning for achievement inevitably aroused – at stake here was not procedural government but substantive democracy.

Rule does come out as the clear winner in the institutional reform presented by the Convention. A visionary project is indeed taking shape, namely the perfecting of the neo-liberal paradigm applied in the European Union. It is now standing firmly on its own two feet: namely, competitive markets and property rights. This new construction, if it were ever to be built, would consist of the juxtaposition of a federal regulatory state becoming increasingly powerful, and a democratic state with increasingly confused legitimacy. However asymmetric their relationship now, it is bound to become even more so in the future as the regulatory state will subjugate the democratic state, while itself being sanctuarized. It seems, therefore, that we are heading for an 'exit' type of an unstable, enlarged Europe which will need deregulating sooner rather than later.

The enlarged Union's future, between exit(s) and voice

Rule-led exclusion: 'hyper', 'hard' and 'soft' exit.[15] After the Intergovernmental Conference of the Autumn of 2003, the Constitution draft went through a first revision process.[16] It now has to receive the approbation of all EU citizens either through a vote in Parliament or by a referendum at best in the Spring of 2005.[17] Rejection will then become a real danger, because the ballot could be used (as is usually the case in representative democracies) as a way of passing judgement in retrospect on both the orientation taken by European integration since Maastricht and the already decided enlargement to include countries in Eastern Europe.

It must be noted first that it has now been more than ten years since EU citizens were asked directly for their opinion on Community matters, and there is no real reason why they should not seize a new opportunity to give an overall assessment of the years that have passed since the 1992 referendums. What is at stake in a democratic consultation covers both past achievements and future prospects. If one assumes that citizens will decide to consider only economic issues before casting their vote – because this is the part of European reality that comes closest to meeting the citizens' own concerns and expectations – how safely can it be assumed that they will give their support to the project? Were the 1990s such a success in terms of growth and employment on the 'old continent' that a 'yes' vote can be taken for granted? Why should the general dissatisfaction with politics, so much decried at national level, not apply also to Europe? Even though the draft constitution may be of dubious quality, the member states would carry a huge responsibility if the project were to fail, because they have credited their national accounts with all the gains from economic integration since 1992, while all the losses have been added to the Community's debit side.

Furthermore, EU citizens could use the vote on the constitution to censor enlargement, since they have not been consulted on this issue and while they are unable to evaluate its benefits but are able to fear its drawbacks. Can it be said for certain that the stakes, or even the modalities, of EU enlargement have been explained clearly to them? In this respect, surveys at the time of writing on the state of European public opinion show that in France, Germany, the United Kingdom, Austria and Belgium, the citizens – the majority of them in some cases – are strongly opposed to enlargement.[18] If the votes to be cast in 2004, just after the membership of the new entrants of the CEE countries' first wave has become effective, are guided by future rather than past projections, then a 'yes' vote is still less certain: even applicant countries which have just escaped from communism have entered the Union only reluctantly.

Out of the twenty-five consultations to be held, one single 'no' return – to within 0.5 per cent – would suffice to bring the European project to a halt. Two or three negative results would put it in jeopardy. The importance of the challenge posed by the failure of the EU's democratization process is assessed quite easily with the risk of 'hyper exit' (whereby the decision of retrospective withdrawal by one or more members would bring institutional chaos to the rest of the Union). It will take more than federalists burning with fervour and passionate conviction (as were Hamilton, Madison and Jay) to talk citizens out of using their power of last resort in a punitive fashion.

Let us imagine that the citizens, being both lenient and idealist, finally agree to ratify the European constitution. What of the equilibrium in this new regime, more than ever subjugated to the Rule? To answer this question, voluntary withdrawal from the Union, a fundamental institutional innovation usually hardly ever mentioned, must be considered. Article I-59 of the draft constitution provides in its first paragraph: 'Any Member State may decide to withdraw from the European Union in accordance with its own constitutional requirements.' This new provision opens up two prospects of what can be referred to as a 'hard exit'. It is first, potentially dangerous because it may bring about a weakening of mutual commitment, a possibility made even more likely with twenty-five members than with fifteen. Because all member states are aware that they are able to exercise this exit clause, they may feel less willing to try to influence EU decisions, or less determined to seek a delicate compromise when confronted with the conflict – or even the sometimes psycho-dramatic – situations of which only the Union has the secret.

Conversely, this possibility, if used subtly by member states, might have the advantage of facilitating the extension of qualified majority voting, since the threat of secession could effectively replace the right of veto in the case of serious infringement of a member state's vital interests. This dynamic and strategic alternative, possibly founded on game theory, is expressly envisaged in the project that provides, in paragraph 4 of article I-59 quoted above, that: 'a State which has withdrawn from the Union' can ask 'to re-join'.

'Soft exit', namely the development of enhanced co-operation between member states, is the third possibility offered by the EU's new architecture. On this point, the historical role played by the Iraq crisis may deserve to be underlined, as the EU's future was probably foreshadowed by the de facto enhanced co-operation that ensued. Even though the future of Europe was long held captive by the dilemma of enlargement and deepening, it will now probably depend on the resolution of the unity versus uniformity dialectic. 'Variable geometry' will undoubtedly lie at the heart of the European debate over both enlargement and freedom of choice. Keeping an equal distance between the federal and the intergovernmental models – in other words, establishing a 'federation of nation states', according to the original formulation so dear to the French but which has now been accepted by virtually all of its partners, is what makes the European project so unique. It is therefore worthwhile to run through the spectrum of all the possible and desirable institutional combinations within this field, but the 'intergovernmental federalism' modalities that would govern this 'differentiated' Europe must first be specified. To date, article I-43 of the draft project provides that 'Member States which wish to establish enhanced cooperation between themselves within the framework of the Union's non-exclusive competences may make use of its Institutions.'

On this matter, it must be remembered that the canonical model of 'variable geometry' takes a geographical approach to diversity and makes the distinction between two political entities. First, there is a core made up of the countries that are involved in the largest number of co-operative projects and are both capable and willing to deepen mutual co-operation. Then, on the periphery, are the countries that either cannot or do not wish to integrate any further, and therefore limit their participation to the schemes relating to the intergovernmental principle. In the 'model of Lamers' named after the former German representative Karl Lamers, countries are placed in concentric circles and the core consists of the countries with the highest functional integration level. The various stages in this polarized distribution process then set the norm and become the single reference for the countries that had originally chosen to stay away and the subsequently decide to become part of the Union. In contrast, the 'Balladur model' named after the former French Prime Minister consists of eccentric circles, in which several centres coexist – one for each of the functional integration spheres. The various integration processes can then become intertwined, but one single process type sets the norm for each integration sphere.

In the end, it would still remain to be seen whether the cross-breeding of these different enhanced co-operation types might result in the merger of the states concerned, and if the possibility really exists of 'going back to Rome' to start all over again, this time beginning with politics. There is currently no sign that we are heading that way. In that case, can we make a return to politics by any other route? Faced with 'exit Europe', does 'voice Europe' stand any chance of being allowed to build up the real democratic skills needed to secure economic stability?

The virtue of 'voice': democratizing Europe, Europeanizing democracies

If such a chance does exist, it demands that gradual and pragmatic reforms be carried out, to allow the return of a government in which freedom of choice takes precedence over the Rule. Europe cannot become our future if it is not grounded in democracy. As has already been advocated by many, it is essential to make the Union's institutions more democratic, which does not imply that we should all be chanting that now famous 'go back to politics' mantra, for what does this claim for more democracy in fact mean? It would be very simplistic to focus only on voting methods or the different types of representative democracy, even though it is obvious that they play a central part. The people's right to question broad economic policy decisions on a regular basis indeed serves as a safeguard against complete loss of contact with everyday reality. It follows from this that democracy enhances pragmatism, whereas a political regime locked into a set of inflexible rules dictated by a doctrine that dominated only a brief moment in history leads to rigidity, or even to dogmatism.

Yet there is more to democracy than the right to vote, as it also involves procedures and achievements. Procedures grant responsibility and credibility to public office-holders and promote the transparent functioning of the system: how can it be justified, for example, that ECB leaders may not be accountable for their decisions to any political authority that has the power to amend their statutes? Achievements are most important too, because credibility stems from accountability and transparency. Furthermore, credibility constitutes a major economic stake that guides the behaviour of investors and other market operators, thus democracy also contributes to economic efficiency.

However, the relationships between democracy and the economy are much more complex than they might at first appear. They more often than not create insurmountable tensions between individualism and inequality (the market principle) on the one hand, or between public space and the quest for equality (the democratic principle) on the other. Whereas the finger of blame is often pointed at market failure, the flaws of democracy are denounced much less frequently. Yet when it is left to the whims of fluctuating majorities to arbitrate and decide on economic issues, democracy can also prove damaging, as it may then harm overall economic efficiency, the interests of minorities and the universal need for social justice. In this sense, entrusting elective democracy with the total command of wealth and employment distribution is bound to produce instability and, in the longer term, put democracy's own future at risk. This explains why democracy progresses along an exclusive, extended time-scale aligned with various sets of principles, institutional provisions and procedures, such as individual freedom and constitutions, for example, which cannot be defeated so easily by a majority vote.

But let us be reassured on this point: it is not an excess of democracy that is currently threatening Europe's economic government. Harsher constraints have been imposed on governments whose distributive power has subsequently been curbed in the name of social and tax competition,[19] all of which has remodelled our societies' system of equality and gradually pared down democracy.

In this democracy versus market conflict, the standard order of values demands that democracy has priority over the economic principle, rather than the reverse. And yet, more often than not, reform policy is assessed against economic efficiency criteria. In 1981, Dan Usher[20] was already suggesting that another criterion be used. Is a specific policy likely to enhance democracy or will it not rather weaken it? Will it rally public support, or is it more likely to bring discredit on the political system? Is any reform workable without popular assent, or is it simply doomed to fail when forced on to the people? What efficiency principle can be erected against people's right to lead their life in the way they choose?

In addition to its intrinsic qualities, democracy is most flexible and proves to be resilient in the worst circumstances. It proceeds from an enlightening and convincing debate over making clear and explicit choices, as a result of which, what used to be taken for granted may well be confirmed as invalidated. However, democracy must handle novelty with a certain amount of discretion because the confines of pre-established rules may cause some disarray. In brief, there can be no governance without sovereignty. The success of the political Union depends on a project for the future whose prioritized objectives are shared by all. Unfortunately, the negotiations on Europe's future borders ignore this principle: they focus instead on the technical requirements – which indeed make room for a minimum standard of democratic rights, but this is the least they can do – for joining the free market economies. Such criteria definitely leave us all in the dark about what is to become of the geographical map of Europe.

The route to political Europe takes the exact opposite direction to the one taken so far. This implies that, instead of reassuring its government with the comfort of the current rules, we should be heading for a government led by freedom of choice. Hence Europe must be made more democratic and national democracies more European thanks to the dynamics of a dual approach. Two pragmatic and yet crucial reforms of the European regulatory state can be considered, as they could act as a lever for improving European unification.

To start with, it is not a sound practice to detach the ECB from all democratic reality, although logic (and economic analysis) suggest that monetary policy should be given a fairly large amount of independence. This is why it must be made accountable to some sort of political assembly: 'it is unsound to leave (ECB) in utter solitude', to paraphrase Tomaso Padoa Schioppa, an ECB executive board member.

It also appears the Bank has decided on too high an inflation target, which will either force it to run an over-tight monetary policy or damage its credibility. It is no secret that EU inflation clearly overshot since 2000 because the ECB kept an eye on both employment and growth, and not just on inflation. So, why not announce it publicly? What of transparency? Of course, virtually all the participants in the debate over monetary policy agree that confessing to having any other objective than price stability is not a good strategy for a central bank (this 'secret/ not so secret' strategy decision was confirmed in the ECB's own evaluation of its monetary strategy presented in May 2003; see Box 2.2). Can democracy live with it, and as time goes by, will this hidden objective be remembered? But, again, referring to the idea that central banks should pursue explicitly a target for growth and employment – which they obviously all watch most closely – is so heterodox that it is better left unsaid. *Eppure si muove.*

Box 2.2   ECB reform, as seen by the ECB

In October 1998 the Governing Council of the ECB announced the main elements of its stability-oriented monetary policy. The strategy consists of a quantitative definition of price stability and a two-pillar framework for assessing risks to price stability. After more than four years, the Governing Council felt it would be useful to evaluate its strategy in the light of its experience. On 8 May 2003 it confirmed the definition of price stability as a year-on-year increase in the Harmonised Index of Consumer Prices (HICP) for the euro area of below 2%. Price stability is to be maintained over the medium term. The Council also clarified that, in the pursuit of price stability, it aims to maintain inflation rates below, but close to, 2% over the medium term. Furthermore, the Governing Council confirmed that its monetary policy decisions will continue to be based on a comprehensive analysis of the risks to price stability, comprising an economic analysis and a monetary analysis. It thereby retains the two-pillar approach to the organisation, assessment and cross-checking of policy-relevant information. The President's Introductory Statement to the ECB's monthly press conference has been restructured to better reflect this approach. Furthermore, the Governing Council decided to no longer review the monetary reference value on an annual basis.

Source: ECB (2003).

Furthermore, the Stability Pact must be reformed, since even the European Commission acknowledges its serious deficiencies (see Box 2.3). A zero norm for structural deficit excluding investment would be preferable to the current provision. As public investment is not really easy to

---

Box 2.3   The European Commission's SGP evaluation since 1999

Seven euro area countries and ten EU Member States reached budget positions of 'close to balance or in surplus' by 2001. Government debt to GDP ratios have generally been on a downward trajectory with large reductions being recorded in several Member States. This created room for the automatic stabilisers to operate during the current economic slowdown, which contrasts with previous downturns when governments had to tighten fiscal policies so as to prevent debt levels from entering unsustainable trajectories. In addition, several Member States have been able to pursue ambitious tax reform strategies and some improvements have been recorded in re-directing public expenditures towards more productive items that are conducive to growth and employment.

Some Member States, however, have failed to complete the transition to the 'close to balance or in surplus' requirement of the SGP. Deficit levels in Portugal reached 4.1% of GDP in 2001 and the Council, on 5 November 2002, adopted a Decision on the existence of an excessive deficit position. Deficit levels have exceeded 3% of GDP since 2002 in France and Germany, and the Commission has adopted a report under Article 104(3) of the Treaty on the risk of an excessive deficit position.

There are also worrying developments as regards government debt where slight increases have been recorded in several Member States. Italy and Greece give most cause for concern as their debt levels remain well above 100% of GDP, very little progress has been made in the past four years to reduce debt levels towards the 60% of GDP reference value. These Member States could have been expected to record significant decreases in the debt ratio, but this did not materialise mainly on account of large and persistent debt increasing financial operations. Moreover, these developments have taken place despite the reduction in interest rates following their membership in the euro area.

Source: European Commission, 'Strengthening the Co-ordination of Budgetary Policies', COM (2002) 668 final, Brussels.

define, the European Council should make a decision on what types of spending come under that category. It is possible to imagine that such a decision may lead the Council to encourage governments to direct public resources towards the spending choices officially designated as most useful at European summits: European networks, research and development (R&D), higher education, new technologies and so on. Besides yielding better results than co-ordination, which always involves a long and difficult process, this political definition could be an effective way of fostering European policy in fields that are essential to Europe's future.

This would put enough pressure on national fiscal policies to keep the ECB satisfied, while leaving European governments with sufficient room for manoeuvre to enable them to withstand cyclical contingencies and run the policies best suited to the societies they have to govern. This rule therefore gives each country some leeway to decide on which part of wealth produced should be allocated to public expenditure, as investment choices may vary from country to country. A common European definition of investment will in future grant the European Council some effective power to promote the development of its own projects. Although it is not necessarily conducive to public debt stability, the new rule implies that all debt increases translate into higher public investment. Within this new framework, the euro area governments would be allowed to stimulate future growth in full compliance with the European Commission's decisions. The rule changes would thus open up a wider range of choices.

Such loosening of fiscal policy constraints would bring a welcome breath of fresh air. Released from the pressure of national governments no longer tightly harnessed under the restrictive provisions of the Stability and Growth Pact, the ECB could then take a more active part in macroeconomic regulation. Besides, the public debt trends presently fuelling the ECB's fears of renewed price instability would then relate to potential growth-inducing investment unlikely to cause inflation.

Conversely, national democracies must be made more European.[21] This calls for the setting up of a largely original system of political institutions that come under neither the intergovernmental nor the federal classification. To ensure the proper functioning of democracy in the Union as well as the legitimacy of the ensuing choices, national institutions must remain at the heart of European issues because they will still be felt as the most legitimate for a long time to come. In this respect, the 'Protocol on the role of national parliaments in the European Union' annexed to the draft constitution presented by the

Convention is far from satisfactory, to say the least. Cautiously 'recalling that the way in which individual national parliaments scrutinise their own governments in relation to the activities of the Union is a matter for the particular constitutional organisation and practice of each Member State', it does not go beyond stating the desire 'to encourage greater involvement of national Parliaments in the activities of the European Union and to strengthen their ability to express their views on legislative proposals as well as on other matters which may be of particular interest to them'.

The Convention ought to have gone much further. Instead of proposing the appointment of a European Secretary of State for External Affairs with an empty portfolio, it should have focused on the fairly minor role assigned at present to the ministers for European affairs in national governments. Europe should not merely come under the authority of foreign affairs but rather be upgraded as a fully-fledged department, headed by a Secretary of State enjoying indisputable prominence. The incumbent would be granted such high-ranking status that s/he would take precedence over all other Cabinet members apart from the prime minister, and might therefore be conferred the title of deputy prime minister. The agenda of national Parliaments also needs reviewing. Too much time is spent on domestic matters, whereas discussion regarding Europe is accorded low priority and is most often relegated to Committee sessions. In-depth debate over Europe's far-reaching options should come first.

Conclusion: the EU, empire or republic?

This entire chapter has been pervaded by the challenge of the imminent eastern enlargement. Is the EU ready for it? The following logic test question should help to reach an answer. After implementing the reforms proposed by the Convention, would the EU, taken as a candidate country, be entitled to join the European Union? Let us clarify the question terms, to be certain that we eventually come to a conclusive answer: what exactly does EU enlargement involve? If this means even more regulation, an extension of the empire of the Rule, then the answer must be that never in its history has the EU ever come close to accepting such a challenge. Assuming reform is about the expansion of democratic rights produces a diametrically opposed answer: the European Union has never been so far removed from the 'ideal republic'.

This inevitably leads to comparisons. Although the USA has recently been described as being endowed with attributes of power and Europe as representing weakness,[22] both share a tendency to fumble their way between empire and republic. Yet, the trajectory they each pursue does not diverge like that of Mars and Venus. The USA is only striving to build a democratic empire, whereas the European imperium offers to substitute human rights for citizens' freedom. As a consequence, the USA will eventually come under threat around the margins of its empire, and Europe is already being struck in its inner core, and deprived of sovereignty.

It is a fact that democracy and sovereignty cannot be dissociated from one another. Far from being the unfortunate result of a specific flaw in the functioning of European institutions, 'democratic deficit' flows from the different logic on which each of our different societies is based. National democracies may agree to being divested of part of their sovereignty to make room for an all-European public space, but if the newly-formed space is not governed according to the principles of democracy at the European level, it will give rise to a twin democratic deficit. This double imbalance is common knowledge among economists: although it stems from only one cause, it brings about many damaging consequences.

Part II
Convergence and Cohesion

Part II
Convergence and Cohesion

3
The Mirages of Nominal Illusion: Variations on Convergence[1]

The euro, the European single currency, was launched in Europe on 1 January 1999, and the subsequent Economic and Monetary Union (EMU) now comprises virtually all European Union (EU) members, namely twelve countries out of fifteen; the United Kingdom, Denmark and Sweden chose to opt out. However successful, economic policy management has never produced a perfect solution to a certain number of fundamental issues. How can a single monetary policy be made compatible with specific economic backgrounds (economic cycles, inflation); independent and yet capped fiscal policies; distinct labour markets; and different economic and social patterns?

The Maastricht Treaty, and later the Stability Pact, have forged a very precise type of economic management to help reinforce the credibility of the euro area. To reach this goal, an independent European Central Bank (ECB) was set up, with curbing inflation as its major objective; public deficits were capped, yet no co-ordination strategy between monetary and fiscal policy was imposed. Even so, the euro area was then deemed to be ready to become an area of monetary and financial stability generating investment and economic growth. Unfortunately, mere compliance with this academic diktat did not deliver the expected results. The period of high growth without significant inflationary pressure that characterized the first euro years was probably related more to the weakness of the euro against the dollar than to any ECB-induced 'virtuous' circle. As became obvious in subsequent years, the European authorities' (the European governments) focus on issues of nominal convergence did not succeed in correcting underlying divergent trends. At the dawn of the twenty-first century, the euro area remains clearly torn between countries with mass unemployment and countries constantly developing new technologies. Even though some of the differences have deservedly resulted in 'smaller' countries catching up with 'larger' ones, it remains evident that current economic policy management cannot both encourage such efforts and bolster declining economies.

The convergence criteria

Basically, it all started with the Maastricht Treaty, if one overlooks the so-called period of 'competitive disinflation' which, despite its well-known negative impact on real convergence, was the first attempt at nominal convergence (Fitoussi, 1995). To a very large extent, EMU institutional provisions, applying from 1 January 1999, were laid out in the Maastricht Treaty, which was signed on 9–10 December 1991. In addition, the Stability Pact was adopted in Amsterdam in June 1997, with the December 1997 Council of Luxembourg dealing with the final details.

Among other provisions, the Maastricht Treaty laid out the EU member states' objectives and tasks: 'The Community shall have as its task, by establishing a common market and an economic and monetary union and by implementing common policies or activities... to promote throughout the Community a harmonious, balanced and sustainable development of economic activities, a high level of employment and of social protection... sustainable and non-inflationary growth, a high degree of... convergence of economic performance' (article 2).

Despite the explicit reference to employment, Article 3A shows the Treaty's marked preference for the fight against inflation:

> [The activities of the member states] shall include... the irrevo-cable fixing of exchange rates leading to the introduction of a single currency... and the definition and conduct of a single monetary policy and exchange-rate policy the primary objective of both of which shall be to maintain price stability and, without prejudice to this objective, to support the general economic policies in the Community, in accordance with the principle of an open market economy with free competition.

The Treaty also laid out the prerequisites for EMU entry. Member states had to fulfil the following five conditions, including four convergence criteria (article 121):

- independence of the central bank (article 108);
- observance of the normal fluctuation margins provided for by the exchange-rate mechanism of the European Monetary System, for at

least two years, without devaluing against the currency of any other member state;

- inflation must not be more than 1.5 percentage point above that of, at most, the three best-performing EU states' average inflation rate;
- long-term interest rates must not be more than two percentage points above that of, at most, the three best performing member states' average inflation rate; and
- government deficits and debts must not exceed respectively 3 and 60 per cent of GDP.

The underlying idea was that all the countries had to prove they could abide by certain sound management criteria before joining the EMU. Launching the single currency at a much earlier date and leaving it to the EMU's in-built mechanisms to produce convergence might have been possible, but this reversed alternative was finally rejected. The original conditions later applied to the new members' (eight CEECs – *Central and Eastern European countries* plus Malta and Cyprus) applications for entry into the euro area, although the reversed alternative could have been selected. It must be noted, however, that, for a time, some countries such as Poland suggested that they might simply adopt the euro unilaterally and merely ignore the Maastricht criteria prerequisites.

Convergence and asymmetry

The Maastricht Treaty selection criteria were applied to decide which countries should be allowed to take part in the EMU. The criteria's economic rationale is fairly straightforward: for exchange rates to remain stable, differentials in inflation rates must be brought down, since differentials are partly responsible for exchange rate levels.

Although monetary union brings in gains – cuts in transaction costs and no exchange rate instability – fixed parities have some costs too, notably because of the theory of optimum currency areas which says that bilateral exchange rates can no longer be used for adjustment when the Union's economies are affected in different ways and hit by so-called 'asymmetrical shocks'.[2] Once deprived of that adjustment tool, the monetary union's governments have to find other ways of absorbing the shocks, if the member states' economies are not to fall out of step. Various market mechanisms may be applied, such as factor mobility and price flexibility,[3] or other centralized mechanisms. It is a fact that worker mobility is extremely weak in Europe, so prices, and more especially wages, are not very flexible. Such adjustment mechanisms are then far from appropriate for absorbing asymmetrical shocks. Centralized transfer procedures between member states may then be considered (Mélitz and Vori, 1993).

Asymmetries are closely related to the economic convergence process. In the event of a transitional asymmetrical shock, economies can steer away temporarily from their natural convergence path and the support of temporary stabilization policies may then be needed. When confronted by a permanent asymmetrical shock, economies can diverge on a longer-term basis. Longer-term redistribution policies can help in going back to the original convergence level.

As far as nominal indicators are concerned – namely, prices, wages and interest rates – it was clear from the start of the euro area that convergence had already made a good deal of progress, although the same can be said for areas outside the European Union. Real convergence, however, was far from effective, and European real asymmetries remained fairly significant.

Convergence and nominal symmetry

Nominal convergence prevailed, but extended beyond Europe

Fuss (1998b) has shown that, over a fairly long period of time (1960–96), macroeconomic shocks had a broad symmetrical impact on nominal variables – that is, inflation rates, nominal interest rates and nominal salary growth rates, in most EU member states, the USA, Canada and Japan.[4] The analysis of nominal convergence was carried out with Germany, France and the USA as 'target countries'. A summary of the results is shown in Figure 3.1, where arrows point to the countries undergoing a convergence process in 1996. The countries sharing a box, without any arrows linking them, had already completed the process.

Overall convergence levels were high: for all indicators and for most countries, the series had been completed or was in the process of converging. Such convergence could relate to progress in European integration, more especially to the discipline induced by the EMU Exchange Rate Mechanism (ERM), or to the economic policies the Maastricht criteria demanded. However, other factors probably also came into play, since convergence occurred between European member states as well as between countries from outside the Union. For example, most (OECD) countries' governments ran counter-inflationary policies after the second oil shock in the 1970s. Inflation rates consequently became much less scattered over the 1980s, as shown in Figure 3.2.

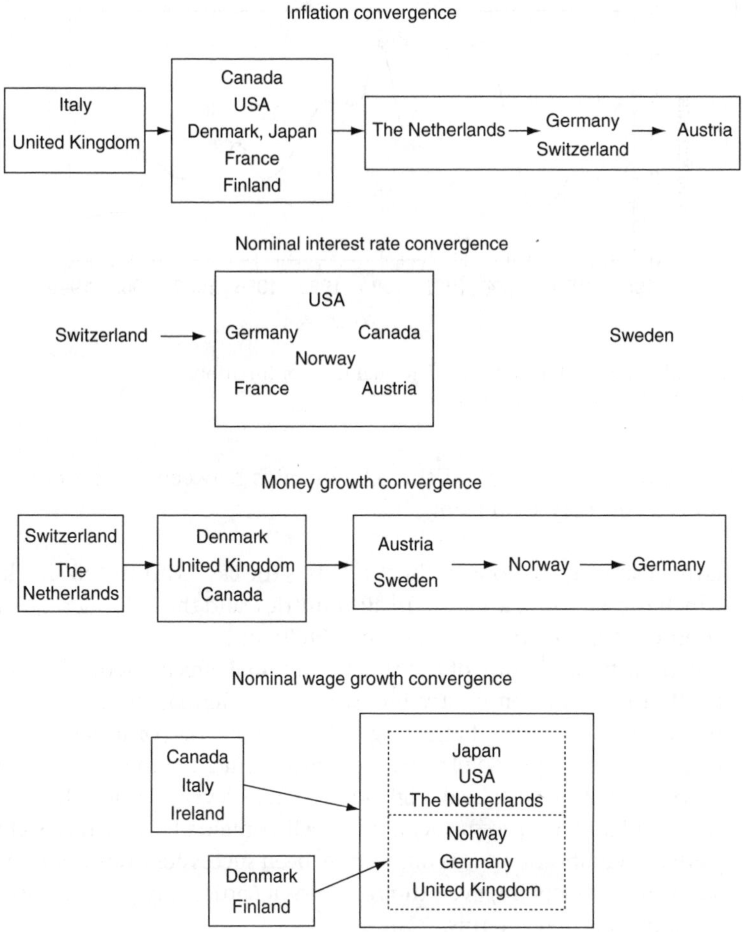

Inflation convergence

Nominal interest rate convergence

Money growth convergence

Nominal wage growth convergence

Figure 3.1 Analysis of nominal convergence

Nominal convergence proved fairly shock-resistant

The nominal convergence process could still be affected by asymmetrical shocks. Among all the major macroeconomic shocks of the past decades – the two oil shocks (outside shocks on the terms of trade) of the 1970s, German reunification in 1990 (a shock specific to one single country), and the 1992–3 speculation crisis on the currency exchange markets – tests prove that only the currency exchange markets crisis seems to have had

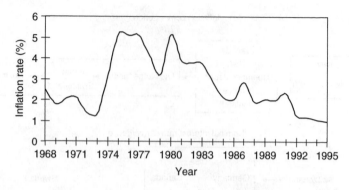

Figure 3.2   Standard deviations of annual rates of inflation
Source: OECD; authors' calculations.

a lasting negative impact on the relationships between the economies reviewed. This may stem from:

- Overall similar reactions to shocks. This is the case with the oil shocks, which caused rising inflation in all countries, and thus the subsequent counter-inflationary policies of the 1980s; and
- The transitional feature of the shocks' nominal effects. German reunification caused a temporary increase in the German money supply (see Figure 3.3) without affecting either interest rate or inflation rate levels over a long period of time. Tight management of the reunification process, such as sustained high interest rate levels, meant that any rising inflationary pressure could be well contained. With hindsight, German reunification turns out to have been successful from a nominal adjustment viewpoint, even though it was a particularly painful adjustment process in real terms.

By contrast, the currency exchange market crisis brought significant changes to the links between European interest rates. Figure 3.4 shows most clearly the convergence of German and French rates over the 1980s an up to 1992, and then divergence as soon as the crisis broke in September. The gap was closed after the fluctuation bands were widened in August 1993. Yet some gaps reappeared in 1995 in tandem with a slight weakening of the French franc. Interest rate convergence seemed to prove irreversible only at the very end of the period – shortly before the introduction of the euro.

There were many reasons for the crisis. As a result, the Italian lira and the British pound had to leave the EMU, and other European currencies

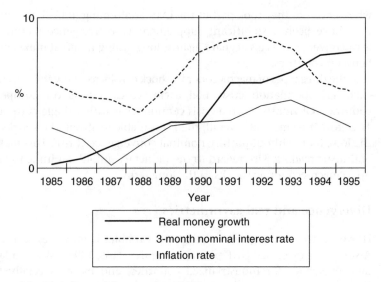

Figure 3.3   The effects of German reunification
Source: OECD.

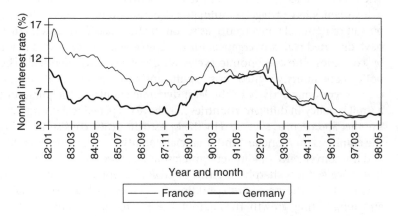

Figure 3.4   The effects of the currency crisis on nominal interest rates

were devalued. This particular example shows the co-ordination problems that might arise when economic cycles become desynchronized. As Germany's economic policy objectives demanded sustained high interest rates to contain rising inflation, they came into conflict with France or Italy, both of which required lower rates.

The part played by European integration in the nominal convergence process is ambiguous. Although all member states' economies converged, whether or not they took part in the EMS, conforming to EMS discipline may have been a significant supplementary convergence factor. At least convergence is a safeguard against long-lasting nominal imbalances between countries.

In the three types of macroeconomic shock considered, only the currency exchange speculation crisis had asymmetrical effects on European countries. Obviously, such a crisis cannot occur with a single currency. Therefore it seems that, overall, the EU was able to absorb the shocks in the long term without putting nominal convergence at risk. This makes optimistic reading with regard to the monetary union's aptitude to face up to macroeconomic shocks in the long term.

Divergence and real asymmetries

However, the convergence of real term variables is much less certain. A similar study of real GDP per capita figures (Fuss, 1998a) shows a lack of convergence for industrialized countries, and more especially for European countries.

There seems to be a complex link between nominal and real convergence. The very existence and nature of the links between money variables and real variables have triggered animated debates among economists. The pursuit of nominal convergence as set out by the Maastricht criteria may have distorted real convergence, for the convergence efforts were made by countries whose economic cycles were not perfectly identical. The policy constraints weighed most significantly in a pro-cyclical fashion on the economic activity of the least dynamic countries: the pursuit of a similar policy in different countries may have deepened real divergence. Another approach, as suggested by the Maastricht treaty, consists in laying the emphasis on monetary and financial stability through price stability and the convergence of long-term interest rates. Subsequently, economies have diverged less sharply in terms of GDP per capita: price stability is deemed to be the necessary condition for achieving high, sustainable and long-lasting growth throughout the EU to the advantage of all participants. At any rate, this is what the rhetoric says.

The European heart is not yet ready to welcome all nations

While debates over the achievement of monetary union focused for some time on the existence of a two-speed Europe, which might demand that monetary union be carried out in two stages, several studies of European countries' asymmetries endeavoured to group together the countries with similar reactions to particular types of economic shocks, and thus distinguish which countries formed Europe's heart. Although this debate is no longer topical, identifying intra-European diversity remains essential, as it clearly shows which asymmetry factors can still play a part now that monetary union is in place.

The origins of such asymmetries are manifold. They can be national – with German reunification being an example;[5] regional – floods in one region depress only that region's GDP, regardless of the rest of Europe's economic prospects; or sector-based – for example, a cut in steel prices on world markets. They can be caused by supply or demand shocks, or even by the desynchronization of economic cycles. A common shock such as a large fluctuation in the dollar or a financial market crisis may also have asymmetrical effects; thus oil shocks have had different consequences for Japan and for the USA, because Japan is much more dependent on the outside world for its supply of oil products. The desynchronization of economic cycles can equally cause asymmetries in so far as countries going through different stages at the same moment in time require differentiated economic policies.

Although it is commonly accepted that Germany, Belgium and the Netherlands form Europe's heart, there is no consensus as regards the heart's exact perimeter, whose size depends on how asymmetries are identified. It seems asymmetries caused by supply and demand shocks have become less frequent over time,[6] and that asymmetries are national rather than sector-based occurrences.[7] Finally, if economic cycles do become more synchronized over time, some find it even this is not enough.[8]

Recent studies of Central and East European Countries (CEECs) (Fidrmuc and Korhonen, 2001) showed that the reference to Europe's 'heart' was a relative notion by trying to assess the pace at which some most recent EU member states, such as Spain and Portugal were able to close their development gap with the 'European heart'. It may therefore not be fanciful to imagine the same could hold true for CEEC countries.

European regions dominated by the divergence of a selective heart

All convergence studies of European regions show that, whatever the method used, convergence first occurred from the 1950s until the oil shocks of the 1970s, followed by divergence in the 1980s and 1990s.[9] Figure 3.5 confirms this diagnosis: real regional per capita GDP standard deviation indeed increased over the 1980s.

As has been noted by numerous authors, regional dispersion rates exceed national dispersion, and regional asymmetries within the same country can be larger than asymmetries between different nations.

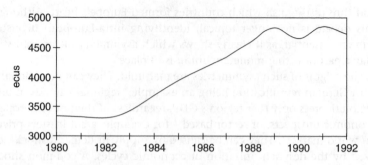

Figure 3.5   Standard deviations of regional per capita GDP
Source: Eurostat.

Conversely, regions of different countries may bear more resemblance to one another than to regions inside a single country, and consequently respond in symmetrical fashion to economic shocks.[10] By the same token, geographically close regions could be linked by externalities arising from the spread of technology, the exchange of information, know-how and human capital, or the use of common networks.[11] The suggestion that shocks travel across borders is not well supported by existing empirical studies. Inversely, common economic policies and institutions link up the same country's regions and the national component does appear to have a significant impact on GDP growth and regional employment.[12]

Asymmetry studies based on the regional approach do not all come to the same conclusions.[13] Yet a distinction can be drawn between highly integrated northern Europe and more loosely integrated southern Europe. It can also be observed that European regional asymmetries are far from being insignificant. In regional terms, the 'European heart' appears to comprise Belgium, most French regions, some of northern Italy's regions, and some German and Dutch regions.[14]

The analysis of current monetary unions – unions in which states have their own independent governments – cannot be transposed rashly to the case of the European monetary union. It must be emphasized, however, that countries are often made up of diverse regions, which tends to indicate that a national monetary union allows for some degree of asymmetry. This applies to Germany, a federal country, but also to the Netherlands and Italy, which both have some extremely specialized regions.

When monetary union causes intensified regional specialization, the occurrence of asymmetrical shocks will become even more likely. Then activity diversification within each country will also increase, so that asymmetry becomes both more intensified at the regional level and more reduced at the national level. Thus some analyses conclude that the situation observed is rather that of intensifying regional specialization,[15] which in turn induces more national diversification and eventually more symmetry.[16]

Regions versus nations: how far should policies become centralized?

Because of these comments on asymmetry levels – whether national or regional – which mechanisms of adjustment to asymmetrical shocks are available and best suited to monetary union? Within a country, regional asymmetry levels can be lowered through a national insurance system, or through either cross-regional or cross-sector labour mobility, because culture and language barriers do not make for any real obstacle. In contrast, the first of the mechanisms described above cannot absorb national asymmetry levels. Only instruments centralized at the European level would be able to address the problem, which means that different shocks need different centralization levels.

Does this not also imply that the option of different centralization levels should be considered? Existing studies come to mixed conclusions regarding this issue too: some show that asymmetrical shocks have national rather than sector-based causes,[17] which tends to advocate that mechanisms centralized at the European level can address shocks that are not strictly sector-based. But others show that regional asymmetry levels are higher than national ones:[18] national states should then be left to play a major part in dealing with the problem.

It must be added that these studies do not include the case of CEECs' application for EU membership. Despite the forced march imposed on them – these countries will have to embrace the entire EU past legislation (the *acquis communautaire*) in less than ten years, whereas it took the longest-standing member states over fifty years to absorb it – CEECs' production and specialization patterns are still different from those of the EU. Their taxation systems are still in embryo, which means that, on the one hand, they are more likely to be confronted with asymmetrical shocks, but on the other hand, and concomitantly, it puts them in a weaker position to respond adequately, as they cannot resort to counter-cyclical tax policies.

Convergence, both nominal and real, thus lies at the heart of European citizens' concerns. Which economic tool can remedy the issue most appropriately? When confronted with unwanted and limited migration flows[19] and some degree of nominal rigidity against a background of fixed exchange rates,[20] euro-area countries, and more generally all EU members, will have no other policy management tool but national fiscal policies, the common monetary policy (for euro-area countries) or a 'follower-type' monetary policy – in the case of ERM 2 members, whose monetary policy must show some degree of exchange rate stability against the euro. These policies should be essential in bringing back harmony and stability in the event of asymmetrical shocks within the EU.

4

Regional Differentials and Policies for Territorial Cohesion in the European Union

Since the late 1980s development gaps between the European Union (EU) member states have been narrowing. In a relatively short period of time, important catching-up events have emerged, alongside ongoing wide income discrepancies between regions within the individual member states. In a period of growing European integration and increasing Community efforts to encourage cohesion, the persistence of significant regional differentials poses two questions.

The first concerns the effects of a closer integration on regional inequalities; and the second relates to the efficiency of the regional policies that the EU has been carrying out with particular intensity since the late 1980s. These questions take on a still greater importance with the prospect of an EU enlargement, when development gaps will further widen and a policy of cohesion adapted to the new European geography will be necessary.

With reference to the consequences of European integration, the prevailing opinion among economists and policy-makers is that it might not encourage the narrowing of regional differentials, but – in some conditions – might widen the gaps. Indeed, the dismantling of trade barriers (including that represented by the exchange rate risk eliminated by the adoption of a single currency) reduces the transport costs of goods and services, and leads to a concentration of production activities in a relatively limited area of the EU, namely the one that is already rich and heavily populated.[1] The reason for the industrial agglomeration at the core of European regions is that 'clustering together' offers an advantage for firms. They benefit from locating close to each other because, for example, this gives them easier access to an ample supply of specialized productive inputs, to large pools of skilled labour, to high-quality infrastructure, and to the technical know-how developed in the nearby firms. Additionally, concentration is favoured by scale economies deriving from production being concentrated close to customers who are not scattered throughout the whole of the European territory; the cost reduction of transport in an integrated Europe makes it convenient for a firm to concentrate its activity in a single area (that is, the one where other firms cluster together), exploit scale economies and reach peripheral markets with low transportation costs.

The mechanisms of concentration/agglomeration resulting from efficiency criteria lead to increases in the distance between the core, where the heart of economic activity lies, and the periphery, where there are few manufacturing firms, apart from those closely linked to the exploitation of local natural resources (typically agriculture) and non-tradable production (mainly services). These tendencies are associated with two specific circumstances characterizing most of the EU territory: that is, a low propensity of the population to move 'between and within' the member states and, because of various types of institutional constraints, an inadequate interregional dispersion of wages according to the differing local labour market conditions. Hence the core/periphery gap, induced by integration, is mirrored in the widening of income gaps and, even more, in the gaps between unemployment and employment rates.

Within this framework, the EU regional policies (Structural Funds and the Cohesion Fund) aim at inverting the widening trend of regional development gaps. An objective based on the (implicit) idea that agglomeration determined by market forces, though caused by efficiency criteria, is too strong and socially unacceptable. Hence the need to oppose the 'natural' trends of localization by attempting to disperse the economic activities on the territory, and thus to contrast the 'unfair' outcome of market forces within the (institutional) targets of the Union.[2]

The approach followed by EU regional policies, particularly in the formulation of its most recent programmes (for the period 1994–9 and, even more so, for the programme concerning 2000–6) consists of creating favourable environmental conditions in the peripheral areas so as to attract productive activities and local development, by leaving to the choices/preferences of single member states those aspects concerning the market institutions that have an impact on domestic regional gaps (primarily, labour market functioning). To this end, the structural funds are well used (more than 60 per cent) to finance infrastructure in the regions that are lagging behind, because the infrastructural gap is thought to represent one of the main causes of geographical economic inequalities and, consequently, the improvement of infrastructure is the main instrument for promoting regional convergence. In this context, the term 'infrastructure' covers a wide area and comprises, apart from physical infrastructure (transport, telecommunications and energy), also education and labour force training (improvement of human capital). The remaining funds committed by the European Union consist mainly of direct aid to businesses.

Starting from these considerations, this chapter analyses the efficiency of regional structural policies – as they have been carried out since 1988 – against the objective of favouring the geographical cohesion of development levels. The main results are summarised below.

Attention is focused on the 'real' convergence of the regions of the twelve-member European Union (EU-12). The estimates (see the next section) confirm that in the latest period (late-1980s and 1990s) there was no regional convergence of real per capita incomes. The dynamics of the per capita income was analysed in its two components – namely, the employment rate and labour productivity. One observes that 'non-convergence' of regional developments is mainly caused by the failed reduction – indeed even to the rise – in the gaps in the employment rate. Labour productivity has shown some convergence. Besides, there is an interaction between productivity and employment rate that tends to widen geographical development gaps. Particularly since the early 1990s, the regions experiencing a productivity level lower than the EU-12 average have also experienced employment rises lower than the rest of the Union. EU regional policies have mainly been aimed at funding the construction of infrastructure, with the conviction that the infrastructural gap represents one of the main causes of geographical economic inequality.

The chapter then surveys the impact of public infrastructure on regional growth. The evidence shows that the infrastructure endowment has a positive influence on regional productivity, but exerts no direct effect on the employment rate. Indeed, there is an indirect effect of employment infrastructure leading to a sort of 'development trap': too low a level of infrastructure favours a relatively low level of productivity, which may imply an employment dynamic that is lower than average.

The regional policy instruments aimed at favouring cohesion are then investigated. Admittedly, the allocation of structural funds committed between 1988 and 1999 has been in compliance with the principles of equity and cohesion that the Community pursues. The funds were distributed according to the principle of inverse proportionality to per capita income, to infrastructure endowment, to population density, and directly proportional to the long-term unemployment rate and the weight of agriculture on the regional economy. Peripheral regions have benefited more from European Union spending than have other regions. Yet this remark may not be valid when one considers the regional distribution of the 'total value or cost of the projects to be financed' which includes – apart from the resources committed by the EU – the contribution of national (either central or regional) authorities, on the basis of the principle of additionality. The amount of this contribution strongly influences the overall value of the projects: about three-quarters of the regions have calculated a national–regional financing larger than the EU-12 average. The consideration of the national contribution falls short of the principle of equity observed in the Union's spending commitments. This stems from the lesser capacity to plan and fund characterizing the administrations of the backward regions. Given the relevance of national contributions, this conditions the regional distribution of the projects, which are correlated only weakly to regional per capita income levels, and have no significant relationship to the infrastructure endowment.

Once proved, the equity of structural fund distribution, but not the equity of the projects considered in their whole value (including national/regional co-financing), it is no surprise that the structural intervention had no positive and significant impact on the dynamics of productivity, employment and per capita income of the less-favoured regions. The framework is even more pessimistic if one considers the real use of the funds committed, which are not distributed uniformly between the different regions. One example is the case of Italy, where the percentage of total resources in fact allocated to the South in the period 1994–9 was smaller than that allocated to the North.

'Real' regional convergence: income, productivity and employment

The level of per capita GDP, measured in Purchasing Power Parity (PPP), is the main indicator adopted by the European Commission, as well as by other international institutions (the World Bank, the International Monetary Fund, OECD, the United Nations), to compare the development levels of different member states and regions. In this section, the investigation of the EU regional development is based on the examination of the member states' per capita GDP (or income).[3]

The development dynamics of the European regions mirror both the specific trends of those dynamics and the trends of the countries to which the regions belong. These two examples of behaviour – either regional or national – exerted different influences on the regional convergence process in the different phases of European integration. The available evidence shows that the per capita income gaps between regions and between European countries diminished gradually during the period of strong interregional and international labour mobility from 1950 until the mid-1970s, a process reflecting the real convergence of specific regional components.[4] In the 1975–85 decade, the development gaps widened and they have not narrowed again since the mid-1980s. Unlike in the period 1950–75, the recent narrowing of regional differences has been caused uniquely by the gradual but considerable narrowing of the gaps between countries. In other words, since the mid-1980s, the differentials between countries have been diminishing again, while those between different regions of a country remained almost unchanged. The convergence between European regions observed in recent years was just the result of the catching-up process started by some member states.[5]

The regional dispersion of per capita GDP may be measured by its standard deviation. This measure clearly shows how the total variability of the overall per capita incomes of the regions tends not to reduce significantly over the years. The analysis by country shows a considerable dispersion rise of per capita GDP levels between Italian regions during the 1990s, and a substantial invariance of the disparities within Germany, France, Spain, and the United Kingdom. A reduction of domestic gaps is observed for the regions of Portugal (limited to the period 1985–98) and for those of Greece (limited to the decade 1975–85). Since 1985, the per capita income dispersion between Greek regions has increased once more. The level of per capita real income of Ireland rose from 56 per cent of the EU-12 average in 1988 to 90 per cent in 1998[6] (see Table 4.1).

The regression estimates of the rate of growth on the initial level of the per capita value added show the lack of a regional convergence process in per capita incomes. The results of single member states (which are not reported here) are substantially in keeping with those of the standard deviation dynamics. Apart from few exceptions, a below-average per capita income does not by itself guarantee a better growth performance than the EU average.

An even more articulate interpretation of regional gaps shows that the EU regions might register not a global convergence process – that is, the convergence of the per capita income of all regions towards a common average value – but rather a convergence by single groupings, named 'clubs', having common geographical (for example, centre–periphery or North–South) or socioeconomic peculiarities (for example, the unemployment level). In other words, the regions might have registered

Table 4.1 Standard deviation of per capita income and percentage ratio between the average income level of each area and the centre*

	1975	1980	1985	1990	1995	1998
EU-12 regions	59.92	60.17	60.17	58.44	59.01	57.76
Italy	24.36	25.53	24.72	27.43	28.63	29.44
Germany	20.73	20.62	21.13	20.30	20.84	22.29
France	15.35	13.80	14.74	14.34	13.76	13.83
United Kingdom	12.42	14.07	13.49	14.67	14.14	14.49
Greece	22.09	17.99	14.37	15.63	17.84	18.44
Spain	22.62	20.61	20.47	21.02	20.67	20.88
Portugal	28.35	30.40	32.87	25.89	18.98	20.33
Benelux	19.20	18.55	18.66	17.33	16.03	16.35
Centre	27.20	28.59	28.52	26.41	24.93	24.57
Intermediate regions	19.83	22.87	22.03	21.28	21.58	20.52
Northern periphery	19.77	23.93	23.18	19.09	14.81	13.60
Northern periphery (without Ireland)	15.89	20.98	18.27	17.43	14.58	14.66
Southern periphery	62.66	59.48	59.25	57.50	59.40	57.71
Intermediate regions/Centre	85.51	88.76	88.66	89.44	90.71	90.01
Northern periphery/Centre	65.96	65.31	65.39	66.80	70.13	71.63
Northern periphery (without Ireland)/Centre	69.60	69.26	69.97	69.97	72.27	71.41
Southern periphery/Centre	47.60	44.77	43.79	45.46	45.98	46.08

Note: * The variable used to compute the standard deviation is the natural logarithm of the 1990 per capita income in PPP (deviation from the EU-12 average). The standard deviation values were multiplied by 100.
Source: ISAE elaborations on Cambridge Econometrics dataset.

a convergence within each club, even though there was no reduction in the development gaps between clubs. Following upon this approach, a regional ranking was made on the basis of a simple geographical criterion. Four regional groups were identified: centre, intermediate regions, southern periphery, northern periphery. The analysis of the longitudinal dispersion of the per capita income levels shows that, since 1985, a clear process of convergence has been emerging within the centre and the northern periphery. The results for the latter club vary significantly according to whether Ireland is included or not. The convergence process within intermediate regions appears to be weaker, while there is no gap narrowing within the southern periphery.

The ratio was also computed between the average per capita income levels of the peripheral areas plus the intermediate regions, and the average per capita incomes of the centre, to verify the presence of catching-up processes between clubs. The results show that only intermediate regions (limited to the period 1975–85) and those of the northern periphery (limited to the period 1985–98) registered a convergence process towards central regions.

More information on the regional gap dynamics may be drawn by subdividing the per capita income into its two components of labour productivity and employed/population ratio, and by extending the analysis of regional convergence. Generally speaking, labour productivity is influenced by capital endowment, by technology and by the regional employment sectoral pattern. The percentage of employees among the population is indeed influenced by the labour market conditions, as well as by cultural, social and demographic factors (population distribution by age and gender). Between the two components there may be a relationship which, in turn, is able to influence the regional gaps of the per capita income.

The examination of the labour productivity convergence shows a process of strong regional gap narrowing between 1975 and 1998, concentrated particularly in the late 1980s (see Figure 4.1). Looking at the single geographical areas (see Table 4.2), one observes how a net convergence process only occurs within the group of regions of the southern periphery: this club of regions has indeed not shown a recovery towards the central regions.

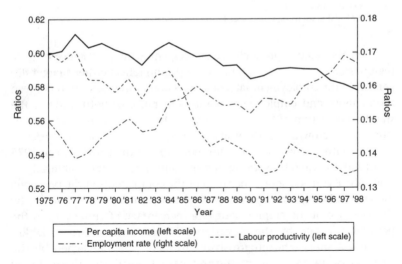

Figure 4.1 EU-12 regions: standard deviation of per capita income, labour productivity and employment rate
Source: Based on Cambridge Econometrics dataset.

Table 4.2 Standard deviation of per capita income and percentage ratio between the average productivity level of each area and the centre*

	1975	1980	1985	1990	1995	1998
EU-12 regions	60.02	57.65	57.82	53.99	53.93	53.01
Italy	15.74	16.52	16.82	17.17	16.45	15.17
Germany	11.49	10.39	10.70	10.72	11.67	12.77
France	12.18	11.18	11.16	9.92	9.91	10.05
United Kingdom	6.69	7.50	4.93	5.65	8.02	6.93
Greece	33.09	22.54	17.55	19.67	17.03	16.05
Spain	22.38	19.22	17.22	15.18	12.61	12.24
Portugal	26.33	30.22	33.98	32.88	24.59	30.26
Benelux	12.04	10.62	11.64	13.18	15.05	16.89
Centre	22.25	23.00	22.30	22.26	22.11	24.35
Intermediate regions	21.42	24.69	21.55	22.52	22.29	21.32
Northern periphery	20.30	24.53	21.75	21.96	20.68	20.33
Northern periphery (without Ireland)	19.49	24.78	21.59	23.31	22.08	21.91
Southern periphery	70.25	67.08	68.47	61.57	62.79	60.35
Intermediate regions/Centre	89.59	94.68	95.32	96.13	96.55	95.51
Northern periphery/Centre	72.52	73.12	76.52	79.42	79.57	79.78
Northern periphery (without Ireland)/Centre	74.2	75.34	78.87	80.46	80.40	79.92
Southern periphery/Centre	56.27	58.72	58.69	59.85	59.74	57.98

Note: * See note to Table 4.1.
Source: ISAE elaborations on Cambridge Econometrics dataset.

Given the relative productivity convergence, the persistence of wide regional gaps in the per capita income should reflect either a larger dispersion in the employment rate, or a reduction in the correlation between productivity and employment/population ratio, or both. Indeed, the standard deviation of the distribution of the employment share signals a dispersion growth over the years. Referring to single areas, one observes for the southern periphery a slight reduction in the gaps between 1975 and 1990, followed by a strong increase during the 1990s (Table 4.3).

Finally, Figure 4.2 shows the trend of the components of the per capita income variance, represented by the labour productivity variance; by the variance of the employment rate (percentage of employees in the population); and by the co-variance between those two variables. Figure 4.2 shows the progressively growing weight reached by the variance of the employment rate and, particularly during the 1990s, by the co-variance between this and labour productivity. This observation makes reference to the positive interaction between labour productivity

Table 4.3 Standard deviation of employment rate and percentage ratio between the average employment rate of each area and the centre*

	1975	1980	1985	1990	1995	1998
EU-12 regions	14.97	14.77	15.66	15.20	16.18	16.67
Italy	14.98	12.02	11.54	11.97	14.38	17.15
Germany	11.22	11.38	11.87	10.87	11.44	11.42
France	7.91	7.69	7.77	7.73	6.67	6.73
United Kingdom	9.38	9.60	11.42	10.62	8.49	9.84
Greece	22.86	13.14	7.45	8.61	14.25	14.66
Spain	11.69	10.99	11.67	11.02	12.05	12.52
Portugal	8.08	1.59	3.04	12.16	10.47	13.34
Benelux	17.31	17.05	17.75	18.26	19.70	21.54
Centre	16.55	17.46	18.15	17.93	17.71	18.85
Intermediate regions	7.75	7.33	7.92	9.02	9.03	9.38
Northern periphery	9.96	8.92	10.02	10.50	10.02	9.67
Northern periphery (without Ireland)	9.89	7.62	7.44	9.22	10.33	10.19
Southern periphery	17.73	13.23	14.48	10.81	13.01	14.32
Intermediate regions/Centre	95.45	93.75	93.02	93.04	93.96	94.24
Northern periphery/Centre	90.95	89.32	85.46	84.12	88.13	89.77
Northern periphery (without Ireland)/Centre	93.01	91.93	88.73	86.97	89.89	89.35
Southern periphery/Centre	84.59	76.24	74.62	75.96	76.97	79.47

Note: * See note to Table 4.1.
Source: ISAE elaborations on Cambridge Econometrics dataset.

and the employment rate: in the 1990s, the employment rate grew more in the high-productivity regions.

All in all, the EU-12 regions have been generally interested by a process of productivity level convergence within each country. The per capita income has indeed not drawn benefits from this process, both because of a divergence effect that has characterized the regional employment rate, and to the 'unfavourable' interaction between productivity and employment, so that the regions with a relatively low productivity level were also those in which the employment rate rose by substantially less than the Union average.

Productivity inequalities and the infrastructural gap

The presence of wide and persistent regional gaps in per capita income and the widening trend that is implicit in the integration process are the main elements of the Union's intervention in favour of regions lagging

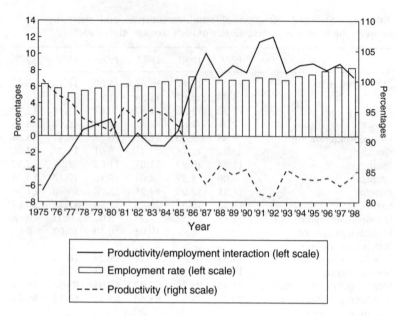

Figure 4.2   EU-12 regions: variance decomposition of per capita income
Source: Based on Cambridge Econometrics dataset.

behind. The structural funds and the cohesion fund helping backward regions mainly finance investment projects in infrastructure, because the infrastructural gap is thought to be one of the main causes for economic inequalities between regions. The dimension and quality of the public service offered to firms may favour economic development. An adequate level of infrastructure is an important prerequisite for the accumulation of private capital and for the birth of new businesses.[7] The social capital stock exerts a positive effect on labour productivity, as it is a production factor complementary to private productive inputs. At the same time, social capital influences the market width by giving room to a larger number of firms; and therefore has a direct impact on employment in the area.

The infrastructure may also have an indirect effect on employment growth. As shown in the previous section, in the 1990s, employment increased more in high-productivity regions and, vice versa, less in low-productivity regions. As its infrastructure has a significant impact on the productivity of a region, the lack of infrastructure lays the basis for a vicious circle between poor infrastructure, low labour productivity and the failure to raise the number of employed (or, symmetrically, the failure to reduce the unemployment rate). These considerations invite one to verify the real impact of social capital (infrastructure) on the level and growth of regional productivity.

The infrastructural gap is measured through an indicator of the infrastructural endowment for 1970 and for 1985 (EU-12 = 100). This indicator derives from the aggregation of numerous elementary categories, which in turn may be regrouped into four major categories: transport (roads, railways, ports, airports); communications (telephones, telex); energy (electric transmission lines, electric plants, oil pipelines, petrol refineries, gas pipelines); and education (number of university students, number of students of high professional schools).[8]

The degree of correlation between the level of labour productivity and the level of infrastructure in the two periods examined (the 1970s and the 1990s) equal 0.59 and 0.61, respectively. The relationship between the two variables is relatively strong and such that a high level of infrastructure tends to favour a high level of productivity and thus a high growth rate.

This observation was verified through an econometric exercise (not reported here), by including the infrastructural gap variable in the equation explaining the regional productivity growth. The result confirms the propulsive potential the infrastructural endowment is able to offer to regional development.[9]

All these results justify a public intervention to finance infrastructural work and thus to prompt productivity in the regions that are lagging behind. The following step is the *ex post* evaluation of the efficiency of structural funds and of the cohesion fund and, in particular, the impact of infrastructural policies carried out within the European Union. Before facing this specific problem, it is useful to review the structural funds allocation criteria and to make a macroeconomic analysis of those criteria.

Allocation of public funds to regions: the macroeconomic determinants

The resources distributed by the European Union for regional and cohesion policies in the period 1988–99 equalled, on annual average, about 3.5 per cent of the GDP of the beneficiary regions. As a reference point, one may add that the Marshall Plan aids, granted in the period 1948–51 for postwar reconstruction in Europe, represent, on annual average, 2 per cent of the European GDP.[10]

What is important is not only the amount (which is, however, considerable) of the funds distributed through regional policies, but also the criteria determining the fund allocation. The allocation principles elaborated by the European Commission specify that the structural funds distribution be inversely proportional to the per capita income, to the infrastructural endowment and to the population density of the area, and directly proportional to the long-term unemployment rate and the weight of agriculture on the economy. It is, however, possible that what is planned 'on paper' is then lost in the bargaining process within and between countries of the EU when elaborating the fund programmes and applications.

A simple empirical analysis shows that the funds committed to finance investment projects in public works in the EU-12 regions in the period 1989–99 were really allocated in keeping with the principles of cohesion and equity advocated by the Commission.

The EU's spending commitments represent, however, only part of the public intervention connected to structural funds. Because of the criterion of additionality – which meets the double need to add the Union resources to national resources and to maintain at the same time the full involvement of local authorities – the European Union commitments are a fraction of the overall resources aimed at covering the total project costs. In other words, they co-finance the global value of the investments approved by adding EU funding to the national/regional resources.

When the projects are considered as a whole (that is European co-financing plus the national/regional contribution), the 'fair distribution' observed at European level falls short. The dimension of the resources committed by national and local authorities to finance the approved projects generally varies according to the Objective within which the European financing is allocated (Objective 1 implies a larger European co-financing and thus the national contribution is lower than for other Objectives), to the kind of project and to the aid modalities (tax allowances for private firms' investments or direct financing of the infrastructure construction and so on).[11] In many cases, the global amount of the national/regional financing exceeds the Union co-financing.

A simple distribution by class of the national contribution rate (meant as the ratio between the amount of resources committed by national authorities and the amount committed by the EU for structural funds) shows that about three-quarters of the EU-12 regions benefited from a national contribution exceeding that from the structural funds. On average, the regions registered a national contribution rate equalling 1.4 per cent. About 13 per cent of regions belong to the national contribution class comprised between 1 and 1.4. About 22 per cent to the class between 1.4 and 2; and about 41 per cent to the class over 2 (thus showing that the national contribution has more than doubled the structural funds) (see Figure 4.3).

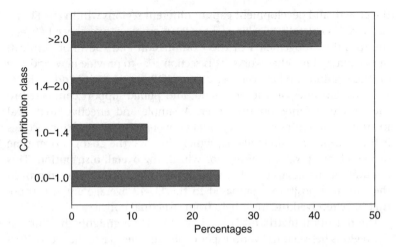

Figure 4.3 Regional distribution by national/regional contribution class (percentages)
Source: Based on OFCE (Observatoire Français des Conjonctures Économiques) data.

The determinant role of national/regional contributions in the financing of projects 'eligible' for structural funds is combined with the fact that less developed regions – in particular those included in Objective 1 – are characterized by a structurally smaller capacity to elaborate projects and attract spending commitments than are other regions. Hence the regional distribution according to cohesion and equity criteria identified for spending commitments (in particular, with reference to per capita income and the infrastructural endowment) diminishes considerably when the overall dimension of the projects is considered. The relationship between the total cost of the project and the initial level of the per capita income seems very weak, and no statistically significant relationship between total cost and level of infrastructure is observed.

Given the particular regional distribution of the total value of the investment projects, doubts emerge as to the effectiveness of public intervention compared to the objective of favouring the convergence of the regions lagging behind. This topic is explored in the next section.

The impact of structural policies on regional convergence, 1989–99

In spite of the growing attention paid to the process of regional convergence in Europe, empirical studies of the structural funds' impact on the growth and development gaps of different regions within the EU are still rare.[12] Generally speaking, there is an ample convergence between the (positive) judgements of the Commission and the (more critical) ones expressed in other works. This section tries to provide new evidence on the relationship between per capita GDP, productivity and regional employment rates on the one hand, and public support connected to the structural funds on the other. A simple and effective analytical instrument to represent the regional convergence/divergence processes is the so-called *transition matrix*, which 'follows' the changes over time of the relative positions of regions within the overall distribution. This instrument enables us to verify whether the regions that have improved their relative positions compared to the EU-12 average are also those that have received the most help from structural policies.

The transition matrix for the per capita GDP highlights the shifts of the regions between the various per capita income classes between 1988 and 1998 (Figure 4.4). Its analysis shows that in the seventeen regions having a per capita GDP 30 per cent lower than the EU-12 average, only one (Notio Agaio, in Greece) improved its relative position in 1998, by passing to the income class between 30 per cent and 80 per cent. The improvement in the relative position of this Objective 1 region is, however, quite small.

In the top income classes there is higher mobility. With a few exceptions, there emerges no improvements in the relative positions of the regions that received the largest assistance from the European Union structural policy. The second class mainly comprises less backward regions than those in Objective 1 areas. Among these, Sterea Ellada (in Greece) falls to join the first income class, while Scotland and Ireland (considered as a region) jump to the third class (between 80 per cent and 100 per cent of the EU-12 average). Within the initial income class comprised of between 30 per cent and 80 per cent of the EU-12 average, there are also some regions with a slightly larger income than that indicated by the Commission for ineligibility to Objective 1. A portion of these regions – together with Scotland and Ireland – passed into the third income class: namely the South West of England, Friesland and some regions of Spain. These latter three, sustained by the cohesion fund but not by the funds of Objective 1, witnessed a considerable improvement of their relative position during the decade being considered.

Other movements concern central and intermediate regions exclusively. Obviously, these regions are not part of Objective 1, but are often beneficiaries of the structural funds of Objective 2, as well as of remarkable national structural aids. Four central regions and one intermediate region passed from the third to the fourth income class; and two central and two intermediate regions (localized in the North-Western area of Italy, the area of industrial districts) passed from the fourth to the fifth class. Conversely, three regions showed a movement in the opposite direction. Finally, for the last income class, there were income regressions for three central regions and for three intermediate regions in Italy.

Admittedly, it is useful to compare the distribution of the per capita income with that of its two components (namely, productivity and the employment rate) (see Figure 4.4). Also in the case of productivity, the

1998 per capita income

Number of regions		0–0.3	0.3–0.8	0.8–1	1–1.2	1.2+
17	**0–0.3**	0.94	0.06[a]	0.00	0.00	0.00
35	**0.3–0.8**	0.03[b]	0.74	0.23[c]	0.00	0.00
22	**0.8–1**	0.00	0.00	0.77	0.23[d]	0.00
24	**1–1.2**	0.00	0.00	0.12[e]	0.71	0.17[f]
19	**1.2+**	0.00	0.00	0.00	0.32[g]	0.68

Figure 4.4 Transition probability matrices of per capita income, productivity and employment rate relative to EU-12 average (ratios)

Notes: 'Ob.' = Objective; [a] Notio Agaio (Ob.1); [b] Sterea Ellada (Ob.1); [c] Scotland (Ob.1), South West England, Madrid, Cataluna, Pais Vasco, La Roja, Friesland, Ireland (Ob.1); [d] Drenthe, Basse Normandie, Gelderland, Oost Vlaalanderen, Noord Brabant; [e] Limburg, Lorena, Zeeland; [f] Veneto, Friuli-Venezia Giulia, Noord Holland, Luxembourg; [g] Berlin, Rheinland-Pfalz, Alsace, Piemonte, Trentino Alto Adige, Lazio.

1998 productivity

Number of regions		0–0.3	0.3–0.8	0.8–1	1–1.2	1.2+
14	**0–0.3**	0.93	0.07[a]	0.00	0.00	0.00
26	**0.3–0.8**	0.08[b]	0.85	0.08[c]	0.00	0.00
23	**0.8–1**	0.00	0.13[d]	0.65	0.21[e]	0.00
33	**1–1.2**	0.00	0.00	0.18[f]	0.70	0.12[g]
21	**1.2+**	0.00	0.00	0.00	0.24[h]	0.76

Figure 4.4   (Continued)

Notes: [a] Alentejo (Ob.1); [b] Ditiki Makedonia (Ob.1), Attiki (Ob.1); [c] Basilicata (Ob.1), Ireland (Ob.1); [d] Gelderland, Navarra, Region Bruxelles; [e] Luxembourg (Belgio), Basse Normandie, Limousin, Abruzzo (Ob.1), Campania (Ob.1); [f] Umbria, Puglia (Ob.1), Zeeland, Luxembourg, Drenthe, Noord Holland; [g] Oost Vlaanderen, Bayern, Niedersachsen; [h] Limburg, Berlin, Piemonte, Valle d'Aosta, Trentino Alto Adige.

movements between classes seem very limited. For the Objective 1 regions, the number of improvements in the relative position is counter-balanced by recedings. There is indeed no clear path of convergence. In this context too, the only exception is Ireland, which registered a strong leap forward in its relative productivity level. Less stability in distribution was registered in the last three classes of productivity, mainly affecting central and intermediate regions. The only exceptions in this context were three regions of the *Mezzogiorno* of Italy.

The less encouraging information on the dynamics of the various development gaps are drawn from the employment rate transition matrix. During the 1990s, the dispersion in the employment rates increased

1998 employment

Number of regions		0–0.8	0.8–0.9	0.9–1	1–1.1	1.1+
13	**0–0.8**	0.69	0.23[a]	0.08[b]	0.00	0.00
27	**0.8–0.9**	0.15[c]	0.48	0.26[d]	0.11[e]	0.00
39	**0.9–1**	0.03[f]	0.15[g]	0.64	0.13[h]	0.05[i]
22	**1–1.1**	0.00	0.00	0.36[l]	0.32	0.32[m]
16	**1.1+**	0.00	0.00	0.00	0.19[n]	0.81

Figure 4.4   (Continued)

Notes: [a] Cantabria (Ob.1), Castilla la Mancha (Ob.1), Murcia (Ob.1); [b] Ireland (Ob.1); [c] Ditiki Makedonia (Ob.1), Ipeiros (Ob.1), Sterea Ellada (Ob.1), Basilicata (Ob.1); [d] Notio Agaio (Ob.1), Madrid, Pais Vasco, Aragon, Cataluna, Valence (Ob.1), Liguria; [e] Attiki (Ob.1), Navarra, Zeeland; [f] Peloponnisos (Ob.1); [g] Dytiki Ellada (Ob.1), Galicia (Ob.1), Bretagne, Poitou Charentes, Abruzzo (Ob.1), Molise (Ob.1); [h] Kriti (Ob.1), Friesland, Drenthe, Lisboa Vale do Tejo, Northern Ireland (Ob.1); [i] Overijssel, Limburg; [l] Niedersachsen, Nordrhein-Westfalien, Rheinland-Pfalz, Saarland, Makedonia Thraki (Ob.1), Ionia Nisia (Ob.1), Algarve (Ob.1), North East; [m] Valle d'Aosta, Trentino Alto Adige, Gelderland, Utrecht, Noord Brabant, Centro (Ob.1), Yorkshire and Humbershire; [n] Berlin, Hessen, Ile de France.
Source: Based on Cambridge Econometrics dataset.

considerably. This widening of the gap was because of a strong polarization of the regional employment rates. As a result of the movement of regions with initial employment rates at an intermediate level towards the extreme parts of the distribution pattern, in 1998 a larger number of regions registered either very low or very high employment rates. In particular, regions with relatively high productivity levels in 1988 moved over a decade towards high employment rate; while regions with initially very low productivity rates moved towards the lowest employment rate. This is perfectly consistent with the evidence of a higher positive correlation between employment rate rises and initial productivity levels.

Only 19 per cent of the regions with initial employment levels exceeding the EU-12 average by 110 per cent dropped to the employment class immediately below. About 70 per cent of the regions with initial employment levels below the EU-12 average by 80 per cent remained at this level. Three Spanish regions participating in Objective 1 reached employment rates of between 80 per cent and 90 per cent. 'Virtuous' Ireland made two leaps forward, jumping to the employment rate bracket ranging between 90 per cent and 100 per cent.

More than 50 per cent of the regions that in 1988 had an employment rate up to 80–90 per cent of the EU-12 average changed their relative positions in 1998: 15 per cent – Greek regions (Objective 1) dropped to a lower position; 26 per cent, mainly Spanish regions benefiting from the cohesion fund but not from the structural fund (Objective 1), moved to the employment class with 90–100 per cent of the EU-12 average; and 11 per cent exceeded the EU-12 average.

About 36 per cent of the regions that in 1988 had an employment rate of between 90 per cent and 100 per cent of the EU-12 average changed their relative positions, distributed equally between 'winners' and 'losers'. Five of the seven losing regions were beneficiaries of Objective 1 funds between 1989 and 1999. Only two of the seven winning regions were beneficiaries of Objective 1 funds.

About 68 per cent of the regions that in 1988 had an employment rate of between 100 per cent and 110 per cent of the EU-12 average changed their relative positions. Three of the eight losing regions were beneficiaries of Objective 1 funds; but only one of the seven winning regions was a beneficiary of Objective 1 funds.

It is worth comparing the employment rate dynamics of the Greek regions with those of the Spanish regions. In Spain, the convergence concerns all regions, with the exception of Galicia, but in Greece, the regions closer to the EU-12 average registered a convergence, while those with higher unemployment rates experienced a widening process.

Therefore, in spite of the effort made to sustain the development of the less-favoured regions through the use of structural funds and through the cohesion fund, regional inequalities between 1988 and 1998 have appeared to show no narrowing.[13] The relative movements in the regional distribution of per capita income, productivity and employment registered no positive relationship with the distribution of funds. Indeed, at first sight the effects of the cohesion fund allocated for Greece, Spain, Portugal and Ireland seem to be different. But in this case too, this was not a process of regional gap-narrowing: the gap reduction compared to the EU-12 concerned single cohesion countries, but there was no narrowing of the regional gaps within them.

Policy implications of the regional analysis

The analytical discussion of the results reported in this chapter leads to some policy indications, which are summarized as follows.

Infrastructural investments, which are the main targets of structural funds, tend to act uniquely on one feature of regional convergence, namely productivity. However, in the presence of a low propension to interregional migration and an insufficient regional wage differentiation, investnents in infrastructure may contribute to the catching-up of poorer regions to only a modest extent. As the experiences since the 1980s shows, these rigidities amplify the unemployment rate gaps and there is the risk also that the improvement of infrastructure connecting the centre with the periphery runs counter the aim of reducing inequalities in geographical development.[14]

As integration grows and transport costs fall, the scarce labour mobility – from whatever causes[15] – may be a favourable condition for the relocation of business firms from the centre to the periphery. Indeed, the industrial concentration implies not only benefits for firms, but also congestion-linked burdens taking the form of growing factor costs (particularly labour costs). The periphery, endowed with a large pool of unutilized labour, again may attract a certain number of firms, provided it offers adequate benefits in terms of wage differentials compared to the more developed regions.

These remarks highlight the need to accompany regional policies aiming at enhancing the infrastructure (thus also productivity) with provisions aimed at reforming the labour market functioning to allow the convergence of the other components underlying real wage differentials, namely the employment rate. Labour market policies aimed at promoting regional convergence should favour the wage dispersion of the area – for example, by shifting the wage determination from a centralized to a firm-level bargaining process.[16]

With regard to the relative inefficiency of projects financed through structural funds, it is necessary to improve the chain linking public financing to infrastructure to the rise in productivity. Indeed, this is influenced positively by the stock of infrastructure, as the evidence confirms. However, structural funds do not always mean *good* infrastructure. Besides, as documented in this chapter, the overall spending commitments for the financing of infrastructures co-financed by the European Union are de facto not distributed on the basis of the cohesion criteria. To improve the quality of public interventions, administrative efficiency and the regions' planning and spending abilities should be enhanced, particularly those of the less-favoured regions. To this end, a changeover of administrative personnel cannot be avoided, and efficiency-improving mechanisms must be adopted. Incentive systems (such as premium reserves), as well as the adoption of careful control mechanisms, might be useful to to encourage the regions' abilities to respect the programmes' ends. This kind of approach, aimed at maximizing the efficiency of the administration of the projects underpins the structural fund programme for 2000–6. It is necessary to take this direction.[17]

Additionally, further decentralization of the decision-making process would increase the efficiency of public intervention considerably, by leaving the 'merit' of the political choices in the hands of local (regional) authorities and operators, with the aim of favouring the creation of development-friendly contexts/environments in order to attract external private resources. The Commission should only take supranational decisions on project financing, on monitoring and on the granting of efficiency premiums (that is, an effective supervision of the best use of distributed funds), as well as on policies aimed at enhancing the infrastructure endowment within the whole Union territory (such as the connecting networks between regions and countries).

The main problem of conceiving a new regional policy within an enlarged European Union remains open. The EU enlargement raises considerable problems for the running of structural funds. With a 27-member European Union, the average GDP per capita decreases considerably and many regions which at present benefit from the funds allocated for Objective 1 would be excluded – not for a real improvement of their situation but for statistical reasons alone.[18]

The new regional support framework should be defined starting from an objective evaluation of the results obtained so far by the regional policies of the European Union. Aiming at the full homogenization of the European territory is already a lost battle and indeed – in its extreme consequences – it is an economic absurdity. The economic activity agglomeration is of itself an efficient result of integration. A realistic geographical cohesion policy should 'limit' itself to laying the foundation of a favourable environment for the territorial development of an area, which means not only quality infrastructure, but also more flexible factor markets, namely labour. It is necessary to take into account the almost 20-year-old experience of the Union's regional policies and make a thorough evaluation of the tasks that a modern policy aimed at restoring a geographical equilibrium within strong economic integration may realistically pursue.

Part III
Macroeconomic Policies

5
The Conduct of Macroeconomic Policies in the Euro Area

With the adoption of the euro, the formal and material macroeconomic 'constitution' of the countries in the European Monetary Union (EMU) has changed considerably. The two major instruments used to regulate the economic cycle – namely, monetary and fiscal policy – were distributed differently among the various economic policy authorities of the EMU, thus creating an unprecedented asymmetry of powers and competences. Indeed, monetary policy is centralized and is left to an independent Central Bank, while fiscal policy remains decentralized and under the responsibility of the national authorities of the member states, though it carries an overall set of common rules.

The different competences correspond to a clear-cut division of tasks. The European Central Bank (ECB), carries out monetary policy, looking at the euro area as a whole and attaching the greatest priority to the control of inflation within the EMU; and, second, considering the evolution of economic activity, provided price stability is safeguarded. Conversely, fiscal policies are aimed at regulating national economic cycles and correcting unsustainable behaviour (overheating or recessions) specifically concerning individual economies as a consequence of asymmetric shocks.

The smooth functioning of this structure requires a complex co-ordination effort, which may be more or less intense but which must exist between fiscal and monetary policies, as well as between the various national fiscal policies contributing to a definition of the overall fiscal stance of the euro area. That need derives from the interaction between policy-makers and from the slight awareness of decentralized authorities of the effects of their public finance decisions on European inflation and economic activity. The existence of the externalities of governments' choices and the need to avoid free riding on the part of individual countries – which might transfer the consequences of their 'non-virtuous' economic policy decisions on to other partners – strongly urges co-operation and co-ordination.

On top of this, macroeconomic policies constructed for the EMU are more likely to function smoothly, the closer the convergence of the economies of the euro area member countries (in their market organization, development, institutions and so on) and, in particular, the more consolidated the process of public finance adjustment in the euro countries. In other words, the framework of macroeconomic policies seems to work better – which means the minimizing of friction and tensions between individual countries – in a fully-operating monetary union not only in terms of definition of general rules, but also in terms of the homogenization of economic-institutional structures of the member states.

In the transition towards a 'fully-fledged' EMU, the euro area is still quite heterogeneous, in that individual economies do maintain important differences in their structures and even in their citizens' preferences, while public finances in many important countries have not yet completed the budget adjustment process that should eventually enable them to fully recover budget policy to an anti-cyclical role.

This chapter examines the monetary and fiscal policies in that delicate transition phase, in the light of the first years of life of the euro. In this period, the macroeconomic policy instruments of the EMU – though not hit by significant asymmetric shocks – were strongly stressed by some major changes in the global scenario; indeed, in 2000, the world and the European cycles reached peaks of expansion followed by a period of strong slowdown. In that same year, oil prices registered a considerable rise, hitting all the importing countries, including those in the euro area. After the terrorist attacks of 11 September 2001, consumer confidence has briskly decreased at the international level by undermining the possibility of a rapid recovery and urging policy-makers throughout the industrialized world to adjust economic policy responses to the new scenario.

The analysis of the euro area monetary policy in the three-year period 1999–2001 undertaken in the first section shows that – while the ECB pursues price stability in the EMU as its prime objective – its behaviour mirrors the influence of the real economic cycle too. Indeed, the profile of the official interest rate 'historically' adopted by the ECB does not differ very much – with the exception of a short phase of a (perhaps) excessive monetary squeeze in 2000 – from the theoretical one obtained through a reaction function (identified through the Taylor Rule), whereby interest rates adopted by the monetary authority in its intervention depend both on the divergence between actual and target inflation and – though with a lower weight – on the output gap both measured at the euro-area level.

This relative sensitivity of the ECB's behaviour to the real cycle derives from two considerations. First, in the presence of demand shocks, such as those connected with marked oscillations of the international cycle, the cycle-regulating monetary policy provisions are no different from the measures aimed at controlling inflation. Conversely, in the case of supply shocks – such as those caused by oil price rises – requiring decisions going in opposite directions according to whether one looks at inflation or at the real cycle, the ECB's approach to evaluating medium-term price trends (so that the core more than headline inflation is controlled) and to consider a vast array of variables indicating the short-term inflation trend as a point of reference for its decisions, introduced a sufficient degree of flexibility and forward-looking behaviour. Thus, the priority attached to price stability does not imply immediate and mechanical reactions to the observed inflation trends on the part of the monetary authority.

All in all, a sufficiently balanced and flexible monetary policy emerged in the first euro phase, given the inflation target pursued by the ECB. This policy contributed to giving more macroeconomic stability to the whole area and to individual countries by providing an 'anchor' to expectations and by reducing the economic system's exposure to external shocks in a much more effective way than national monetary policy perhaps might have done.

Admittedly, one might wonder about the impact of that policy on individual economies, because of their persistent structural heterogeneity. These differences – which are related to their different cyclical positions, with development gaps and, more generally, with institutional factors – may affect both the degree of strictness of the single monetary policy in the different countries and the intensity with which the same monetary provisions affect different economic systems.

This chapter provides evidence showing that, in some countries, the ECB's monetary policy, when compared to the policies that single economies would have adopted on the basis of simple monetary rules, has led to the adoption of interest rates different from the theoretical rates obtained through a national-level reaction function having an inflation objective similar to that of the ECB. In particular, the greater differences observed in the three years 1999–2001 can be witnessed in Germany, on the one hand, and in Ireland, on the other. In Germany, the reaction function to the domestic cycle and to inflation would have brought about lower interest rates compared to those of the ECB; but in Ireland, the theoretical interest rates – computed on the basis of national conditions – would have been higher.

However, this kind of heterogeneity highlights only one aspect of the different impacts of a centralized monetary policy on different countries. Indeed, the structural features of the various economies do influence, at the national level, the transmission mechanism of the common monetary policy, so that a provision that seems in theory suitable for all economies – which are in the same cyclical position – may have completely different effects according to the different degrees of responsiveness to monetary measures characterizing the euro countries. In particular, one has to consider, for example, the weight of the manufacturing sector on the economy, the firms' dimensions, the role of the banking system in the financing of the productive system, and the relevance of both short-term and long-term credit in financing economic activity.

These differences related to monetary transmission mechanisms may add up to, or be offset by, those stemming from the different cyclical economic positions, thus diversifying the national-level impact of the ECB's actions. This chapter describes the results of an estimate of the composed effects deriving from the two main reasons for divergence – that is, the gap between theoretical interest rates and actual ones, and the countries' different responsiveness to interest rates. The exercise is carried out without considering any possible interactions and reactions that might emerge in a fully-specified multi-country model. However, it does provide some useful indications on the sign and dimension of the heterogeneous effects of the European Central Bank's actions. The estimate shows that, by assuming that the ECB monetary policies were 'optimal' for all countries at the EMU's inception (1 January 1999), the impact on the interest rates in the three years 1999–2001 has determined in most economies – taking into account the different degree of responsiveness to monetary impulses – GDP trends roughly in keeping with those that might have occurred if the rates had been decided upon on the basis of national conditions alone. In six economies out of ten, the growth gap did not exceed (or fell short of) 0.1 per cent of the theoretical one. Furthermore, growth was marginally less in Germany (0.2 per cent per year) and slightly larger in Portugal and Austria (0.4 per cent per year). In Germany, the stricter ECB monetary policy was partly offset by the decreased responsiveness to interest rates of the German economy. Conversely, Ireland shows an expansionary reaction, as its GDP trend was one percentage point higher than the one that might have emerged had its interest rates followed the (higher) profile 'dictated' by domestic conditions. Obviously, the impacts on the euro-area of the recessionary or expansionary consequences of the single monetary policy at the national level are different, since Germany (because of its dimension and economic relationship with partner countries) plays a more decisive role for Euro economic activity than Ireland.

Apart from problems of heterogeneity, other kinds of dyscrasia may disturb monetary policy (see the second section). Among these, there are certainly the inflationary consequences of the price convergence process between different countries induced by the adoption of a common currency; indeed, this alignment implies that countries that originally had the lowest prices registered higher inflation compared to the other economies.

In fact, within the EMU, there are countries with very different price levels. Since the 1980s, Germany has been one of the 'most expensive' countries, while Portugal had much lower prices than the averages. There are, however, many reasons to expect that those gaps will gradually narrow as European integration continues – even more so since the introduction of the euro. The elimination of trade barriers between economies, the creation of the single market and the removal of intra-European exchange rates, should gradually narrow differences in euro area prices, at least for tradable goods. Indeed, there are ample margins for further convergence between the economies, since the conversion rates chosen for the old national currencies *vis-à-vis* the euro did not level out the prices of tradable goods between the EMU countries.

An inverse relationship between the initial price level and the inflation rate is justified – apart from a re-balancing need between national prices because of integration – by the so-called Balassa–Samuelson effect, whereby the countries with the lowest prices are identified as the least developed ones. In these countries, the catching-up process should favour speedy growth in productivity and wages in the sectors more responsive to international competition, as well as a process of wage catching-up in the shielded sectors (mainly services). This would cause a cost-driven inflation typical of countries characterized by initial lower prices, by a rapid productivity growth in sectors exposed to competition, and by a less dynamic service sector.

The convergence caused by integration or catching-up is – in the long run – an autonomous cause that modifies relative prices. Other reasons may in the short run determine such changes and affect the dynamics of national inflation rates. Sometimes it may be necessary to make an adjustment to asymmetric shocks hitting one economy by modifying national prices. In the presence of a flexible exchange rate, these variations take place through the depreciation or appreciation of national currencies; if there is no national currency, they may occur through diversified national price dynamics compared to the rest of the area.

Short- and long-term variations in relative prices would be no problem for the setting of an objective inflation rate for the euro area if the price levels and the production factor costs could decrease for sufficiently long periods of time. However, in the presence of nominal rigidities, such as those characterizing the European economies, the adjustment of relative prices between countries necessarily takes place through a higher inflation on the part of those countries that – because of the need for convergence or reactions to specific shocks – 'have to' increase their prices compared to their partners'. The average inflation rate of the euro area should thus take into account this need, by accommodating any necessary relative price adjustment. Indeed, a 'too low' inflation target might be a 'straitjacket' limiting natural adjusting processes, with a negative impact on resource allocation and on the functioning of mechanisms accompanying the convergence paths. This chapter tries to quantify the average European inflation that is necessary to accompany the relative price changes caused by convergence, but without causing long deflation processes in any of the EMU countries. According to these estimates, based on the experience of the convergence process that has been taking place between the euro countries since the 1980s, the 'underlying' inflation ranges from 0.8 per cent and 1.7 per cent. The lower limit of this range seems substantially compatible with the ECB inflation target (less than 2 per cent in the medium term), while the upper limit seems to absorb that target completely, leaving no room for price variations resulting from reasons other than long-term convergence or the shifting connected to cyclical fluctuations.

The centralization of the EMU monetary policy with the ECB goes hand in hand the decentralization of fiscal policy, which is left to national governments for the stabilization of national cyclical fluctuations. However, that competence is necessarily subject to constraints and conditions. Because they belong to a monetary union, the euro countries' actions interfere with other economies and may undermine the overall monetary stability of the area. For this reason, the Treaty establishing the European Community sets Community-level Rules and co-ordination procedures for the implementation of national budget policies. The fundamental principle is that, while adopting their national fiscal policies to regulate the economic cycle, the EU economies must not create excessive deficits – that might have negative repercussions on the rest of the area – by raising market interest rates and conditioning the conduct of monetary policy (see the fourth section of the chapter).

As many important European economies have not yet completed their budget adjustment processes, the idea that fiscal policy is not, at the time of writing, a fully-functioning instrument for stabilizing national economic conditions is implicit in the general provisions forbidding excessive deficits. Only when the public finances of different countries reach stability, and medium- and long-term sustainability, will the public budget again be a fully-fledged economic policy instrument. Before that time (and for a lengthy transition phase) the macroeconomic policy framework in the euro area will continue to be unbalanced. On the one hand, there is monetary policy, already operating with full autonomy in pursuing its targets, in spite of the problems deriving from the heterogeneity of the EMU economies. On the other hand, there are national fiscal policies oscillating between the need to complete the financial adjustment, and the temptation to disregard the need of fiscal consolidation to start again using the public budget as a cycle-regulating tool in weak cyclical phases and to implement reforms aimed at easing national fiscal pressures in view of the more intense competition in the European area.

These temptations are faced by a complex co-ordination mechanism drawing inspiration from principles of consensus, by adopting incentive/disincentive systems and peer pressure rather than strict criteria. Its complex nature derives from the intertwining of institutional sources comprising objectives and commitments (the Broad Economic Policy Guidelines, the Stability and Growth Pact and the annual Stability Programmes); from the number of actors involved in different positions and competences in the co-ordination process (national governments, the European Commission, the Ecofin Council, the Eurogroup and the European Council); and from the procedures necessary to fully perform the control mechanism (there are nine official steps from the March meeting, when the European Council approves the implementation report of the economic policy commitments of the previous year, until the moment when it decides on the priorities for the following year).

The evaluation of the first years of fiscal policy co-ordination – the first Stability Programmes were presented in 1998 – is mixed: after positive results in the very beginning (up to 2000) problems emerged in the latest period when the economic cycle weakened.

In the phase of slowdown that started in 2001 European fiscal co-ordination mechanism showed shortcomings requiring the reconsideration of some of its aspects. The first is that the pace of the deficit reduction has proved to be slower than expected. Given that the objective is to reach a balanced or surplus budget so as to give back to public budgets their roles in the stabilization and reform processes for a better functioning of the economic systems, time becomes a considerable cost for the countries involved, which witness a postponement of the possibility to better survive the adjustments to negative shocks and to draw an advantage from the progress in terms of the general efficiency of their economies. Even more important is the fact that many of the the adjustments made in recent years were as a result of cyclical phenomena, to temporary/extraordinary measures, and to a reduction in their interest expenditure. The structural interventions indicated in the programmes have often been postponed, thus gradually losing credibility as the proposing governments have got close to the end of their mandates.

Also the statement – which *per se* is correct – to let the automatic stabilizers work in slowdown phases – such as that of 2002 – considerably loses its effectiveness if the smooth functioning of these stabilizers is not allowed in expansionary cyclical phases as well. This generally does not take place. Primary structural surpluses – that is, net of the interest expenditure and of the cyclical effects – decreased in the EU (and in the EMU) in 2000; that is, in a year of strong economic growth that should have brought about a rise in those budgets, had the stabilizers been functioning well. This means that 'dividends' deriving from favourable economic cycles – far from being used to accelerate budget adjustment – have eventually been devised to loosen the fiscal rigour. It is therefore necessary for fiscal policies to be stability-orientated over the whole economic cycle. This is not necessarily true with the Stability and Growth Pact in its shape at the time of writing, as it contains an implicit pro-cycle bias, and envisages no deterrents towards national policy-makers who want to raise expenditure and/or decrease taxes in the 'high' cyclical phases.

Finally, the experience of recent years has highlighted the limit of the short-term view implicit in the Stability and Growth Pact, as the lapse of time covered by stability pacts does not usually exceed four years. This approach neglects the fundamental question of the long-term sustainability of the countries' fiscal positions in connection with the public budget imbalances deriving from population ageing.

Shortcomings, limits and imperfections that have been emerging during the experience of fiscal co-ordination over the years have led the Commission to study some devices to correct the monitoring and control mechanism, which seem to be moving in the right direction. It is worth emphasizing that they do not question the spirit and foundation of the procedure – a central EU budget maintained within limits and fiscal policies left to individual economies co-ordinated and monitored by the EU bodies – which substantially work, though they could improve.

The first aspect concerns the need to reduce the opportunity for the arbitrary evaluation of public finances of the various countries through a more precise identification of what are real or anticipated 'significant divergences' from both the medium-term objectives and the intermediate targets indicated in the stability programmes. Such divergence gaps must be measured against the structural budget to exclude the effects caused by automatic stabilizers.

These remarks hint at the second proposal advanced to improve the effectiveness of the control mechanism and, in particular, to eliminate the risk of the pro-cycle bias in decisions regarding public finances. Governments should be asked to present, alongside the objectives on the nominal budget, also those concerning structural budgets. However, as the computation of the structural budget introduces a factor of uncertainty – since the output gap, on which the structural budget evaluation is based, is not observed, but only estimated – it is necessary to avoid this if it means that a larger discretionary power to decide whether the position of an economy is deviating or not. One, or even two, criteria used to evaluate the structural budget, based on different methods and valid for all countries, might contribute towards reconciling the need to have more thorough information and to reduce uncertainty.

Furthermore, the exclusive attention the Stability and Growth Pact attaches to the public budget leads to the neglect of equally important factors in determining the fiscal sustainability and overall efficiency of a country. In particular, these may be more influenced by the composition than by the sign of the budget. To give an example, a balanced budget with revenues and expenditure exceeding 60 per cent of the GDP may be qualitatively worse and potentially more distorting for the economy than a deficit budget with an acceptable fiscal pressure. For this reason, it is equally important that, apart from the budget dynamics, the *quality* of national public budgets also be monitored in terms of taxation on productive factors, of non-efficient public expenditures, of long-term trends influenced by the demographic evolution, and of the public debt situation and dynamics, including the hidden one caused by the pension system. To this end, the monitoring and control of public finance quality would be greatly helped by the awareness that, alongside budget balances, annual objectives are also important in terms of primary public expenditure dynamics, golden rule adoption (exclusion of investment expenditure from deficit computation) and closer links between deficit evolution and debt trends while evaluating the national adjustment paths.

The conduct of monetary policy

The European Central Bank

Objectives and strategies of the European Central Bank

The primary objective of the common monetary policy is price stability. Apart from that, the European system of central banks – Eurosystem (comprising the European Central Bank and the national central banks of the European Union member states) – supports the general policies of the Community, among which there is a harmonious and balanced development of economic activities, sustainable growth, the convergence of living standards, the maintenance of a high employment level and, finally, economic and social cohesion.

The ECB defined price stability as the 'annual increase in the Harmonised Index of Consumer Prices (HICP) of below 2%' underlining that 'price stability is to be maintained over the medium term' throughout the whole euro area.[1]

The strategy to achieve this objective is based on two 'pillars': 'A prominent role for money, as signalled by the announcement of a quantitative reference value ... for the growth rate of the broad monetary aggregate' (first pillar); and 'Broadly based assessment of the outlook for price developments and the risks to price stability using financial and other economic indicators' (second pillar). Through its stability-orientated monetary policy strategy, the ECB 'eschews "mechanistic" monetary policy responses to deviations from a specific target or developments in a specific indicator variable'.

Thus the formulation of decisions is not automatic, but takes place through a complex elaboration and synthesis procedure of the information coming from the two pillars. As for the first pillar, the definition of a reference value different from the concept of an intermediate objective, outlines that a deviation of monetary growth from that value does not necessarily imply a reaction, as happens in the case of a monetary-targeting strategy. Indeed, the evaluation of monetary dynamics as against the reference value implies that – given the way in which it is computed – the money gap, namely the deviation of the money growth from the one compatible with the medium-term equilibrium, is the leading indicator of the future price dynamics. In this sense, it might be considered as part of the second-pillar indicators and the strategy subdivision into two pillars made by the ECB might reflect the will to emphasize the responsibility of the Eurosystem for monetary impulses to inflation and the wish to provide a 'nominal anchor' to monetary policy.

The reference value was derived by using the monetary quantitative equation, on the basis of the medium-term objective of the inflation trend, of the real GDP trend and of the velocity of circulation of M3.[2] It is based on the long-term relationship between money and prices and on the awareness that any deviations of the monetary growth from the reference value gives an anti-cyclical feature to monetary policy. As the ECB itself underlines, a deviation of monetary growth from the reference value does not automatically affect interest rates, but it requires further analyses to identify and interpret the economic factors responsible for the deviation, to discover the existence of a threat to price stability.

With reference to the second pillar, the ECB assesses the price prospects in the euro area by making reference to a wide range of economic indicators, including 'many variables that have leading indicator properties for future price developments. These variables include, *inter alia*, wages, the exchange rate, bond prices and the yield curve, various measures of real activity, fiscal policy indicators, price and cost indices and business and consumer surveys'. One should also add the inflation expectations and forecasts upon which the Eurosystem evaluates 'the full range of inflation forecasts produced by international organisations, other authorities, market participants, etc. and will also produce its own assessment of the future inflation outlook'.

All this leads to different considerations enabling a 'formal' definition of the ECB strategy. The first point is that it is a price stability-orientated strategy attaching overriding importance to the control of price dynamics, and which may be therefore labelled 'inflation targeting'. Indeed, the monetary role defined in the ECB strategy does not imply monetary targeting elements, and the two pillars are comparable to one – namely a group of indicators of price prospects.

The second consideration derives from the fact that the statute states explicitly that monetary authorities have to contribute – apart from price stability – to the Community's economic and social objectives – that is, to the maintenance of a stable but sustained growth rate in the economic system, guaranteeing a high level of employment and a better quality of life for citizens. Theoretically, the ECB strategy might be classified as flexible inflation targeting, which differs from inflation targeting in a narrow sense[3] because of the presence in the preference function of the monetary authorities, along with the maintenance of price stability, of real overall economic stability target.

Finally, the definition of price stability adopted, particularly the fact that price stability is maintained over the medium term, introduces, *per se*, as it is meant for future developments, elements of flexibility compared to 'pure' inflation targeting, which show some advantages. First of all, the fact that the monetary authorities' behaviour responds to the target variable determinants rather than to the target variable itself, brings about a more efficient monetary policy.[4] Indeed, this goes beyond one of the major criticism to pure inflation targeting – that this approach (as it does not distinguish between demand and supply shocks) does not enable a consideration of the trade-off between growth and inflation generated in the latter case, with negative consequences for output and interest rates stability.[5] Indeed, a forward-looking strategy allows a price oscillations in the short term in the presence of movements in the economic variables that cannot be controlled by monetary policy, therefore guaranteeing more macroeconomic stability. In this way, the Central Bank may implement a gradual and balanced response, avoiding the introduction of elements of uncertainty and reducing any financial stability risks.

To summarize, one may state that, first, the ECB's mandate and strategy may be interpreted as the task to stabilize inflation around the long-term objective, and the real variables around their natural or equilibrium levels. This is represented by a preference function that includes – along with the inflation target – the target of income stabilization at the maximum levels allowed by the available resources and technology. Second, monetary authorities have ample margins of flexibility in performing their monetary policy. The ECB is not constrained – exactly like any other 'modern' central bank – by a fixed code of conduct, but it adopts its own decisions on the basis of the evaluations made, using every relevant information drawn from a wide range of variables and instruments.

The performing of monetary policy in the first three years of EMU

This section evaluates the ECB's strategy on the basis of a theoretical reaction function known as the *Taylor Rule* (see Box 5.1). This is a simple rule

Box 5.1   The Taylor Rule

A way to evaluate and interpret ECB policy is by making reference to a theoretical reaction function. One of the most adopted rules in the literature is the Taylor Rule (TR). It was suggested for the first time by John Taylor in 1993,[6] as an instrument to define the optimal monetary policy for the USA. According to the TR, the real interest rate is affected by three variables: namely, the output gap, the deviation of inflation from the targeted level, and the real equilibrium ('neutral') interest rate.[7] Its formula is as follows:

$$rt = r^* + 0.5^* \, (pt - p^*) + 0.5^* \, (yt - y^*)/y^* \qquad (5.1)$$

where r is the real interest rate, p is the inflation rate, y is the potential output, t indicates time, and the asterisk indicates the long-time equilibrium level (thus, for the inflation rate, it indicates the targeted rate). When the economy is in equilibrium – i.e. when the inflation rate equals the targeted rate and the output equals the potential one – the real interest rate is also in equilibrium. Whenever inflation exceeds the target and/or the output exceeds the potential level, the real interest rate must rise beyond the 'neutral' level. Whenever the opposite takes place, the real interest rate falls short of the 'neutral' figure.

Taylor did not estimate the equation, but the parameters and the equilibrium levels were chosen in such a way that the equation roughly describes Federal Reserve behaviour in the period 1987–92.

Equation (5.1) may be transformed by setting the nominal interest rate (i) on the left side as follows:

$$(^*) \; i_t = i^* + 1.5^* \, (p_t - p^*) + 0.5^* \, (y_t - y^*)/y^* \qquad (5.2)$$

Equation (5.2) represents a simple rule that identifies the policy interest rate, which moves in response to inflationary shocks to such an extent that it brings about a correct variation of the real interest rates (inflation gap coefficient >1).

Ball (1997) and Svensson (1997) demonstrated that the TR overlaps with a formula whereby the inflationary target is forward-looking and may be optimal provided the current output gap and inflation are sufficiently able to forecast future inflation. To this end, one might adopt a price index net of the components that are most volatile in the short term, and which are non-significant to

Box 5.1 (Continued)

forecast the medium-term inflation rate. Thus, the TR – particularly in its version with core inflation – shows no elements running counter the ECB mandate and strategy, and therefore it may be used as benchmark to evaluate its monetary policy.

Figure 5.1 presents the results obtained by computing a Taylor Rule for the euro area as a whole in the first three years of the ECB's life. The adopted weights are traditional ones, the medium-term targeted inflation equals 1.5 per cent and the output gap is computed against a potential output obtained by applying the Hodrick–Prescott filter.[8] In the last quarter of 2001 a dummy was introduced that attaches the utmost importance to the output gap alone for monetary policy decisions, while neglecting price trends to take into account risks for growth prospects following the events of September 11.

The interest rate is computed on the basis of the following equation:

$$i_t = i_0 + 1.5* \ (p_t - p_0) + 0.5* \ (y_t/y_t* - y_0/y_0*) \tag{5.3}$$

where p is the core inflation[9] and the time index 0 refers to the first quarter 1999.

Equation (5.3) is the difference between Equation (5.2) computed at time t and the same equation computed at 0. The hypothesis at the root of this formula is that at the beginning of EMU (1st quarter 1999) the ECB fixed the interest rate 'in keeping with' the Taylor Rule applied to the euro area, which avoids the making of assumptions on the neutral interest rate and is tantamount to considering variations more than the level of variables.

of behaviour of a monetary authority that may be used as benchmark to interpret the policy implemented by the ECB in the first three years of the EMU. According to this approach, the optimal interest rate depends on objectives of inflation stabilization around a target value, and of income around its potential value (the output gap). The validity of this rule – in the presence of forward-looking inflation targeting strategy, as the one adopted by the ECB – depends on the capacity of the current inflation rate and output gap to anticipate future price dynamics. For this reason, it is better to make reference to the inflation rate adjusted for volatile components, such as the so-called core inflation, obtained from the consumer price index net of energy products, foodstuffs, alcohol and cigarettes. The inflation objective upon which the deviations of consumer price dynamics current at the time of writing are computed, is set at 1.5 per cent, which is 'in keeping' with the ECB's medium-term target.

The results (see Figure 5.1) indicate that the monetary policy the ECB performed in its first three years closely resembles the Taylor Rule formula as computed for the euro area as a whole. The 'flexible' ECB behaviour towards the current inflation rate emerges clearly from the comparison with a similar reaction function which, however, considers the deviation of inflation from the Harmonized Index of consumer prices (HICP), which is subject to more volatility. Indeed, in the latter case, the ECB's reaction would have implied more restrictive manoeuvres than the ones that were enforced.

Finally, one might provide some more detailed evaluations of the monetary policy performed by the ECB during the first three years by comparing it with the 'theoretical' policy suggested by the Taylor Rule.

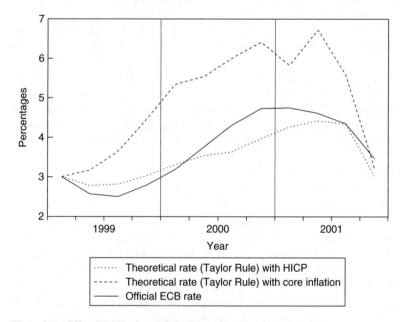

Figure 5.1   Official ECB rates and theoretical rates
Sources: ECB, ISAE elaborations on ECB data and datastream dataset.

After fixing the interest rate level at 3 per cent on 22 December 1998, the ECB modified it twelve times during its first three years of life. Two changes were introduced in 1999 (a 0.5 per cent reduction in April, and a 0.5 per cent increase in November); six in the year 2000 for an overall rise of 1.75 percentage points; and four in 2001 (a cut of 1.5 percentage points).

During the first year (that is, 1999) the interest rate modifications suggested by the Taylor Rule and the ECB's actions were very similar. The decrease in the first half of the year mainly mirrors the actual trends, characterized by weak economic activity and by the absence of signals of recovery with no inflationary risks. The HICP inflation rate was smaller than the targeted one, even though it was growing, particularly with the early-1999 oil price increases, and core inflation – which was also less than 1.5 per cent – was falling. In the second half of 1999, there was a strengthening of the economic cycle, and the core inflation reduction process came to a halt.

In 2000, the theoretical rule suggested the adoption of restrictive measures, though smaller than those adopted by the ECB, particularly in the second half of the year, when a considerable economic growth slowdown occurred in the presence of a core inflation which – though growing moderately – was still below 1.5 per cent.

In the first months of 2001. The ECB adopted a wait and see approach related to growth perspectives' uncertainty. In that period, a still-positive cyclical phase and an above-1.5 per cent core inflation dynamic (and still growing) caused a rise in the theoretical interest rate by about 0.5 per cent. After that, the two curves indicating the theoretical interest rate and the ECB manoeuvres decreased,[10] because of a deterioration in the macroeconomic situation which worsened after the September 11 attacks and in the presence of a core inflation growth slowdown.

Different effects of the single monetary policy on member countries

As mentioned above, the European Monetary Policy had led to a common monetary policy for all member states, formulated by taking into account the prices and economic stabilization in the euro area as a whole. The interventions introduced by the monetary authority on this basis may be more or less suitable for the individual economies, because of existing differences in growth and inflation rates and in the transmission mechanisms of the monetary policy itself. These differences – which are going? bound to diminish only in the long term, as integration goes on and the economic structures of member states converge – are mirrored in a diversification on the effects of the ECB's actions at national level, as they may prove to be 'too expansionist' for some countries and 'too restrictive' for others. This is a potential source of distortions that may not be attributed to real 'mistakes' by the European Central Bank, but rather to the fact that a single monetary policy is adopted in a currency area not yet optimal. The degree of divergence between 'optimal' monetary policies may be evaluated by considering the difference between the ECB's interest rate, fixed at supranational level, and the 'theoretical' interest rate obtained by applying the Taylor Rule (see Box 5.1 above) to national situations. An evaluation is made of the most suitable monetary policies after 1 January 1999 for individual EMU countries (excluding Luxembourg) on the basis of national conditions, represented by inflationary pressures (expressed by the core inflation deviation from a 1.5 per cent target, the same in all countries) and by the output gap. Some simplifying hypotens are introduced: the neutral interest rate and the inflation target are the same in each country; the initial interest rate was settled by EBC in an optional way, according to eq. 5€(*) in Box 5.1.

The results show – as expected – a divergence between optimal national theoretical rates (Figure 5.2). During the first year, for example, the 'optimal' interest rate for income and inflation stabilization around the long-term values in Ireland should have been two percentage points higher, and in Germany should have been about 0.8 per cent smaller. Among other countries, Portugal and Spain should have had an 'optimal' theoretical rate considerably higher than that of the ECB.

Apart from that, it is worth considering the possibility that each economy reacts in a different way to the same manoeuvre on interest rates. Useful indications to this end come from Van Els *et al.* (2001), where an analysis is carried out of the effects in the different euro area countries of a rise in the policy interest rates based on an *ad hoc* econometric exercise involving individual national central banks and the ECB. Figure 5.3 summarizes the main results, referring to the three-year effects on the real GDP dynamics of a one-percentage-point rise in the first two years, and back to the initial level in the third year. Admittedly, the same monetary policy has a larger effect (compared to the EMU average) on the real GDP growth in Greece, Portugal, Spain, Ireland, Italy and Austria, and a smaller one in the remaining countries. Thus the first group of countries would have a stronger restriction in the case of an interest rate rise, and larger expansionary effects in the case of a reduction.

It is interesting to try to estimate, for each country in the three-year period 1999–2001, the joint effect deriving, on the one hand, from the discrepancy between ECB policies and those that would have been asked for on the basis of the individual national situation [results

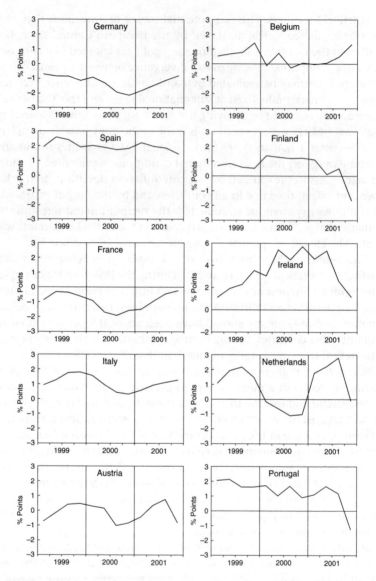

Figure 5.2 Gap between the variations of adjusted theoretical interest rates and those of the official ECB rate[a]

Sources: ISAE elaborations on ECB data and datastream dataset.

Note: [a] The differential is computed by adjusting national theoretical interest rates to take into account the different cyclical conditions of the euro area member states at the beginning of 1999.

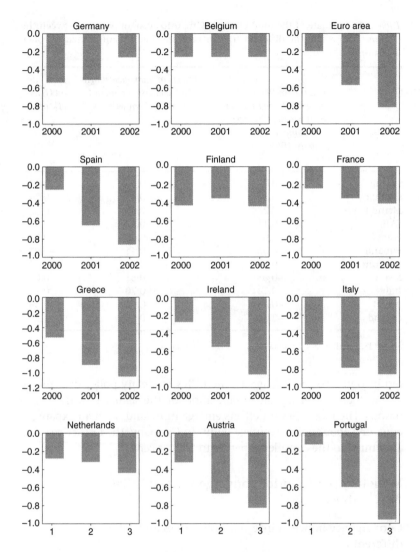

Figure 5.3 Effects of increase of interest rates by one percentage point on real GDP growth (percentage variations from basic scenario)
Source: Van Els *et al.* (2001).

obtained by the first exercise] and from the different transmission mechanisms on the other. This is a 'mechanical' exercise which does not take into account the interactions, but it is useful to highlight at least the sign and direction of the phenomena. On the basis of the

Table 5.1   Estimate of the joint effects taking into account the gap between the ECB provisions and the different transmission mechanisms of monetary policy measures in the euro countries

	Average gap between the variation of the official interest rate and that of the theoretical interest rate, compared to January 1999 *(1)*	*Effects of a one-percentage point increase on interest rate on GDP growth* *(2)*	*Joint effect on GDP* *(1)*(2)*
Portugal	0.77	−0.56	−0.43
Germany	0.54	−0.44	−0.24
Netherlands	0.23	−0.35	−0.08
EMU	0.15	−0.52	−0.08
France	0.09	−0.33	−0.03
Finland	0.05	−0.41	−0.02
Belgium	0.06	−0.26	−0.02
Spain	−0.03	−0.61	0.02
Italy	−0.14	−0.70	0.10
Austria	−0.58	−0.62	0.36
Ireland	−2.30	−0.55	1.27

Source: ISAE elaboration on data from Van Els *et al.* (2001).

results obtained (see Table 5.1), the ECB's monetary policy determined in most cases a marginal modification of the actual growth of real output. The most relevant effects emerge in Ireland, with an expansion equalling about one percentage point. In Germany, the restrictive effect amounted in the considered period to 0.2 per cent.

Monetary policy, price convergence and inflation differentials

Convergence between international prices and inflation differentials

The integration of the euro area economies, strengthened by the adoption of the single currency and by the intensification of intra-area trade favours the price uniformity of goods and services traded between the EMU countries. If the initial price level is different between economies, admittedly, this process of convergence justifies, *per se*, inflation differentials. European policy-makers recognize this aspect publicly,[11] but it is often neglected while analysing the inflation differentials between different countries – though it is generally considered in the explanation of the differentials between areas within the same country. Only recently the problem of price convergence was indicated explicitly as being among the main factors determining the inflation rate dispersion within the EMU. According to a recent study,[12] the convergence effect accounts for most of the inflation differential compared to the European average, particularly in low-price countries, while it seems to have a smaller influence on the originally 'more expensive' countries. This would confirm that the convergence process led to higher inflation only in low-price countries, with prices remaining substantially stable in all other areas.

In a perfectly competitive market without trade barriers and with one single currency, the price of the same product should differ from country to country only because of transportation and trading costs. Any further difference would be cancelled out by a more or less speedy arbitrage mechanism. In turn, international price homogeneity implies homogeneous profits and wages, under quite similar conditions between countries concerning the available technologies. All in all, one might expect that the convergence between final product prices favours a convergence between wages at the same productivity level. As that result is socially desirable to strengthen cohesion within the Union, the convergence between national prices should not be hampered. From this perspective, an underlying inflation associated with these processes of price convergence would hence be tolerable.

Indeed, arbitrage becomes convenient only when the price difference exceeds a minimum threshold, which is mainly determined by the unitary cost of transactions and of the payment instruments adopted, by the risk premium on the exchanges and by the actual goods divisibility (measured by the value of the minimum quantity that is traded). Hence the so-called 'law of one price' presents numerous and significant exceptions that justify considerable differences between the prices practised within each country also for internationally tradable goods.[13]

The law cannot be applied to non-tradable goods and services that cannot be moved from one country to another, and on which no arbitrage is possible. Indeed, in a modern economy, most products are non-tradable: they range from almost all public services to many private services, up to typically local goods, such as fresh foods. Hence, the general price level (including both traded and non traded goods) may differ significantly from one region to another, within the EU area without activating rapid and automatic offsetting mechanisms. Similarly, the simple intensification of trade within the EMU is unlikely to bring about convergence between wages and profits, let alone for sectors that are particularly exposed to international competition.

In this scenario, each national inflation rate would depend, on the one hand, on the common price dynamics of tradable goods and, on the other, on strictly domestic factors linked to efficiency and to the degree of protection of non-tradable sectors. Because of lower competition in protected sectors, productivity is likely to grow much less there than in sectors exposed to competition. However, in a system of centralized industrial relations, wages are substantially similar over the whole economy, and workers' productivity and wage gains in exposed sectors are also likely to trigger wage rises in protected sectors. This might increase the inflationary pressure – the Balassa–Samuelson effect – which is typical of least-developed economies experiencing catching-up processes. Productivity acceleration in tradable sectors of the least developed economic systems, compared to the rest of the area, go alongside a higher general price dynamic. Thus, for the whole of the European Union, there would be a portion of inflation caused simply by the different levels of member states' development, by their different industrial structures, and by the productivity differentials existing between exposed and protected sectors. Recent studies[14] estimate that, in Europe, the Balassa–Samuelson effect justifies a minimum annual figure of 1 per cent inflation. Below that threshold, the adoption of a common inflation objective for the whole Union would be too restrictive, because it would require reduction of the price level in the most developed high-price countries that are more orientated towards tradable sectors. In the presence of a nominal price rigidity, a similar scenario would hamper the necessary adjustments of the actual trade relationships between member countries, with an evidently negative impact on the overall performance of the area. The danger of deflation would have negative effects, particularly on investment and on the consumption of durable goods.

The price convergence in the EMU

To evaluate the inflationary impact of the process of convergence between national prices it is necessary to verify whether prices in the different countries have really shown signs of convergence towards a common level in recent years. Unfortunately, the quality of the available statistical indicators on absolute prices ('spatial' indicators) is bound to be harshly criticized, at least for the objective difficulty of comparing prices in substantially different economic situations. It is therefore necessary to be cautious in interpreting the spatial indicator dynamics and, in particular, to compare these to the other deflators of the national accounting aggregates and to other inflation indicators. What follows provides an examination of the convergence between prices of tradable goods and services by resorting to the purchasing power parity (PPP) indicators of GDP computed by the OECD for the EMU countries. Unlike what happens with indicators computed for consumer goods alone, these indicators take into account the prices of all goods and services demanded in an economy (private and public consumption, investments, exports and inventories) and thus mirror the wage dynamics of all national factors of production. PPP indicators are therefore useful in studying the overall process of convergence of prices of both tradable and non-tradable goods, and to evaluate the impact of price variations on the relative purchasing power of EMU citizens.

The examination of data (Figure 5.4) suggests that, from 1980 till 2001 – if one excludes the pause linked to the exchange rate realignment that occurred between 1992 and 1995 – national prices showed signs of convergence towards a common level (represented by a PPP value equal to 100 in the graphs). In particular, the graphs (a) and (b) show that, in countries with a higher price level (all located in northern and central Europe) the differential compared the European average has gradually been reducing. The situation was reversed in southern European countries, where prices remain below the average. In Ireland and Finland, the PPP indices continued to widen during the 1980s and eventually showed some signals of realignment in the following decade.

On the basis of the dynamics and level of the PPP indices, one might identify a group of countries witnessing a kind of autonomous convergence among the present EMU member states, namely the countries of northern and central Europe. In other countries the process was more diversified, though it is possible to recognize a common trend in southern European countries. Price levels have become ever more homogeneous over time, both within that group and in general between other countries (though to a lesser extent there), as shown by the trend of the dispersion of indices computed for all countries and for the two subgroups (north–centre and south of Europe) (see Figure 5.5). The reduction of the average gap between prices has undergone only one (though significant) interruption coinciding with the EMS (European Monetary System) crisis of 1992–5. However, that event apparently had no influence either on the ongoing process of convergence within the group of northern–central countries, or on that occurring within the group of southern economies. In particular, price dispersion in the northern–central countries

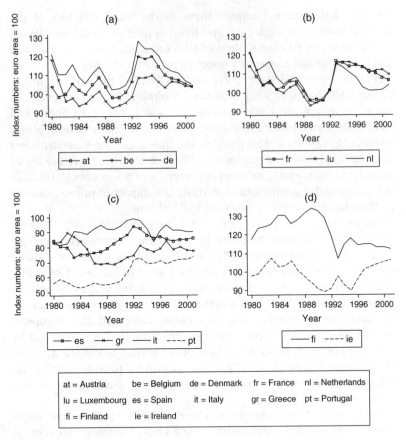

Figure 5.4 Purchasing power parity (PPP) indices in euro countries (weighted average in euro countries = 100)
Source: ISAE elaborations on OECD dataset.

has been reducing gradually since the late 1980s. In the south of Europe prices began to be homogeneous only since the middle of the nineties in coincidence with the acceleration of the adjustment process to enter the EMU. This evidence suggests that the anti-inflationary policy performed by national central banks before 1999, and by the ECB afterwards has not been so restrictive as to halt the process of price convergence.

A further confirmation comes from the examination of the relationship between the initial price level and its average annual variation. Figure 5.6 shows that, since 1980, the relationship between the two figures

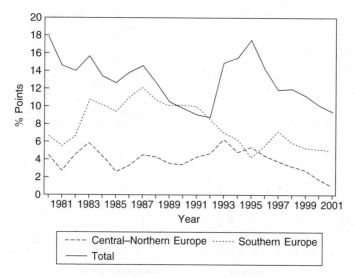

Figure 5.5 Dispersion between PPP indexes (average weighted squared differences)
Source: ISAE elaboration on OECD dataset.

has been negative in all the twenty-two years taken into consideration, as well as during the various sub-periods, all characterized by anti-inflation measures with different degrees of stringency. This means that prices in euro countries registered a convergence towards the average value of the area. The sign of the ratio did not change even after the 1999 adoption of a regime of 'irrevocably fixed' exchange rates. Such behaviour could indicate that the common monetary policy might have accelerated the natural trend towards price levelling through the more rigid discipline imposed by countries with above-average prices. It is no coincidence that in Germany, whose price level is among the highest in the EMU, the GDP deflator remained substantially unchanged in 1999, and even decreased in 2000. The constraints imposed on the more advanced (high-price) countries have thus enabled catching-up economies to gain ground more rapidly without resorting to high inflation rates.

Indeed, the degree of homogeneity between national convergence rates, in turn, has changed. Throughout the twenty two years examined, almost all the countries seem to respect the same relationship between price level and its average annual variation. In graphical terms, the points representing the different EMU members lie along the regression line between the two variables. The overall average dynamic of the PPP

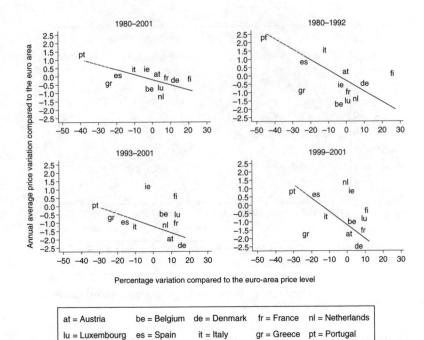

Figure 5.6   Price convergence in the euro area
Source: ISAE elaborations on OECD dataset.

indices in that period is rather modest, with annual variation rates ranging between 1.3 per cent for Portugal and 0.7 per cent for Belgium.

This result underpins situations that are diversified over time and mirrors the brusque PPP adjustment that occurred between 1992 and 1993. In particular, the stability of the inverse relationship between the variation rate and the price level has changed. Indeed, up to 1992, it was valid for almost all countries: only in Greece and Finland did the differential tend to remain substantially constant compared to European average prices, though it was still quite ample (25 per cent). In contrast, relative prices in Benelux tended to decrease, although they were already very close to the European average. After 1992, most countries readjusted to the inverse relationship between variation and PPP levels, with the exception of Ireland and Finland. In fact, the price differential compared to Europe as a whole increased in those countries, though both had price levels equal to or above the average. Finally, since the changeover, the dispersion of countries around the regression line has grown considerably, which testifies to some uncertainty in the process of convergence.

In all the cases, the process of price levelling has been very gradual, so that in none of the years examined has the average variation of the PPP indices exceeded the annual figure of 2.5 per cent, not even in countries presenting a significant price differential compared to the European average. At this rate, it would take twelve years to halve the initial difference between national prices and average EMU prices. Indeed, it would take twenty years if one took as a reference point the highest PPP variation rate computed over the whole period, which is about 1.5 per cent per annum.

In spite of the slow convergence process, national prices tend to move towards a common level and together with their scarce downward flexibility, probably exert some inflationary pressure within the EMU. This poses a lower limit on the inflation objectives the ECB can realistically fix without causing a deflation in high-price countries. Table 5.2 provides some estimations of such a limit; it shows the average

Table 5.2 Dynamics of national PPP and minimum inflation in the EMU (percentage average variation rates on annual basis)

Countries	1980–2001	1980–92	1993–2001	1998–2001	1999–2001
Austria	0.00	0.20	−1.75	−1.28	−1.51
Belgium	−0.69	−1.68	−0.58	−0.87	−1.16
Germany	−0.66	−0.77	−2.40	−2.04	−2.54
Spain	0.09	0.98	−0.93	0.76	0.60
Finland	−0.21	0.08	0.54	−0.84	−0.39
France	−0.34	−1.02	−1.13	−1.54	−1.76
Greece	−0.34	−0.91	−0.53	−0.43	−1.78
Ireland	0.41	−0.59	1.14	1.20	0.98
Italy	0.38	1.50	−1.07	−0.42	−0.49
Luxembourg	−0.52	−1.62	−0.62	−0.26	−0.89
Netherlands	−0.80	−1.57	−1.37	0.97	1.33
Portugal	1.29	2.28	0.01	1.09	0.86
*Minimum inflation rate for the EMU**					
Overall figure	0.80	1.68	2.40	2.04	2.54
Excluding the country with maximum PPP reduction	0.69	1.62	1.75	1.54	1.78

Note: * Computed under the hypothesis that in no country nominal prices may diminish in absolute value.
Source: ISAE elaboration on OECD dataset.

PPP variation rate in each country in different significant periods. Admittedly, wherever the rate is negative (in Belgium, Germany, France and Luxembourg in the whole sub-period considered), a relative price fall takes place compared to the European average. Had that fall brought about a reduction in absolute prices, this would have led to a deflation in those countries. Each PPP average annual variation (with inverted sign) may thus be interpreted as the minimum inflation rate for the euro area (computed in terms of GDP deflator) which would have enabled the observed process of convergence without causing the absolute price reduction in the economy considered.

In the whole period between 1980 and 2001, the Netherlands is the country that would have required the highest price reduction (0.8 per cent) to realize the convergence with the euro area followed by Belgium, Germany and Luxembourg. In order to avoid deflation in the Netherlands, national central banks and the ECB should have tolerated a price rise above 0.8 per cent. However, that threshold would prove to be insufficient to avoid a deflationist adjustment of some economies, both in the 1980s and after 1992. Indeed, in the former period, the minimum inflation rate in the euro area should have reached 1.7 per cent (to avoid a deflation in Belgium) and, after 1992, should have reached 2.4 per cent (to avoid deflation in Germany). The threshold exceeded 2.5 per cent in the period of irrevocably fixed exchange rates (1999–2001). In all the sub-periods examined, a price rise of between 1.5 per cent and 1.8 per cent would have caused deflation limited only to the countries most 'at risk' (Belgium before 1992; and Germany in the following periods).

The figures indicated in the last two lines of Table 5.2 can be interpreted as estimates of the minimum threshold for the ECB inflation objectives that can be hardly overcome. The thresholds computed since 1993 and those reported for the two most recent sub-periods are necessarily affected by the adjustment following the 1992 shock and thus represent an extreme value, not representative of the long- and medium-term PPP dynamics. Conversely, the minimum inflation rate estimated for the whole period implicitly embodies the hypothesis that the PPP realignment in 1992–5 is not an isolated episode, but is the expression of the long-term trend towards European price levelling. However, this seems to be contradicted by the fast recovery of price convergence that has been taking place since 1993. For the same reason, the PPP variations registered before 1992 cannot be considered 'sustainable' in the long- and medium-term, because of the subsequent realignment. A realistic estimation of the EMU inflation justified by price levelling alone should be made between the maximum of 1.7 per cent (based on the experience of the 1980s) and the minimum of 0.8 per cent (based on the average of the twenty-two years under consideration). The ceiling of 1.7 per cent seems to be confirmed substantially by the minimum inflation rate required since 1992 to limit any possible deflation for Germany, where the rapid adjustment in PPP has probably been affected by the reunification shock of the 1990s.

The conduct of fiscal policy

Co-ordination in the EMU fiscal policy

The process of convergence in the institutions and policies of nations belonging to an integrated area – as in Europe – may generally take place along two major lines, namely co-ordination or, alternatively, competition, between countries. In turn, to reach convergence, these two options may be more or less stringent (or more or less 'loose'), according to whether they aim directly at the general rules to which individual behaviour and national policies should adhere or at the policies pursued by single member states. Both paths draw inspiration from very different principles and may lead to completely different results in terms of intensity and overall efficiency of the convergence process between structures, policies and institutions of the countries participating in the integration process.

This co-ordination tends to impose on individual countries the choices made between member states, or between them and the supranational bodies of the integrated area. This overlapping is strongly binding whenever it aims at setting not only the objectives, but also the policies to be adopted for their implementation (policy co-ordination). It is less invasive when it encourages convergence by co-ordinating general rules (the fixing of objectives, defining recommendations, identifying guidelines and codes of behaviour), to give a common guide for national decisions, leaving to individual countries margins of autonomy to set the specific modalities to pursue their own objectives (rule co-ordination).

Conversely, competition between countries leads to convergence that stems from market incentives. This may happen on the basis of a minimum common denominator, namely very general rules shared by all countries (competition of policies), or of direct competition between the same basic rules (competition of rules). The final result of this mechanism is not a priori uniformity, nor is the deepening the result of a mediation between national partners.

Though they are strongly opposing principles, co-ordination and competition represent guidelines that may be applied to different situations at the same time, according to the areas where convergence is pursued. Whenever market incentives prove to be unsuccessful, or the propensity of national policy-makers to adopt short-sighted behaviour is strong – perhaps because they are swayed by lobbies or vested interests – then more or less binding forms of co-ordination may offset the market failure. Conversely, whenever the market plays its role of arbitrage – as indeed is possible in all areas connected with supply policies – then forms of competition based on a set of minimum common rules might favour an effective process of convergence. With regard to the carrying out of European budget policies, the adopted approach – taking into account the risks of opportunistic behaviour on the part of policy-makers – is based on the co-ordination of rules. At first, rules were represented by the Maastricht parameters on the deficit-to-GDP and debt-to-GDP ratios of the general government, and then by the objectives concerning the medium-term budget balances listed in the Stability and Growth Pact, strengthened by control procedures and hypotheses of sanctions for behaviour deviating from the target of macroeconomic stability for the area.

The idea of a co-ordination of the budget policy rules is part and parcel of the Treaty establishing the European Community.[15] To this end, art. 4 states that 'the activities of Member States and of the Community shall include ... the adoption of an economic policy which is based on the close co-ordination of the Member States' policies'. Co-ordination becomes a necessity for EMU countries, as the performing of a single monetary policy would be undermined, or at least be less effective, if national economic policies paid no attention to the externalities of the rest of the currency area, particularly in their impact on price dynamics.

The pursuing of the correct policy mix is thus a fundamental prerequisite in the EMU, not only for those countries leaving to the ECB their national sovereignty on monetary policy, but also for the EU members that have not adopted the single currency. Indeed, the Treaty imposes on them a compliance with the euro area policy and, in particular, with the single market smoothing functioning.

The main instrument for co-ordination foreseen by the Treaty consists of the Broad Economic Policy Guidelines, introduced with art. 99. The Guidelines represent a reference framework for the carrying out of the economic policy in the Community and in individual member states, to ensure a long-lasting convergence of economic results and facilitate the monitoring of the economic evolution of the Union. According to the Treaty, member states communicate to the Commission information on their economic policy interventions. The Ecofin Council – on the basis of the Commission's reports – controls the economic policies in the Union and, should it identify any inconsistency between economic management in a member state and the Guidelines, it issues the member state with a Recommendation that may be made public.[16] To make its control over public budgets more stringent, art. 104 of the Treaty defines the 'excessive deficit procedure' by specifying reference values for the budget deficit and for the government debt, equalling 3 per cent and 60 per cent, respectively (art. 1 of the Protocol on the excessive deficit procedure). The aim is to avoid any form of loosening of the fiscal stringency, once a country has joined the EMU. The Stability and Growth Pact, which the member states signed in 1997, sets out the rules for the functioning of budget policies and fixes a procedure of rigorous and timely fiscal policy surveillance.

Since 1997, the debate on economic policy co-ordination between EU member states has become more intense and has also involved sectors that used to be part of supply policies, for which – as has already been noted – a competition-based approach seemed to be more suitable. In particular, the Luxembourg process (December 1997), the Cardiff process (June 1998) and the Cologne process (June 1999) define the procedures for a close co-operation in the sectors of employment policies, of structural reforms and of macroeconomic dialogue with social parties, respectively.

Alongside those initiatives involving different sectors of economic policy, the need is growing for greater consistency between the various procedures adopted by the different Council bodies. Thus the Guidelines take up an ever more important role in the co-ordination process: on the one hand, they provide a unitary vision of the effects of national economic policies, trying to exploit positive externalities and eliminate negative behaviour; and on the other, they are a link between the different processes, so as to make the economic policies implemented in different sectors consistent and highlight their interactions.[17] The whole co-ordination process is led by the Ecofin Council. It also includes a smaller body, the Eurogroup, consisting of members of the euro area alone, which deals at an informal level with all aspects linked to the monetary union. The full Ecofin Council is involved when decisions need to be taken.

The economic policy co-ordination between member states must take place in full respect of four main principles recognized by the Treaty, namely (i) the principle of *subsidiarity*, whereby member states maintain their responsibility on economic policy, with the exception of monetary policy for countries adopting the euro; (ii) the principle of *independence* of the various policy-makers, which defines the relationships between institutions and, in particular, between member states and the ECB, which are called to debate and discuss the economic prospects and the policies adopted, but without exerting *ex ante* pressures and interferences; (iii) the principle of an *open and competitive market economy* underlining the central role of the single market; and (iv) the principle of *close co-ordination*, leading member states to consider domestic economic policies that would be interesting to the whole Community.

The approach underlying co-ordination is based on consensus, to avoid imposing necessary provisions on a member state, but trying to convince its government to adopt an economic policy approach that is considered more suitable.

The role of the Stability and Growth Pact within the co-ordination process

The Stability and Growth Pact stems from the need to clarify and enhance the Treaty rules on budget policy. In particular, the pact sets the rules for economic policy co-ordination and defines the conditions for the enforcement of the excessive deficit procedure.

It consists of three components: (i) the Resolution on the Meeting of the European Council on the Stability and Growth Pact (17 June 1997); (ii) Council Regulation (EC) n. 1466/97 of 7 July 1997 on the strengthening of the surveillance of budgetary positions, and the surveillance and co-ordination of economic policies; and (iii) Council Regulation (EC) n. 1467/97 of 7 July 1997 on speeding up and clarifying the implementation of the excessive deficit procedure.

To ensure sound public finances, the Resolution of the European Council commits the member states to pursue budget balances close to parity (or positive) in the medium term. The first Regulation foresees a monitoring and control procedure of the budget policies on an annual basis through Programmes of Stability (for EMU countries) and Convergence (for the remaining EU countries) and subsequent updating procedures monitored by the Ecofin Council. The second Regulation sets the circumstances in which a deficit exceeding 3 per cent of GDP may not be considered excessive[18] and sets schedules and deadlines for the monitoring procedure of the financial positions of member states and of the modalities and amount of sanctions. In particular, the Council Regulation n. 1467/1997 envisages that a government with an excessive deficit will create a non-interest-bearing deposit for an amount given from the sum of two components, namely a fixed component equalling 0.2 per cent of GDP and a variable component equal to one-tenth of the difference between the deficit as a percentage of GDP in the year in which the deficit is deemed to be excessive, and the reference value of 3 per cent of GDP.[19] The annual amount of deposits may not exceed the upper limit of 0.5 per cent of GDP. A deposit is converted as a rule into a fine if, in the view of the Council, the excessive deficit has not been corrected after two years.

The prerequisite of a budget 'close to a balance or in surplus', foreseen explicitly in the Stability and Growth Pact, draws inspiration from the need to pursue three main objectives, namely (i) avoiding excessive deficits and reversing the past trend to accumulate high public debt as a percentage of GDP; (ii) enabling automatic fiscal stabilizers to operate freely in the various cycle phases; and (iii) making the constraint of a deficit not exceeding 3 per cent of GDP more credible. Additionally, a stringent budget policy allows the accumulation of resources to face the impact of the ageing population on public finances. However, a budget balance implies a constant decline of the debt-to-GDP ratio that might not be a desirable outcome for every country in the long run.

However, the Stability and Growth Pact provides no operative indication on the computation of the budget objectives. In a first approximation, the European Commission computed minimal benchmarks for each of the member states. The balances indicated are those that allow a smooth functioning of automatic fiscal stabilizers by avoiding, in normal cyclical conditions, deficits exceeding 3 per cent of GDP. This is a minimum prerequisite for the fiscal objectives. It must be respected on average along the economic cycle and must thus hold true for that part of the public budget net of economic fluctuations. The consequence on the balance in nominal terms is an oscillation mirroring the anti-cyclical nature of the budget components, without discretional interventions.

Table 5.3 reports the minimal benchmarks for member states computed by the European Commission, together with the structural budget balances registered in 2001 and the coefficients of sensitivity of the cycle. These represent the impact on the public deficit of each percentage-point deviation of GDP from full employment.[20] As Table 5.3 shows, Germany and Portugal were the only countries that did not respect the minimum prerequisite for structural budgets, and thus were unable to

Table 5.3 Coefficients of sensitivity and minimal benchmark, 2002

	Coefficients of sensitivity	Minimal benchmark (as a percentage of GDP)	Structural budget balances of 2001 (as a percentage of GDP)
Belgium	0.60	−0.7	−0.4
Germany	0.50	−1.6	−2.5
Greece	0.40	−1.7	−0.7
Spain	0.40	−1.5	−0.7
France	0.40	−1.7	−1.6
Ireland	0.35	−1.3	2.4
Italy	0.45	−1.5	−1.5
Luxembourg	0.60	0.1	3.6
Netherlands	0.65	−0.7	−0.3
Austria	0.30	−2.1	−0.2
Portugal	0.35	−1.2	−3.2
Finland	0.70	0.8	3.6
EU-12	0.50	−1.4	−1.5
Denmark	0.80	−0.3	2.6
Sweden	0.70	−0.8	4.2
United Kingdom*	0.50	−1.2	0.6
EU-15	0.50	−1.4	−0.9

Note: * Data refer to the financial year.
Source: European Commission (2002c).

face the ongoing economic slowdown by resorting to the automatic flexibility margins contained in the public budget structure, and they reported deficits equalling 2.7 per cent of GDP, that is, close to the critical threshold.

Table 5.3 shows that the structural budget balance of all the EU countries satisfies the minimum prerequisite, but not the euro countries alone: indeed, countries not adopting the single currency in 2001 registered ample structural surpluses. Table 5.3 also indicates that, for most countries, a deficit of between 1 per cent and 2 per cent of GDP is sufficient to make automatic fiscal stabilizers function without causing excessive deficits. Belgium, the Netherlands, Denmark and Sweden should aim at obtaining smaller deficits (below 1 per cent of GDP), while Finland and Luxembourg should maintain a surplus budget.[21]

Better results than the minimal benchmarks may be obtained, both to manage the variability of the erratic budget components not linked to cyclical fluctuations, and to finance further economic policy objectives, among which a quicker reduction of the debt-to-GDP ratio, higher costs caused by the ageing population, or possible discretional policies.

A cyclically adjusted balance respecting the objective of a budget close to a balance or in surplus means that, in expansion phases, the budget positions in nominal terms are positive. This causes a public saving enabling greater scope for manoeuvre in the face of further factors influencing the fiscal policy.

Apart from the objective of a balanced budget, the Treaty establishing the European Community and the Stability and Growth Pact requires a public debt-to-GDP ratio below 60 per cent or, should that ratio exceed the reference value, that it decreases 'sufficiently' and gets close to the reference value 'with a suitable pace'. The meaning of 'sufficiently' and 'suitable pace' is not specified, and this means that the only reference is the sign of the change of the ratio, should it exceed the reference value.

Debt levels below 60 per cent of GDP may move freely in both directions, under the only constraint that the 60 per cent threshold is not exceeded. However, a different relevance of the objectives in terms of deficits between countries with very different debt-to-GDP ratios (as those registered in the EU) emerges from that perspective. The convergence towards the objective of a balanced or surplus budget (though within the upper limit of 3 per cent of GDP) would indeed be less stringent for countries with low debt levels (below 60 per cent).

Among countries with either nominal or structural high deficits (above 0.75 per cent)[22] – Germany, France, Italy and Portugal – only Italy has the problem of substantial debt, which indeed causes growing pressure to accelerate its reduction. Germany, with a debt equalling 59.8 per cent of GDP, is closer to the reference value, and the Commission predicted that the 60 per cent threshold would be slightly exceeded in 2002–3.[23] France and Portugal, in turn, are very interested in interpreting the Stability and Growth Pact in such a way that the stress is laid more on the debt level: this would reduce the urgent need to reduce the deficit quickly.

Table 5.4 shows that, among countries with debt levels above 60 per cent of GDP, Belgium has reached a budget balance in nominal terms, while Greece and Austria are close to it. Renewed attention to the public debt level is emerging because of the impact of the ageing population on public finances. Debt reduction is one possible measure to expand financial resources in view of future demographic trends. Thus the debt level is likely to be monitored more closely in the evaluations of the stability and growth programmes in the near future.

At the time of writing, the procedure of multilateral surveillance foreseen by the Stability and Growth Pact was undergoing its fourth round.

Table 5.4 Budget balances and public debt, 2001 (as a percentage of GDP)

	Budget balance	Structural balance	Public debt
Belgium	0.0	−0.4	107.5
Germany	−2.7	−2.5	59.8
Greece	−0.4	−0.7	99.7
Spain	−0.2	−0.7	57.2
France	−1.5	−1.6	57.7
Ireland	1.7	−0.1	36.3
Italy	−2.2	−1.5	109.8
Luxembourg	5.0	3.6	5.5
Netherlands	0.3	−0.3	52.9
Austria	−0.1	−0.2	61.7
Portugal	−2.7	−3.2	55.5
Finland	4.9	3.6	43.6
Euro area	−1.3	−1.5	68.6
Denmark	2.8	2.6	43.3
Sweden	4.6	4.2	52.6
United Kingdom*	0.9	−0.2	37.6
EU-15	−0.7	−0.9	60.5

Note: * Data refer to the financial year.
Source: European Commission (2002c).

If one looks at the original stability programme and at its three updated versions, one notes that the budget objectives were satisfied or improved, and the adjustment profiles became more ambitious. Besides, the changes emerging from the latest updating (not in all countries) relates to the economic slowdown and thus stems from the very rules of the Stability and Growth Pact. Therefore, making reference to the nominal balance trend, the co-ordination and surveillance process in the first three and a half years seems to have functioned well.

However, if one goes beyond the exclusively quantitative aspects, one may identify some shortcomings in the ongoing process. The first problem is that the adjustment process seems to have been longer than was foreseen. Indeed, the adjustments made were left mainly to cyclical or temporary phenomena and to the reduction of interest expenditure. The structural interventions indicated in the programmes have often been postponed to the end of the period under consideration, thus implying a lesser political credibility, particularly in the cases in which the governments involved had a shorter 'residual' life than the time horizon envisaged by the programme. Furthermore, in periods of economic cycle expansion (particularly in the year 2000), the growth dividends were not fully exploited to accelerate the balance restoration.

Table 5.5 Structural budget balances[a] (as percentage of GDP)

Euro area	1997	1998	1999	2000	2001[b]
Structural budget balance	−2.2	−2.1	−1.3	−1.3	−1.5
Primary budget balance	3.0	2.7	3.0	2.7	2.4
Interest expenditure	5.1	4.8	4.3	4.1	3.9
EU-15					
Structural budget balance	−2.1	−1.6	−0.8	−0.7	−0.9
Primary budget balance	2.8	3.1	3.3	3.1	2.8
Interest expenditure	4.9	4.6	4.1	3.9	3.7

Notes: [a] Structural balances exclude revenues from mobile phone licences (UMTS).
[b] Data for 2001 are estimated.
Source: European Commission (2002c).

Table 5.5 shows the cyclically adjusted balances and the expenditure for the debt financing in the euro area and in the EU-15 for 1997–2001. In the face of constantly decreasing interest expenditure, the EU structural deficit falls until 2000, but rises again in 2001. Conversely, the primary surplus inverts its trend, which had been growing since the previous year. Structural primary balances are the best variable to measure the fiscal stance (that is, the fiscal policy direction), as they are not affected either by variations in the economic cycle, or by the interest expenditure representing a component that is not controlled directly by fiscal authorities.

The loosening of the fiscal strictness observed during the economic recovery of the year 2000 brings about the risk of pro-cycle policies and raises doubts on the credibility of budget objectives close to a balance or in surplus. Indeed, while the excessive deficit procedure makes the 3 per cent threshold a stringent constraint, the lack of enforcement instruments weakens the medium-term objectives required by the Pact, which are a type of reference point.

If the member states could complete the restoration of their public accounts until they reached sufficiently robust budget positions, the fiscal policy would again be an effective instrument, not only to reduce the impact of cyclical fluctuations but also to finance economic reforms and implement targeted discretional policies. Indeed, with structural budgets close to a balance or in surplus, the member states' governments might support the economic activity stabilization with robust public finances. The implicit principle in the Stability and Growth Pact is that automatic fiscal stabilizers are cycle-regulating instruments more effective than discretional interventions. The fundamental criticism levelled against discretional policies is that – because of the parliamentary procedure necessary for their approval – they risk being enforced when cyclical conditions have changed. Thus discretional provisions tend to have pro-cycle effects by amplifying economic fluctuations.[24] These interventions seem to be more suitable for introducing structural changes in public finances, or responding to exceptional events. Conversely, automatic fiscal stabilizers have the advantage of acting spontaneously as soon as economic activity weakens.

The efficacy of automatic fiscal stabilizers depends on their dimension, which, in turn, mirrors the structures of the taxation system and of public expenditure. Indeed, a higher public expenditure/GDP ratio means more protection for the economy against cyclical fluctuations and, on the revenue side, a growing tax progression enhances the stabilization effect.[25] Hence the reduction in the public-sector weight pursued in many European countries should guarantee the maintenance of a minimum dimension for the smooth functioning of cyclical stabilisers.[26]

To be effective in the medium-term, automatic fiscal stabilizers must operate symmetrically in both phases of the cycle; this would allow the exploitation of the expansionary phases to accumulate reserves for slack periods.

New proposals for better co-ordination

The first years of the Monetary Union were very useful to identify, on the one hand, the limits of the present co-ordination procedure and, on the other, the needs that are to be considered in the process. Against this background, agreements and conventions become part of the procedure and integrate with it, even though fiscal strictness remains the main objective; indeed, as new targets take up importance (long run sustainability, structural reforms, growth supportive measures) better evaluation instruments are needed (structural deficits, sustainability of pension systems and so forth).

To make multilateral surveillance and budget policy co-ordination more effective, a whole series of improvements was proposed, both within and outside the Commission. Some of these have already been included in the new code of conduct, and member states are about to adopt it. Among these improvements, it is worth mentioning:

- the simultaneous submission of programmes and *ex ante* co-ordination;
- the improvement of the contents and drafting of programmes;
- the improvement of the evaluation instruments; and
- more attention to the qualitative aspects of the budget.

New timing for programme submission

The Commission and the Council are sometimes accused of being unfair when they examine programmes. Among the reasons recognized by the Council, there is the long period of time that the two Community bodies need to examine all the programmes. A simultaneous submission on the part of all member states would enable a fairer discussion to be carried out in a single Council meeting. This would enable all countries to have the same level of updating of data and forecasts, and to evaluate whether the macroeconomic hypotheses contained in the programmes are consistent. Thus the new code of conduct approved by the Ecofin Council requires member states to present the updating of their programmes within one and half months (15 October–1 December). Hence, the Council commits itself to evaluating all programmes within a maximum of two sessions' time between December and January.

Definition of structural objectives

Among the problems of programme interpretation, there is the fixing of objectives. If objectives are set in nominal terms, as happens at present, there is the risk of pro-cycle behaviour: thus the need emerges to monitor structural budgets. Unfortunately, the reference to cyclically adjusted budget balances – though provided by some countries – is still limited as a medium-term objective. In particular, this is because of the discretionality of the construction of that indicator.[27]

Thus the need to identify a reliable parameter to compute structural budget balances seems ever more urgent. The indicators generally used to this end present a series of shortcomings and practical and theoretical difficulties. The definition of a structural budget needs the identification of two components, namely the output gap and the parameters of budget sensitivity. To compute the former component, there are two

Table 5.6   Output gap (deviation of actual from potential output)

Euro area	1997	1998	1999	2000	2001	2002	2003
European Commission HP[a]	−1.0	−0.4	0.0	1.1	0.3	−0.6	0.0
European Commission PF[b]	−0.8	−0.2	0.1	0.9	0.0	−0.9	−0.5
OECD	−1.9	−1.3	−0.9	0.2	−0.5	−1.4	−0.8

Notes: [a] HP refers to a methodology based on the Hodrick–Prescott filter.
[b] FP refers to a methodology based on the production function.
Source: European Commission (2002d); OECD (2002b).

prevailing methods: (i) a statistical approach utilizing a Hodrick–Prescott (HP) filter to identify the growth trend; and (ii) a structural approach based on the estimate of a production function. The former was utilized currently by the European Commission, while the latter is the basis of the output gap measurement provided by the IMF and the OECD. Unfortunately, the output gap levels generated by the two procedures are not so consistent (see Table 5.6). The Commission has therefore begun to estimate the output gap with both methods and used them from the financial year 2002–3.[28] Table 5.6 shows the output gap values computed by the Commission using both methodologies, alongside the figures estimated by the OECD through the production function method.

Not only do the two procedures lead to different results, but also the output gap computed by both institutions on the basis of the production function shows even more divergent results. This happens because the evaluation of the potential product through the production function depends strongly on the way in which capital and labour are estimated. Both variables show deep limitations: on the one hand, it is difficult to obtain a reliable measure of capital; and on the other, the potential employment level estimated through the NAIRU implies a number of discretional assumptions.[29]

Qualitative aspects of the public budget

To go beyond a merely quantitative evaluation of the budget policy, and while recognizing the role that public finances may play in promoting growth and employment, the member states are invited to provide in their annual programme updatings some indications of the economic policies they have enforced or planned to reach the following objectives:

- reduce the fiscal pressure on labour, with particular attention to low-skilled labour, and improve the incentives implicit in the fiscal and social security systems to encourage high employment rates;
- restructure public expenditure by increasing the role of (both physical and human) capital accumulation, and stimulate research and development; and
- guarantee the long-term financial sustainability, particularly in the light of the demographic evolution.

Constraints to the public expenditure growth

One of the main difficulties of the process of convergence towards the a budget close to a balance or in surplus is maintaining strict fiscal rigour during expansion phases without yielding to the temptation to use growth dividends to loosen budget constraints. To this end, the Commission and the Ecofin Council are paying more attention to structural balances. It is, however, rather difficult to provide a thorough evaluation of them – all the more so because, in order to be useful in carrying out current fiscal policy, the current estimate of the position of the economic cycle should be available.

A more effective instrument of fiscal rigour is to be found in rules to control public expenditure. These rules appear more effective in controlling the budget for several reasons: (i) they address directly the main source of pressure on deficits, which is generally the public expenditure/GDP ratio; (ii) they apply to the budget component that is controlled directly by the government, which is directly responsible for the respect of objectives; (iii) they are conceptually easy and simple to verify; and (iv) they enable the use of automatic fiscal stabilizers, at least on the revenue side.[30] Indeed, the constraints on the expenditure growth rate do not offer protection from the emergence of excessive deficits caused by drastic fiscal cuts. Thus budget balances must be kept under control, particularly if a balanced or surplus budget has not yet been reached. Above all the introduction of these rules is part of national sovereignty of individual states and, at Community level, this may be at the best suggested rather than enforced.

The reform of the Stability and Growth Pact

Finally, the need to modify the very approach of the Stability and Growth Pact has grown since slowdown of the economic cycle in 2001. Draft reforms are necessitated in the main by the public financial difficulties of major European countries, because of worse-than-expected economic trends. However, these proposals go beyond the mere cyclical 'occasional' phenomenon. Generally speaking, they aim at making the pact more focused on the target of relaunching development and increasing incentives to work and invest in Europe.

Two main indicators emerged in the recent debate on the modification of the pact. The former states that public balances should be computed on the basis of the golden rule – that is, net of investment expenditure. These expenses would create a debt burden, which could be 'covered' thanks to higher productivity and growth. This procedure is justified by the consideration that sacrificing investments for budget reasons might mean penalizing long-term growth, with negative effects for public accounts. Particularly, investments have long run positive effects on the economy and, for this reason, their finnancing can be fairly shared with future generations that will benefit from those effects. Last but not least, an implicit 'golden rule' was behind the 3 per cent threshold when the Maastricht Treaty was signed: indeed, it was (implicitly) assumed that current expenditures should have been fully financed with corrsponding revenues, while investments, up to an amount of 3 per cent of GDP, could be financed in deficit. The second draft modification is based on the principle whereby – given the technical relations existing between deficit formation and debt trends (both as a percentage of GDP) – the process of debt reduction and budget balance should be evaluated while taking into account the distance separating the general government borrowing of each country from the objective parameter of 60 per cent indicated in the Stability and Growth Pact. Thus, according to this approach, the amount of the deficit-to-GDP ratio has a different weight according to the debt-to-GDP ratio that accompanies it.

Addendum

This chapter was written in 2002. At that time, the phase of European economic slowdown had been going on for one-and-a-half years; since the time of writing, another year and a half passed before seeing some moderate improvement in the economic situation of continental Europe. This long period of stagnation shed more light on the drawbacks of the architecture of macroeconomic policy of the euro area, particularly as far as the limits of the coordination processes are concerned. Dissatisfaction with the use of the European policy instruments was further accentuated by the comparison with the US coeval experience: in that country an activist approach on the sides of both monetary and fiscal policies allowed a much more rapid recovery, though at the expense of increasing domestic and external imbalances.

As to the European monetary policy, the ECB approach remained basically consistent with that depicted in this chapter, with interest rates determined on the grounds of both inflation and output gap of the euro area. However, in this period of prolonged deceleration, asymmetric repercussions at the national level became more pronounced with respect to what could be detected in the first three years of EMU. In particular, monetary policy proved more restrictive for Germany, given the dimension of the this economy and its trade links with the European partner countries, with some consequences for the whole euro area. According to some econometric evidence,[31] the ECB interest rate in this period (2002–3) was higher by almost one percentage point than the one that would have been appropriate for Germany considering its domestic cyclical conditions (regarding inflation and output gap); on the grounds of these estimates, had the ECB adopted in this phase a more Germany-oriented interest rate policy, the outcome for the euro area as a whole could have been a slightly higher inflation, but also a stronger GDP growth.

The three-year stagnation also revealed the weakness of the Stability and Growth Pact as a 'coordination device'. Some member states had the incentive to relax their budget policy to stimulate domestic demand while tax revenue was reduced by economic downturn. As a result the deficit to GDP ratio worsened in most countries. General government's budget balance moved from –1.7 per cent of GDP in 2001 to –2.4 in 2002 and –2.7 in 2003, for the euro area as a whole (it was respectively –1.1, –2.1 and –2.7 in the EU15); structural deficit also increased in 2002 but not in 2003. In particular, France and Germany broke the 3 per cent threshold in 2002 and 2003 (with a deficit to GDP ratio equal to 3.2 and 4.1 in France, and to 3.7 and 3.8 in Germany, in the two years respectively), while Portugal had showed a previously unexpected deficit of 4.4 per cent of GDP in 2001. In the year 2003, the Netherlands and the UK also exhibited public deficits above the Pact limit, with values of 3.2 and 3.3 per cent of GDP respectively. Moreover, the multilateral surveillance appeared quite weak in its ability to control budgetary data provided by member states: when a new government took power in Greece in 2004, it turned out that the country had suffered from an excessive deficit since 2000 (this episode followed the already mentioned case of Portugal where a higher than expected deficit emerged only with a new government in charge). Debt to GDP ratios also grew in many countries, reaching 70.6 in the euro area and 64.2 in the European Union in 2003; it also rose above the 60 per cent reference value in France and Germany.

An important feaure that emerged during this period was the hetero-geneous nature of the euro area: large and small countries, when facing a symmetric shock, react with different strategies due to divergent incentives and constraints.[32] In particular, during negative phases of the cycle large countries have a strong incentive to use the fiscal tool to stimulate the economy as domestic demand plays a major role in supporting growth; conversely, small and open economies can easily give up public spending to support the cycle as their economies rely mostly on external demand. Moreover, a limited public budget and debt, with low tax burden, can be a source of a further stimulus to growth for the smaller countries, thanks to better business incentives and increased competition.

These two positions emerged clearly in the Ecofin Council of 25 November 2003, when the Council opposed the Commission proposal to move a step further in the 'excessive deficit procedure' against France and Germany. Institutional conflict occurred with that decision and opened a large debate on the appropriateness of the Stability and Growth Pact and its current application. Major proposals that emerged from this discussion still reflect those discussed in this chapter (basic-ally, golden rule and more focus on debt burden); however, because of the required unanimity of 25 member states for any formal change, it is quite unlikely that a modification would be the outcome. Most probably, an informal agreement will be reached on the interpretation of the Pact.

6
The European Policy Mix:
Law and Order

The rite of money

The euro area triggered the launch of a yet-unheard-of economic policy architecture. Unlike a US-style monetary union, Europeans decided they did not need the federal financial clout that would allow them to carry out an effective redistribution policy between member states on a vast 'European' scale. With an upward limit of 1.4 per cent of European GDP, the Community's budget does not allow – far from it, in fact – for far-reaching policies. Torn as it is between the Common Agricultural Policy (CAP) and structural funds, it finds it hard to make its mark on either agricultural revival or the realignment of poorer regions.

Although the USA's common monetary policy is independent, it is yet accountable to elected bodies such as the Federal government or Congress. In addition, as US fiscal policy has proved, it was powerful enough to face shocks as devastating as the bursting of the early twenty-first century's financial bubble or the Middle East wars (Afghanistan and Iraq), it can at the time of writing afford to redistribute wealth between the richer and poorer individual, and wealthier and needier regions. With the help of state budgets, the Federal budget can play its part in resolving asymmetrical shocks, since the links with monetary policy are complements rather than close substitutes, and foster the exchange of information for which there is no replacement (Debrun and Wyplosz, 1999). So, while it originated in the USA [the 'rational expectations' revolution in macroeconomics and the widespread credibility and reputation status to ensue, the macroeconomic dogma] is hardly ever applied there.

Consequently, Europe seems to be best characterized by its shadowing of US theoretical modes and models – it did grant the ECB independence, but without being held accountable to voters. Budgetary policy was capped to prevent its inflationary tendency jeopardizing the ECB's objectives. Governmental power was distorted to such an extent that it sometimes had to turn to the Commission for recommendations on public finance (the Stability and Growth Pact), or even on structural reform (Broad Guidelines for Economic Policy): the institutional provisions that each contributed to the democratic deficit affecting Europe make a long list. When one is confronted with a most debatable policy mix, it becomes necessary to think of possible reforms, which will be dealt with later in the chapter.

But before we do that, the economic policy underpinning Europe's architecture and rationale must be scrutinized. It will become obvious as a result that there *was* an alternative; it may not be too late to go back and adopt it.

Institutional provisions for...

...*monetary policy*

The European system of central banks (ESCB) comprises the European Central Bank (ECB) and the national central banks. The ESCB is entrusted with the euro area's monetary policy, whose prime objective is 'to maintain price stability' (art. 105 of the Treaty). The ECB and the national central banks are independent of both the national governments and the Commission; and they are not required to take instructions from the latter organisations (art. 107 of the Treaty). 'Overdraft facilities or any other type of credit facility in favour of... public authorities shall be prohibited, as shall the purchase directly from them by the ECB... of debt instruments' (art. 104 of the Treaty). The governing council of the ECB comprises the governors of the national central banks and six members of the executive board, including the president. They are chosen by national governments for a term of office of eight years 'from among persons of recognised standing and professional experience in monetary or banking matters' (art. 109 of the Treaty). The ECB is required to prepare an annual report to be delivered to the European Parliament, the Council and the Commission. The European Parliament will be addressed by the president of the executive board four times a year. The president of the executive board and other board and Council members will not be involved.

...*exchange rate policy*

The European Council may conclude exchange rate agreements following a recommendation from the Commission, after consulting the European Parliament and the ECB 'to reach a consensus consistent with the objective of price stability'. It may 'formulate general orientations for exchange-rate policy... These general orientations shall be without prejudice to the primary objective... of price stability' (art. 109 of the Treaty). Further to exchange rate agreements, the European Council reserves the right to decide on an exchange rate policy. Strictly speaking, this provision removes the ECB's independence, since the Council can impose on the ECB a loosening of monetary policy – for example, a cut in the euro against the dollar. This could become a source of conflict. The Council of Luxembourg made it clear, however, that the European Council could interfere only in rare instances, and then only if this did not encroach upon the ECB's independence and primary objective.

...fiscal policy

Fiscal policy remains within the competence of the national states. However, the criteria put absolute limits on public deficits and government debt. They also set up a recommendation and fines procedure applicable when member states do not comply with the limits set. It is thus provided that: 'Member States shall avoid excessive government deficits' (art. 104c of the Treaty), which are defined in the following terms:

- a government deficit above 3 per cent of GDP 'unless either the ratio has declined substantially and continuously and reached a level that comes close to the reference value; or, alternatively, the excess over the reference value is only exceptional and temporary and the ratio remains close to the reference value'; and
- a government debt above 60 per cent of GDP 'unless the ratio is sufficiently diminishing and approaching the reference value at a satisfactory pace'.

Exceptional government deficits are subject to fines until they are corrected. As government entities are barred from privileged access to financial institutions, neither the Community nor any member state can be liable for another member state's government debt.

...economic policy co-ordination

Two authorities are to co-ordinate economic policy. Member states co-ordinate economic policy within the Ecofin Council, which is composed of the national states' finance ministers. The Council may make the necessary recommendations to a member state running a policy that it deems to be hazardous (art. 103 of the Treaty). Moreover, the Maastricht Treaty made provision for an Economic and Financial

Committee composed of representatives from the national states, the Commission and the ECB. This Committee is responsible for keeping under review the national states' economic and financial positions, and for preparing the decisions regarding the functioning of the financial systems and financial relations with third countries and international institutions (art. 109c of the Treaty). This Committee was to replace the Monetary Committee; the Eurogroup has, in fact, replaced it.

Initiated by France and Germany at the Munster Ecofin Council of 14 October 1997 and later confirmed at the Luxembourg summit, reinforced economic policy co-ordination among euro-area countries is closely related to the creation of the Eurogroup, an informal consultative body. The Euro group was assigned the following tasks: promoting the exchange of information on the economic developments and political projects with a likely impact beyond national borders; the close monitoring of member states' macroeconomic developments, keeping under review the member states' fiscal situation and explaining national labour market policies. In addition, the Eurogroup is a forum for discussing what decisions may be made regarding the functioning of ERM2 (to include Denmark, and eventually, the United Kingdom and Sweden as well as the new EU entrants as of Spring 2004); it will also become the place where G7 summits are prepared. The Eurogroup will therefore contribute to the preparation of the broad economic guidelines decided at the Ecofin Council.

Finally, as part of informal economic co-ordination policy, the president of the European Council and a member of the Commission may partici-pate, without having the right to vote, in meetings of the Governing Council of the ECB. As for the ECB president, s/he 'shall be invited to participate in council meetings when the council is discussing matters relating to the objectives and tasks of the ESCB' (art. 109b of the Treaty). The Council of Luxembourg acknowledged the need for 'continuous and fruitful dialogue between the Council and the European Central Bank, involving the Commission and respecting all aspects of the independence of the ESCB'.

The Stability and Growth Pact

The Stability and Growth Pact consists of the European Council Resolution of 17 June 1997 and Council Regulations No. 1466/97 and No. 1467/97. Derived from the Maastricht Treaty, these instruments complete the Treaty's provisions with regard to government deficits, and strengthen fiscal policy surveillance and co-ordination. The Resolution details preven-tion and deterrence, the Stability and Growth Pact's two fundamental objectives: the former is developed in the first regulation; and the latter, together with its repressive corollary, in the second.

The first Regulation is intended to increase the economic policy surveillance procedures introduced by the Maastricht Treaty, and requires each member state to publish a yearly 'stability programme' (for euro-area countries) or a 'convergence programme'. The programmes present medium-term macroeconomic forecasts with forthcoming trends in fiscal expenditure and revenue. They are clearly aimed at overall fiscal positions 'close to a balance or in surplus', leaving the automatic stabilizers plenty of room to manoeuvre and allowing the amassing sufficient savings to finance the pensions of the future.

On the basis of the Commission's recommendation, the Council examines the stability or convergence programmes to detect any significant divergence from the medium-term objective. Since the regulation does not provide a strict definition of what must be understood by 'significant divergence', the Commission has since then specified three criteria: to what extent the objective was missed, how much is from discretionary causes, and the probability risk of running excessive deficits. When significant divergence has occurred, the Commission can initiate the 'early warning' procedure, writing a proposal to the Council, which may then decide whether to send recommendations to the countries veering away from their programmes.

The second regulation strengthens the provisions of Article 104c of the Maastricht Treaty on public deficits above 3 per cent of GDP. The Commission must tell the Council whether the excess over 3 per cent of GDP constitutes an excessive deficit, or if it can be included under the provisions covering 'unforeseen circumstances beyond the control of the Member State concerned'. In the latter case, 'the deviation from the reference value is judged temporary if the Commission's fiscal forecasts can establish that the deficit will fall below the reference value when the unforeseen circumstance or the severe recession vanishes'. 'In principle', the same logic applies when the excess is caused by a severe recession, namely a yearly GDP fall of 2 per cent and over. Apart from these mitigating circumstances, the country concerned will have to make up the deficit in the course of the following year. Otherwise, it may be subject to a non-interest-bearing deposit of 0.2 per cent of GDP, plus one-tenth of the amount in excess of 3 per cent, up to a maximum of 0.5 per cent of GDP. This can eventually be transformed into a fine if the deficit still endures after two years. Another sanction can be the suspension of all European Investment Bank operations with the country at fault.

However, this procedure is not initiated systematically. The Council must decide via qualified majority voting by all member states (including the non-euro area countries) whether a deficit above 3 per cent of GDP must be regarded as excessive. In view of the observations made by the country concerned, the Council may judge that a 2 per cent GDP setback qualifies as a severe recession. 'In principle', member states have pledged not to call upon the latter possibility unless they have suffered a minimum 0.75 per cent GDP setback. The pledge is non-binding legally, since it is mentioned in the Council resolutions but not in the Council regulations. When the deficit is deemed to be excessive, the Council may make economic policy recommendations to the country at fault. If the recommendations are not acted upon, the council may decide to impose penalties. Such a decision requires a two-thirds majority vote, taken only by the euro-area countries, excluding the country at fault.

Why should fiscal policy be capped?

Capping government debt and deficits stems from the various public finance threats to the macroeconomic equilibrium.

On the one hand, there is the risk that government debt might be absorbed through monetization

In theory as well as in praxis, public expenditure can be financed in three ways: taxation, borrowing, or money creation (read 'printing money'). Therefore, according to the neoclassical macroeconomics underpinning the Maastricht criteria, fiscal policy must be financed through money creation – that is, inflation – as propounded by the quantity theory of money. When interest rates over top growth rates, as has been the case in Europe since the early 1980s, government debt snowballs to such an extent that it becomes almost impossible politically to finance it through taxation. At that point, there is no other way out than money creation. Once this is completed, increasing inflation expectations causes both long-term interest rates and real inflation to rise; and investment decreases, since interest rates are now higher than the expected return on capital; subsequently, monetary and financial stability subsides under the over-mighty weight of the state which crowds out the wealth-creating private firms. At least, this is how it looks from a theoretical standpoint.

Classical school economists advocated central bank independence and supported the appointment of 'conservative'[1] central bank governors, as they thought this was the best means of killing the public and inflationary hydra and encouraging a return to monetary discipline. Because the central bankers' primary economic policy objective was the fight against inflation, they were not likely to give a complacent and sympathetic ear to 'the sirens of monetisation and seignorage'. Central bank independence may indeed reduce the threats of systemic crises in the European financial systems by alleviating the (justified or unjustified) fears the financial markets may feel about each European country's public finance management, and the subsequent knock-on effects such mistrust can cause to the markets. Yet independence may also have harmful economic consequences when it brings about, for example, poor co-ordination between fiscal and monetary policy, and therefore higher unemployment and inflation levels than economic adjustment would have required had co-ordination been more effective. This lies at the heart of the debate over whether a more formal body for economic policy co-ordination is needed, the Eurogroup being just a first step.

As there was no such co-ordination, if governments wanted to get round the deflationary bias initiated by the ECB conservative stance, they might be tempted to increase their public deficit and debt. Therefore forcing governments to comply stood out as the solution to EU monetary stability. Thus, in so far as they help independent and conservative central banks in their fight against inflation, the public finance criteria seem to be justified. It is double-edged support, though: it certainly makes sure no circumstance will ever jeopardize the objective of price stability. It also reveals that, as they were contributing to the Maastricht Treaty, European governments did not believe that the ECB would reach the objective on its own. The fiscal safeguard was added to avoid permanent victory or quick defeat on the credibility front. Although the first impression was that the ECB was not powerful enough to fend for itself, the Bank was granted the possibility to of arguing *ad infinitum* that its own assignment prevailed over that of national governments!

The preconceived need for capping fiscal policy therefore falls into a rather specific framework stemming from the threat from such constraints to the equilibrium of the goods and services market and the subsequent repercussions on relative prices and the nominal interest rates shared by all EU members. It then seems obvious that the economists who advocated this type of policy mix did not regard fiscal policy as an adjustment tool for allocating and redistributing countries' wealth, but rather as a costly and necessarily ineffective government effort.

Monetization can hardly justify the public finance criteria. Although the banks are the only institutions responsible for money creation, their statutes bar them from financing public expenditure. So justification has to be found elsewhere.

The 'crowding out' fear

If one EU country runs too loose a fiscal policy, the consequences may spread to other EU members through trade and financial crowding out. Such a policy would indeed cause EU interest rates and the euro to rise and the whole euro area would subsequently undergo a cut in net exports. The lack of co-ordination between both authorities – national states are responsible for fiscal policy; the EU for monetary policy – would induce a cut in growth for the EU members that did not increase their budget deficits.

Because of possible feedback effects from one EU country to another through crowding out, the fiscal policy run by one EU country can well turn out to be harmful for its EU partners. The situation can be described as sub-optimal as it brings out the lack of co-ordination between the different EU budget authorities. Box 6.1 illustrates the situation.

Within monetary unions, however, the 'crowding out' argument soon fails to justify the public finance criteria. To start with, the less open the Union's cross-border commercial relations, the fewer the repercussions

---

Box 6.1   The prisoner's dilemma

Let us imagine two countries in a monetary union; that is, with a common interest rate. It can be assumed that each country will have to arbitrate between budget discipline – to keep interest rates down – and the political cost attached to it. Obviously, while it is running a loose fiscal policy, each country would rather its partner ran a tight budget policy, hence the temptation of the 'stowaway' strategy. The two countries' mutual gains read as follows: the country running the tight fiscal policy will gain a full percentage point in growth, while the other country only gains half a point; in the case of a loose fiscal policy, the country running it gains two points while the other loses one. Such a situation is usually referred to as 'the prisoner's dilemma': if the two countries' governments do not harmonize their policies, they will both select the one that serves their own interests best, given that they have no say in the policy run by the other country, and so they will both opt for a loose fiscal policy. This results in a sub-optimal Nash equilibrium: both countries only score one growth point, whereas, had they taken the other country's economic policy into account and shared information, they would have both gained an extra half a point in growth by running a tight policy concomitantly.

Table 6.1 Trade openness rates, 1996* (as percentage of GDP)

	Imports	Exports
United States	13.0	11.4
Japan	9.4	10.0
Germany	24.2	23.0
France	21.4	24.0
The euro 11	27.3	29.8
The euro	13.4	14.4

Note: * Trade in goods and services.
Sources: OECD, figures by Creel and Sterdyniak (2000).

on trade: increasing disposable incomes will not be enough to prompt European households to spend a larger amount on imported products. Table 6.1 clearly shows that despite the euro-area countries' high level of trade integration, customer penetration within the zone remains lower than that of, say, France or Germany before monetary union. Moreover, trade partners, namely EU members in this particular instance, will also benefit from improving economic conditions in the country running a larger deficit (see the first part of this chapter on European cycle synchronization). The appreciation shock caused by one EU member's increased budget deficit may therefore be set off by the positive impact on the trade of the members that do not run a loose fiscal policy. Finally, it must be noted about crowding-out that euro-area countries borrow on *globalized* financial world markets, not just on European markets. There is then no real reason why any of the above should urge the ECB to raise its intervention rate. The situation that prevailed in Europe at the end of 2002 leads one to questioning seriously that the borrowing country's financial status may affect both long and short interest rate levels. The increasing government debt and deficits run by so diverse a range of countries as Germany, Portugal, France and Italy did not have a bearing on long-term rate levels at all, or cause these countries' rate spreads to widen in any way.

Better deterrence from easy excessive government deficits and greater incitement to higher economic policy co-ordination

Can governments not avoid accuring the excessive public deficits that induce long-lasting macroeconomic imbalances – inflation and current account deficits? If so, capping government financing powers seems justified. Some support this view, albeit in two different ways. In the first place, the criticisms levelled at politicians usually point to their

		Country B	
		Tight policy	**Loose policy**
Country A	**Tight policy**	1.5; 1.5	0; 2.5
	Loose policy	2.5; 0	1; 1

Figure 6.1   The prisoner's dilemma: gains matrix
Note: The first figure in each box stands for country A's growth gain in point terms; the second is that of country B.

		Government	
		Tight policy	**Loose policy**
ECB	**Tight policy**	4; 2	−1; −1
	Loose policy	0; 0	1; 3

Figure 6.2   The game of 'chicken' gains matrix

incompetence and over-generosity. This is undoubtedly not the rationale underpinning the Maastricht Treaty. It was probably worried more about the harmful effects of poor fiscal and economic policy co-ordination, especially how it would affect the already underlined primary objective of EU price stability.

'The prisoner's dilemma' has previously been used as an illustration of noncoordination between fiscal authorities (see Figure 6.1). The macroeconomic repercussions caused by the lack of co-ordination between the ECB and euro-area governments also need to be examined. They are explained in Box 6.2.

Since the ECB and European governments may have different sets of preferences, the question of macroeconomic equilibrium must be raised. Will the authorities persist in fighting conflicting battles, inflation for the former and unemployment for the latter? To put the matter at rest, the Maastricht and Amsterdam Treaties set out that the ECB should prevail over the European policy mix: fiscal policy was capped and thus the co-ordination between the members states' fiscal policies and ECB monetary policy had to emerge somewhat by default. The objective of fiscal policy is balancing the budget, which gives it

---

Box 6.2   Playing chicken[2]

Let us have two authorities responsible for EU economic policy: the ECB is in charge of monetary policy with price stability as its objective, while the national government is in charge of economic policy with economic growth as its objective (see Figure 6.2). The ECB opts for a tight policy because of the subsequent high interest rates and the strong euro, while the national government goes for a loose policy with economic reflation and low unemployment. The problem lies in that the national government is not content with the ECB's tight policy and the ECB is not content with the government's loose policy. Thus the loose/tight policy mix leads to constant outbidding between high interest rates and over-large deficits, for both authorities are trying to cancel out each other's harmful impact on their own policy. The higher the inflation-boosting government deficits, the tighter the monetary policy; the higher the growth-depressing interest rates, the looser the fiscal policy. This model of policy mix is therefore totally ineffective: there is no point in the ECB running a tight policy when the national government runs a loose one, and vice versa. This comes to what is usually referred to as a lack of dominant strategy for both authorities.

As the lack of dominant strategy leads the two authorities to co-operate, two co-ordinated equilibriums can be reached. Yet, given their different sets of preferences, each authority will try to impose its own preferences on the other. Hence the game of 'chicken': the first authority that overthrows its opponent is left free to impose its own policy and decide de facto what the other authority's policy shall be. The first is called a 'conservative' equilibrium, whereby both the ECB and the national government run tight policies. In this case, the ECB is said to exert domination. The second is called a 'social' equilibrium, whereby both authorities run loose policies; the national government is then said to exert domination.

---

only a small part in macroeconomic management, whereas the independence of monetary policy is clearly asserted. This authoritarian drive towards avoiding conflicts between monetary and fiscal authorities only confirms that support for the ECB's credibility is written into the Treaties.

Action!

The game of 'chicken' probably enjoyed a short hour of limited glory during 2002 and 2003. Although Germany, the most stalwart original champion of the Stability and Growth Pact, had initially favoured a 1 per cent of GDP limit on government deficits rather than the 3 per cent that was eventually agreed upon, it was in fact among the first of the large European countries to go over the limit. Unlike France, it didn't even try to plea for the European authorities' clemency or sympathy. Germany made amends at once, swore it would not be caught out a second time and promised it would not dare to affront the Commission by submitting a large public finance deficit two years in a row. As for France, it could pride itself on being utterly 'unrepentant'[3] since it had already forecast a deficit above 3 per cent of GDP for the following two years. But Germany's strict observance of the Maastricht Treaty's outer limit was nevertheless interesting. For a time, the German authorities even seemed to have braced themselves to be duly sanctioned in accordance with the Stability and Growth Pact's provisions for the countries that did not fulfil their obligations. So Frankfurt was the 'chicken', not Bonn.

Another major event in early 2003 was the ECB's feeble response to poor economic conditions in Europe and the world. Even though deflationary pressure outweighed inflationary threats, the ECB refrained firmly from cutting interest rates. Such a strategy of keeping some leverage for even harder times was part and parcel of the game of chicken. Since the ECB was concerned not to let the macroeconomic balance be tipped to the national governments' advantage and the euro area be shifted from a 'conservative' equilibrium – 'price stability first' – to a social equilibrium – 'fighting unemployment first' – it ran a limited intervention policy to show that it was not supporting irresponsible national governments. Because of reduced interest charges, low interest rates make the financing of increasing public deficits much easier when inflation is high: real debt will in fact decrease provided government bonds are not price-linked. Given the interaction that the launch of the euro has brought into play between the ECB and European governments, suspicion seems *de rigueur*. This unbalanced and rigid policy mix blatantly shows it has not yet been fully realized that the co-ordination of all member states' economic policies is a prerequisite for the achievement the optimum welfare of all European citizens.

The ECB

A promising start that gave way to too much inertia

The ECB's early stages leave a mixed impression. The Bank's legal statutes combined with the economic conditions of the time bore heavily upon the objective of very low inflation set to it. It would be unfair to say the ECB in fact failed in its mission. In 1999, it quite adroitly helped the European economy wrestle out of the 'air pocket' formed by the Asian crisis. Strengthened by this episode, the ECB could prove its real concern with deflationary threats and dare to fix a tangible, though uncertain, target level for its lower inflationary limit: keeping the euro area's yearly consumer price rises at under 2 per cent ruled out immediately negative inflation at once.

Procrastination, however, did not really turn to the ECB's advantage as about six months were needed in May 2001 to come to a decision on a one quarter-point cut in its key intervention rate. The next move was also a one-quarter-point rate cut, but did not come into force until the end of August 2001. From the end of 2000 it had indeed been feared the US cyclical downturn might affect European growth. Those limited and far between cuts did not establish clearly enough what course of action the ECB intended to take. Faced with lingering outbreaks of inflation, the Bank decided to make caution a priority and stuck to a rigid interest rate management policy that did not allow for advance reaction to the European economic drop of 2001.

Assessing ECB policy since the launch of the euro area none the less remains difficult. It is too early to draw conclusions about a policy for which no performance time reference is currently available. However ECB policy seems to have completed a full cycle over four years, if its key intervention rate trends are anything to go by (Figure 6.3).

The full swing taken by the intervention rate reflects the shortened cycles that European fluctuations underwent. It is most striking that this mini-cycle seems to reproduce, albeit at a later time and with less force, the phase the USA went through towards the end of the 1990s, in a totally different historical context.

As for the euro exchange rate against the dollar (see Figure 6 .4), it appears to respond to two factors: (i) the anticipated growth difference between the USA and the euro area;[4] and (ii) the subsequent interest rate divergence. Regarding this last point, it must be noted that the change in uncovered interest parity seems to apply roughly to the euro/ dollar exchange rate. For the parity to be covered, 'the return on European

152

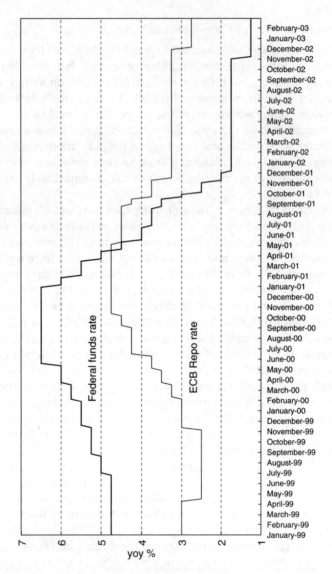

Figure 6.3 Short-run interest rates: the Fed and the ECB

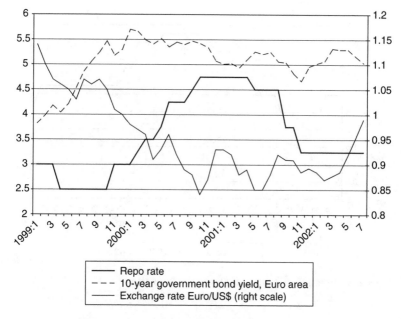

Figure 6.4 Short-run and long-run nominal interest rates in the Euro area and the Euro/US$ exchange rate

assets must equal that of US assets plus or minus the anticipated exchange rate losses, otherwise investors seize on arbitrage opportunities'.[5] Yet, from January 1999 to May 2001, the positive nominal return difference between US and European assets demanded that operators anticipate a euro increase, which translated into an immediate and persistent fall in the euro against the dollar.[6] When the difference in the two nominal return rates was reversed from May 2001, the euro went up, in accordance with the anticipation of a future fall in the euro.

Even though this theory may help to forecast the euro/dollar parity trends, it is of no help with the actual impact of the trends on economic activity. Yet it must be emphasized that the original euro fall was beneficial to the euro area, since it contributed to the redressing of the area's trade account deficits. Recent trends are therefore more alarming, as they indicate that European growth will find it difficult to be pulled up by net exports.

The timing of European monetary policy can be appraised according to various terms of reference: (i) the data available for economic activity in the euro area; and (ii) US monetary policy trends and their impact on financial world markets. The ECB took rapid action against rising inflation (Figure 6.5). The first rate increase took place in November 1999 at a time

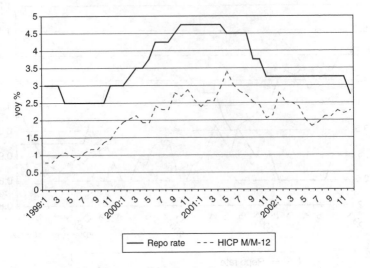

Figure 6.5 Inflation and interest rates in the Euro area

when the retail price index had gradually been going up since the summer period from 1 per cent to 1.5 per cent. Subsequently, the oil and food price shocks fuelled the price index, which kept on rising until Spring 2001. It then almost reached a 3.5 per cent annual peak before dropping back to a 2 per cent threshold. Until Autumn 2000, rising inflation prompted a more than proportional increase in the refinancing rate, and consequently a rise in the real short rate. From late 2001, monetary policy remained dull, though inflation topped 2 per cent: given the euro area GDP's continual slackening in 2001 (see Figure 6.6), it was obvious that the medium-term inflation rate could not stay above 2 per cent for very long.

It then becomes evident the ECB was running a tight policy (see Figure 6.6). After European economies managed to put the Asian crisis behind, it reached a peak between late 1999 and the beginning of 2000. As early as Spring 2000, the slowing down in European GDP started to become gradually more noticeable. Until the start of 2001, European monetary policy tightened significantly against the background of a downturn in European growth in a process governed by domestic priorities. The expansion drive was never quite consistent or long-lasting enough to place European output markedly above its potential (that is, non-inflationary) level, as was commonly assumed.

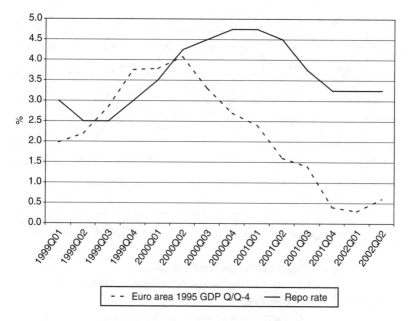

Figure 6.6 Nominal interest rate and economic growth in the Euro area

It is also possible simply to compare euro-zone short- and long-term rates with their US equivalents (see Figure 6.7). First, one can examine Figure 6.3, which plots in weekly terms the ECB's refinancing rate and that of the Fed funds. This figure shows that European decisions follow a monetary policy prompted by the USA, though in a somewhat looser fashion and after a lag time of up to six months.

Naturally, one must be cautious not to jump to the conclusion that the ECB merely shadows the Federal Reserve. At the time, the USA and Europe did witness a phase of partial resynchronization during which both economies concomitantly went through, first, a growth upturn and then a later downturn. It is also true that the US economy had started from higher economic activity levels, so it remained more dynamic than the euro area until the end of 2000, because of a more favourable growth and economic activity differential. It is then no surprise that US short rates pulled ahead of Europe's, and the euro had long remained rather weak against the dollar, given the disparity in growth prospects or interest rate levels.

Questions arise, however, from Europe's decision to raise its interest rate significantly during the year 2000 in pursuit of the Fed funds

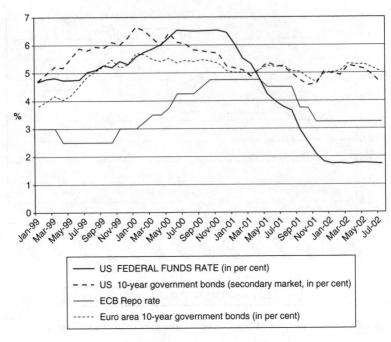

Figure 6.7 Long-term and short-term interest rates: USA and the Euro area

increase, when European growth had not yet caught up with that of the USA. It may not necessarily be a case of mere shadowing, since the ECB's decision probably also considered the inflationary risks posed by a world economy more in line with US dynamism. The 'real' inflation imported by the tensions between supply and demand on a global scale – for example, oil prices – and imported money inflation – for example, the fall in the euro – are believed to have had a strong influence on the ECB's underlying decision motives. The economic situation within the euro area did not seem to be at any real risk of an imported inflation-boosting wage/price spiral. While this analysis of the ECB's behaviour complements the first approach, it also emphasizes for the ECB's difficulty in striking the right balance between the conflicting demands of both the world and Europe's economy.

Regarding long as well as short rates, the euro zone seems to be reacting more to world economic constraints rather than forming an economically independent unit, although the consequences should not be overrated. On average, the zone's monetary policy was much looser than it had been in the years prior to monetary union, provided both interest rate levels and the fall in the euro were taken into consideration. This loosening fuelled a renewal of European expansion, which then started to become more sustainable because of job creation.

However, the impact of ECB policy on long rate levels is less convincing than that of the Fed. From late 1999, European long rates became hesitant and the upward trend came to an end. Moreover, although the fear of renewed perceptible and persistent inflation remained legitimate, the monetary tightening that should have accompanied inflationary pressure only took place in late Autumn 2000. Conversely the rates did not drop markedly either until Autumn 2000, which should have happened if ECB's tightening in its monetary policy had been perceived as a quick and efficient response. The rates did follow the bearish US trend, but in a somewhat looser manner. From early 2001, it is quite remarkable how close US and European long rates became, whereas the short rates cuts implemented by both the Fed and the ECB diverged very widely; the ECB appears to have found it most difficult to steer long rates towards the course it desired.

One is then tempted to conclude there is some inertia on the ECB's part compared to the most decisive monetary loosening stance taken by the USA when threatened by recession throughout 2001. It must also be noted that the Fed's strategy is compatible with a gradual approach in its decision-making: a series of consistent measures taken over a short time point clearly to the direction in which it is heading. By contrast, the ECB's inertia in monetary policy management may give way to inconsistent and disturbing stops and starts.

The ECB's so called 'two-pillar' strategy is meant to blend a medium-term quantitative target (M3) with the close scrutiny of the manifold causes of inflation. It is the result of the unresolved ambiguity produced by the desire of both sticking to the Bundesbank legacy and adopting the Anglo-US central banks' 'good practice'. This is not such stuff as steady relationships are made on. The strategy's second pillar tends to lead the ECB into deciding on a specific target for future inflation: this objective would certainly require more ECB transparency as well as the adoption of an target inflation range.

ECB inertia is just another obstacle in the way of its achieving policy credibility. It seems to allow itself ample time to gather the relevant information before it changes its key intervention rates. Although such inertia is fairly common among central banks, it can cause market impatience, especially with the ECB, whose moves are rather abrupt. What is at stake here is not so much the risk that markets may be caught off-guard – the Fed has already acted in such a fashion in the past – but rather the difficulty for the ECB in providing clear and convincing guidelines on both its own analysis of the economic situation and on the subsequent action it intends to take.

Market reactions to information from central banks

Credibility has become some sort of central bankers' holy grail; a source of eternal youth. Yet by letting the financial markets be the only judges of whether the quest has indeed been achieved, it can result in a pusillanimous monetary policy which cannot do other then constantly stifle growth or bring all expansion phases to a premature end. What does 'credibility' mean, exactly? Three definitions coexist among economists.[7] Another definition taken straight from the dictionary can be added to the list: 'credible' means believable, worthy of belief, convincing (Oxford) or 'capable of being credited or believed; worthy of belief; entitled to confidence; trustworthy' (Webster). To become credible, any institution should bridge the gap between official statements and reality.

More precise academic definitions of credibility introduce specific terminology, such as inflation aversion, precommitment or incentive contracts. The first phrase justifies the appointment of 'conservative' central bankers: their inflation aversion warrants that the price stability objective will be hit, hence the credibility of the institution of which they are in charge. With precommitment, discretionary economic policy is denied the opportunity to improve, in a wide sense, the welfare of all the citizens that either central bankers, or the institutions that have appointed them, represent. The economic policy rule serves as a panacea of sorts compared to the latent mess caused by governments' inconsistent practices. The latter – incentive contracts – bears witness to the suspicion that still hovers over the heads of these expert citizens-central bankers, whose entire lives everyone believes are totally devoted to fighting inflation. If, as ill-luck would have it, their CVs were not evidence enough we should place our trust in them, there is nothing left for us but to sign an explicit contract that stops them steering away from the optimal course.

Transparency is another element which contributes to the building up of a central bank's credibility. The best of situations in that case most probably consists in 'doing what you say and saying what you do', as former French Prime Minister Lionel Jospin said in investiture speech in Spring 1997. The second part of the quotation lays the emphasis on the complex notion of transparency, which lies at the heart of a certain number of recent discussions on ECB members' communications skills.

If it is to be most efficient, transparency according to Winkler (2000) must carry out the following three tasks: (i) clear communication with the public at large; (ii) honesty – which means external communication patterns must conform with those of internal communication so that the public does not have to fear any (or the least possible) strategic manoeuvring on the central bank's part; and (iii) effective internal communication. It is obvious that this new 'triangle of compatibility' may either enhance or undermine credibility. In an ideal context – the central bank sends clear, honest and efficient signals – transparency may avoid confusion in all available information, objectives and the adopted strategy in the bank's relation with the public. However, transparency may also help to disclose *ex post* the inefficiencies in the decision-making process when the context is not 'ideal'. In the first instance, credibility will be enhanced, in the second it will be undermined.

Torn between credibility and transparency, the ECB seems to have opted for the lowest level of transparency. While the Bank's objectives are perfectly known, its strategy cannot really be described as 'clear': the two pillars do not constitute a perfect model in that respect. External communication often appears to be more style than substance, as shown by the following example: in May 2001, the Bank's governor said the interest rate cut had not been prompted by gloomier economic prospects – although such a striking economic situation had been reported extensively by all European economic research institutes and the media – but was caused by the previous overestimation of the broad money aggregate, M3. And prior to this, at the very time that Otmar Issing, the ECB's chief economist, forecast that inflation would peak in 2001's second quarter, the Bank stubbornly refused to change its rates, claiming it might cause inflation. When one bears in mind the time lag before monetary policy changes come into effect, it is difficult to understand the reasons for such obduracy unless it is meant to show how little store is set by 'in-house' economic forecasts.[8] If so, this is an obvious case of major discrepancy between honesty and efficient internal information.

Beyond these few comments on the ECB's communication strategy, it may also be useful to assess its impact on the decisions taken by financial market operators and to distinguish, among all the information disclosed by central banks, the data that operators feel is most important. In a recent study on central banks' communication, Marie Brière (2001) listed the topics that ECB and Fed members claim to be of concern to them. From econometric models, she set up a taxonomy of media events such as speeches and statistics, ranked according to their impact on the financial markets' average anticipation levels[9] in Europe and the USA, as well as the corresponding anticipation deviation rates.

The first major conclusion drawn by the author concerns the main differences in the ECB's and the Fed's communication modes. Fed members communicate extensively about all finance-related matters: banks, markets and crises make up 43 per cent of speeches by Fed members. If the 'new economy' is added to the list, the figure tops 45 per cent (see Table 6.2), without any mention of the exchange rate, whereas financial topics are mentioned in barely 10 per cent of speeches by ECB members, against over 25 per cent concerning the euro (see Table 6.3). Part of the focus on the euro in the ECB members' external communication could be explained as follows: the Bank was persevering in its attempts to win over the financial markets to the charms of the euro with speeches attempting to (re)assure them about the European currency's 'potential rise prospects', which should in turn convince the markets about the ECB's strict anti-inflationary policy stance. It can also be suggested that, in the absence of a clear dividing line between the European Council and the ECB regarding which is responsible for the European single currency's external parity, the Bank was led to urge its members to proclaim themselves the only real 'Mister or Madam Euro' so as to discredit the governments and make sure they did not run an exchange rate policy that could eventually impugn the European monetary policy.[10] After all, Willem Duisenberg did attach the 'Mr Euro' title to his name![11]

Table 6.2　Fed members' speeches distribution list, January 1997–November 2000

Speeches about:	A. Greenspan's (%)	Other Fed members' (%)	Total (%)
The financial system	9.4	23.3	32.7
The US economy	7.3	3.0	10.3
Monetary policy	4.3	12.1	16.4
The world economy	2.7	2.1	4.8
Financial markets	1.2	2.7	3.9
Financial crises	3.3	3.1	6.4
The new economy	0.9	1.5	2.4
Others	9.1	13.9	23.0
Total	38.2	61.8	100.0

Source: Brière (2001).

Table 6.3 ECB members' speeches distribution list, June 1998–November 2000

Speeches about:	W. Duisenberg's (%)	Other ECB members' (%)	Total (%)
The financial system	1.8	3.5	5.3
The euro zone economy	5.7	9.3	15.0
Monetary policy	6.6	15.9	22.5
The world economy	0.4	1.8	2.2
Financial markets	1.4	2.6	4.0
Financial crises	0.0	0.4	0.4
The euro	5.7	21.5	27.2
Others	21.5	2.2	23.7
Total	42.5	57.5	100.0

Source: Brière (2001).

Moreover (but this is undoubtedly related only to the ECB's recent past), 23 per cent of the Bank's speeches bear on monetary policy, against the Fed's 17 per cent. More specifically, it must be noted now that, while the share of both governors in the speeches of either institution is comparable – 38 per cent for Greenspan as against 42 per cent for Duisenberg – the topics of the speeches are rather varied, though fairly well focused in the case of A. Greenspan: the financial system, the US economy and monetary policy make up 55 per cent of the Fed governor's speeches, with only 20 per cent relating to less clearly defined topics. With Duisenberg, the figure is a mere 50 per cent. Monetary policy, the euro zone economy and the euro make up 40 per cent of the ECB governor's speeches, which shows how little interest is given to financial markets and the economy of countries outside the euro zone, except when the speeches deal with the exchange rate.

Regarding the events, which seem to influence market estimates (and their deviation) most, several results are particularly revealing of the 'operational modes' these markets adopt, especially when European interests are at stake (see Tables 6.4 and 6.5). In the USA, Greenspan's announcements are the two events that influence markets most, after which come employment and inflation figures, in that order. It can also be noted that inflation tends to increase estimate deviation. In Europe, Duisenberg's speeches rank only third in the hierarchy of influential events, and tend to increase market uncertainty. Besides, German statistics are always ahead of European figures as factors both influencing anticipation and decreasing market uncertainty. EU statistics – M3,

Table 6.4   Ranking of events according to their importance to the markets

The USA	The euro zone
1 A. Greenspan's statement to Congress on 'Humphrey Hawkins' report	1 German inflation
2 Speeches by A. Greenspan	2 Changes in key ECB interest rates
3 Statistics on employment (and wages)	3 Speeches by W. Duisenberg
4 Inflation	4 Germany's unemployment rate
5 Retail sales	5 Europe's M3
6 Changes in key Fed interest rates	6 Europe's CPI
7 Speeches by other Fed members	7 Germany's retail sales
8 NAPM surveys on industrial activity	8 Germany's industrial output
9 Industrial output	9 Europe's industrial output
	10 Europe's unemployment rate
	11 Germany's IFO (Institut für Wirtschaftsforschung)
	12 Speeches by other ECB members

Source: Brière (2001).

Table 6.5   Ranking of events according to their impact on market uncertainty

The USA	The euro zone
Events decreasing uncertainty	*Events decreasing uncertainty*
1 A. Greenspan's statement to Congress on 'Humphrey Hawkins' report	1 Germany's unemployment rate
2 NAPM surveys on industrial activity	2 Europe's unemployment rate
3 Retail sales	3 German inflation
4 Changes in key Fed interest rates	4 Changes in key ECB interest rates
5 Speeches by A. Greenspan	5 Germany's IFO
6 Statistics on employment (and wages)	6 Europe's M3
	7 Europe's industrial output
	8 Germany's industrial output
Events increasing uncertainty	*Events increasing uncertainty*
7 Industrial output	9 Speeches by W. Duisenberg
8 Inflation	10 Speeches by other ECB members
	11 Germany's retail sales
	12 European inflation

Source: Brière (2001).

inflation, industrial output and finally unemployment – rank fifth, sixth, ninth and tenth, respectively, lagging far behind Germany's inflation (first) and unemployment (fourth).

Three explanations can be put forward to explain why markets favour information about Germany. First, market operators have fallen victim to strong behavioural inertia and have not realized what real changes the introduction of the euro has meant for Europe. They have continued to think as though Germany still benefited from an exclusive advantage, as used to be the case when the DM could exert its domination over the other member states' currencies within a fixed parity system such as the EMS: the Bundesbank was then able to set monetary policy for the rest of Europe without taking into account other member states' macroeconomic situations. However, the launch of the European single currency has cancelled out Germany's currency advantage. The part played by Germany's economic situation in setting EU monetary policy should not be mathematically heavier than its real weight in the euro zone – German current GDP came up to 31 per cent of the EU-12 area's GDP in the year 2000.

Second, market operators were in the process of gaining familiarity with the new European monetary system until late 2000. As European economic indicators had at that time only recently been set up, financial operators preferred to stick with the former indicators that they probably deemed to be 'beyond suspicion' until the new statistics were properly tested. The fact disclosed in 2001's second quarter, that European aggregate M3 had been overestimated, tends to bear out such reasoning and justify the financial markets' relative and necessary caution in using the new European indicators.

Finally, the financial markets' attitude was consistent with the discrimination principle with imperfect information. Grouped together in the euro zone, the twelve countries sharing the euro can neither be checked on an individual basis because of a glut of information, nor globally for lack of information – see the previous two points. Therefore, as commonly practised by banks for country risk management, operators tend to monitor more specifically the country that is reckoned to be representative of the whole area. A look at the trends in long-term interest rates and stock market prices will suffice to prove the point. Regarding long rates (see Figure 6.8), the European rate shadows most closely the German rate, considered as the benchmark, albeit always on a higher curve, which bears witness to the risk premium attached to the euro zone as a whole, since it is believed to be less 'safe' than Germany. Stock market prices also follow a similar trend in both Germany and the euro zone (see Figure 6.9), yet German prices are naturally higher this time.

In the European case, the fact that markets give priority to one specific country's economic trends over those of countries within a larger zone cause at least two serious difficulties. On the one hand, the zone is vastly diverse – economists still claim that it does not constitute an

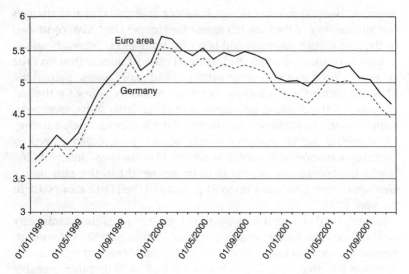

Figure 6.8 Interest rates on 10-year government bonds (in %)

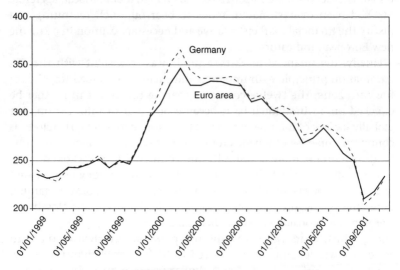

Figure 6.9 Stock market prices (1995 = 100)

optimum currency area[12] – and it cannot be fully understood if the entire zone is subsumed into only one of its components. On the other hand, selecting Germany as the representative country for the euro zone is a particularly poor choice, at least, this is the case as long as the country's economic prospects remain persistently poor. Germany can no longer be described as Europe's economic engine, and the German economic model is finding it hard to take on a new lease of life.

In the circumstances, it is important to ponder over what mechanisms are at work in Europe, if one is to avoid the spreading of Germany's economic sluggishness to other member states, and if Germany is to pull out of its present crisis. In the absence of a formal authority in charge of fiscal and monetary co-ordination (see above), even the ECB may run the risk of being mistaken about the causes of the European crisis because of its lack of independence from financial markets. The Bank may overestimate the importance of the German economy and fail to understand that the structural reforms Germany needs very badly do not necessarily apply to the other euro zone countries. These countries would certainly be better off economically if the ECB cut its key interest rates. Finally, it is desirable that financial markets are able to fine-tune their information about the euro zone so that they can make the distinction between the trends specific to single countries and to those of the entire zone.

The Stability and Growth Pact

The marked and prolonged economic slackening that has hit Europe (and more especially the euro zone) since early 2001 has revealed the weaknesses of the institutional framework designed for national fiscal policies and their co-ordination. Although discussed heatedly and criticized fiercely by some when it was first introduced in 1997, the Stability and Growth Pact has appeared to be less constraining than was expected since 1999, and it even emerged as a useful instrument. In times of sustained growth, the Stability and Growth Pact encouraged the continuation of the fiscal adjustment policies initiated by the dynamics of the famous 'Maastricht criteria' in all euro-zone member states. In some of the smaller euro-zone countries, shrinking public deficits eventually turned into significant budget surpluses, while public debt ratios (gross public debt to GDP ratios) started to drop in all EU countries.[13] As a global framework for improved medium-term national policy planning and better co-ordination within the euro zone, the Broad Economic Policy Guidelines (BEPG) were supposed to make the zone more coherent, while, in theory, maintaining the taxation and fiscal autonomy of national governments.

The first sign of weakness inherent in the institutional provisions capping fiscal policy in the euro zone goes back to February 2001. As the Irish economy was overheating, consequently pushing Ireland's inflation above average, the European Commission felt tighter fiscal policy was needed. On the Commission's recommendation, the fourteen finance ministers of Ireland's partner member states decided to send the Irish government a recommendation, even though that country's budget met all the European regulations in force. The Irish government ignored the recommendation: its reaction was legitimate on two counts, since an economic slowdown also set in, which confirmed that the Irish determination was justified.

The year 2002 witnessed a surge in the tensions and controversies about fiscal policy orientations between the European and national authorities. This highlighted the inbuilt limits and serious flaws of the euro zone's fiscal policy regulations. As early as February, the Commission urged the Council to initiate an excessive public deficit procedure against Germany and Portugal: the Council decided not to take action. The finance bill the France's government introduced before the French National Assembly in September forecast a pro-cyclical policy, which nevertheless included a budget deficit. Although the original deficit did not breach the 3 per cent of GDP threshold stipulated by the Stability and Growth Pact, gradual increases were planned for both 2002 and 2003. This triggered both the first open debate on the Stability and Growth Pact[14] and the Commission's recommendation of an early warning procedure against France. Despite a 3.6 per cent deficit in 2002, Germany has not faced the same sanctions as countries with excessively high budget deficits.

Given all these excesses, the permanence of the provisions capping national finance policy in the euro zone is being challenged by the setbacks inflicted on them by the larger EU countries. Should unsustainable regulations be applied, come what may, as the Commission is trying to do simply because it must fulfil its mandate? Conversely, should all attempts at regulating national fiscal policy be given up? If some budgetary discipline must indeed be imposed on member states, it then becomes desirable to reform the Stability and Growth Pact so as to remedy the major flaws that hamper the credibility of its action.

Unsustainability, externalities and financial markets

What could justify the regulations imposed on national budget policies, since the current interpretation of the subsidiarity principle gives national governments the upper hand in that field? Besides, the major economic argument for this partition is that national governments should be compensated for being divested of their exchange rate policies, the other instrument formerly part of their economic management toolkit.

The logic behind this distribution of responsibilities needs clarifying, and the objectives thereby pursued must be scrutinized to bring out the major flaws in the current regulations and ascertain what reforms could best address the issue.

The institutional decision of maintaining decentralised budgets within the monetary union – a small-sized budget at European level complemented by large, self-contained national budgets – was meant to leave national governments with an adjustment instrument for macro-economic stabilization policy when their countries were hit by, for example, asymmetric shocks – shocks that only affect a single country or a group of countries within the euro area. Some distrust democratically elected governments because they tend to manage public finances irresponsibly. Therefore it is believed that government's room for manoeuvre should be bound by strict regulations. This argumentation is thought to have become all the more relevant since the euro replaced national currencies, as markets can no longer sanction the national governments guilty of excess by taking on their exchange rates. Yet beyond this 'technocratic' approach, the validity of budget ceilings and the pleas for national policy co-ordination rests on the possible existence of strong interdependence or externalities between national economies within a monetary union.[15]

Regarding fiscal policy, the negative externalities commonly referred to comprise, first, the induced impact of deficits on interest rates over the whole of the euro area and on the euro exchange rate; and second, the long-term risks run by excessive and unsustainable debt on the independence of the central bank and consequently on the zone's monetary stability. In an 'ideal' world, efficient financial markets should be able to impose sufficient spontaneous financial discipline on governments to avoid such excesses. Yet in pratice, and most especially in the euro area, markets do not seem to make any distinction between the member states' various debt instruments, as shown by the euro zone's near-perfect convergence of nominal long-term interest rates. Hence, because of their poor judgement, markets cannot really anticipate or prevent any type of financial slippage.[16]

The experience of the first four years of the euro does not indicate that the 'sanctions' imposed by the markets on all euro-area members because some of them had run increased public deficits bore heavily on long-term rate levels – which hardly responded to the new fiscal measures – or on the euro's external exchange rate – which tended to go up along with the growing public deficits in major euro zone countries. It then appears that the fear the some rising public debt trends may become unsustainable in the long term must have been the major reason behind the need for fiscal ceilings. If so, it becomes essential that the public debt ratio (the public debt – preferably in net terms – to GDP ratio) does not get out of control. From now onwards, the ratio's long-run stability needs to be watched, which involves deciding on its appropriate level, just as stipulated in the Maastricht Treaty.[17]

At given spending and revenue levels, public or private debt sustainability results from the difference between future growth and interest rates. With growth higher than the interest rate, all debt levels become sustainable. In the opposite situation, debtors must strive to show a revenue surplus if they wish to avoid debt explosion. The logic of this argument would suggest that the capping of public deficits currently stipulated by the Stability and Growth Pact takes it for granted that fiscal policy has no impact on the workings of the debt ratio apart from the increase in interest rates generated by excessive deficits.

There are, however, reasons to think the opposite, and to suggest that fiscal policy *can* affect the 'potential' rate of long-term economic growth. It can either have a negative effect, if taxes and social contributions cause such distortions that resources are insufficiently or badly mobilized, or a positive impact, if part of public spending – on infrastructure as well as education, research and development and so on – achieves gains in private sector productivity and hence a higher growth path in the long run.

A Stability Pact in need of reform?

Criticisms of the Stability and Growth Pact in its current form before 2003 usually did not question the need for the sustainability regulation of public national debt. In fact, they most often focused on flaws in the regulations, where the lack of credibility attached to regulations that go unobserved naturally figure prominently.

The second flaw regards the pro-cyclical bias to the regulations. 'Nest eggs' built up at the top of the cycle are hardly likely to be spent on reabsorbing deficits, so when recession returns, the 3 per cent of GDP ceiling is soon reached. Counter-cyclical policies cannot be made to work in such a situation, nor can the 'passive' built-in stabilizers.

When the Commission belatedly became aware of the problem, it proposed in June 2001 that the 'budgetary position close to a balance or in surplus' should no longer be assessed in terms of total balance in the medium term, but rather in cyclically adjusted (or structural balance) terms. The medium-term objective would then no longer include deficit increases caused by a drop in tax receipts, or to rises in social spending, since such moves are deemed to be temporary, and therefore reversible.

The advantage of the new rule is obvious: a structural deficit target allows automatic budget stabilizers to operate fully, since the norm becomes mechanically looser as soon as economic activity enters under its potential growth path. Thus more expansionary fiscal policy may also be run in times of growth downturns and not just in 'severe recessions', as currently stipulated by the Stability and Growth Pact. Conversely, the target automatically becomes more constraining as recovery strengthens.

Yet the proposal has at least two flaws. First, the Commission has not planned to review the 3 per cent ceiling in terms of total deficit, which includes the impact of economic vagaries; and second, the euro zone's national governments must agree on a potential growth path level since, in this instance, the current account varies according to the output gap, namely the difference between actual and potential GDP. So, as the underlying growth path is derived from policy orientation, notably fiscal policy, potential GDP consequently becomes an endogenous variable dependent on fiscal policy. The Commission's recent output gap calculations do not take into account the endogenous factor and are based on the assumption of very low potential growth.

The Stability and Growth Pact's third negative impact in this respect stems from the attitude of governments. As they are concerned about keeping up some appearances of financial orthodoxy by meeting the 3 per cent criterion, governments tend to prune their public investment projects rather than their operating expenditure, or even raise some taxes, as recently announced in Germany, all of which result in structural problems that depress growth. A possible remedy would be to introduce public deficit rules similar to those implemented in the United Kingdom.

Since 1997, the UK government has applied a medium-term rule – 'the golden rule' – to bring public finance into balance. This rule stipulates that public deficits from operating expenditure (that is, exclusive of public investment expenditure) should be in balance over the cycle. Adopting such a constraining rule naturally implies that governments reach an agreement on a definition of public expenditure that distinguishes clearly between operating and public investment spending.

Ideally, it is advisable to advocate a rule on structural deficits that excludes public investment. Such a rule would leave each country free to act independently, as stipulated by the subsidiarity principle, and decide what role each society is prepared to assign to the state in macro-economic management and the redistribution of wealth output, notably through education. What is indeed at stake here is the setting up of a new convention on the classification of public spending, emphasizing what type of expenditure is likely to affect potential GDP in accordance with the debt sustainability objective. This concept of public investment therefore extends well beyond that of physical capital.

In use, the rule would not affect growth, and yet it would allow the free operation of the built-in stabilizers. European governments could then afford to opt for strict-looking ceiling specifications: thus, for example, banning all structural deficits – namely, setting the ceiling level at zero, which allows for the building of surpluses in times of economic upturn – would be less constraining than the current rule of 3 per cent of GDP. It would also appear to be less arbitrary, hence legitimate and more credible.

Moreover, the new rule would provide European countries with signifi-cant room for manoeuvre and thus allow them to carry out far-reaching reflationary policies to offset the effects of the recession current at the time of writing. Less advanced countries, namely entrant countries, could then seize on the opportunity to catch up on their partners' economic development by improving their supply of public infrastructure and education.

The European policy mix and time management

The move to monetary union has altered the scope of public and private decision-making. The transitional period was bound to deliver a rather limited and uncertain view of the future, and this still holds true for CEECs. Over the transitional period to monetary union, priority was given to achieving questionable convergence criteria within a strict schedule, one which widely restrained macroeconomic policy and totally confused private operator anticipation. The union, once in place, is intended to be irreversible, which demands government action on the fundamentals of European growth without regard for the unevenness of economic developments. Within the union, it is both possible and desirable to introduce more consistent timing of economic policy harmonization; namely, long-term rules and objectives should interlink smoothly with the cyclical policy required by economic circumstances. This long-term intertemporal approach calls for an unprejudiced review of the criteria underpinning the sound governance of public affairs. Thus, as public debt sustainability is affected by operator anticipation over future growth, it must be assessed in conjunction with the real financial constraints of long-term growth. Even though it cannot be described as being unrelated to effective public spending, this aspect is rarely mentioned in national or EU fiscal forecasts. The direction to be taken by European structural policies – technological, regional or sector-based – deserves to be discussed and settled with this viewpoint in mind.

The assessment of the euro zone's institutions, and more particularly its economic governance, must take into account the need for the widest scope, with wise arbitration between structural policy constraints and long-term European growth factors. This reordering of priorities involves political union, as it implies that the fundamental objectives of European unification are set out clearly and serve as guidelines to the everyday running of the EU by the European authorities. Political union was written into the Maastricht Treaty as a complement to monetary union, yet the unsatisfactory compromise that had to be struck between supranational, intergovernmental and federal constraints did not encourage the advancement of political unity. The subsidiarity principle – that is, the rational and democratic distribution between the different institutional tiers of power, was approached so unilaterally that, until recently, possible EU measures to tackle unemployment were looked upon as a breach of the principle. The strengthening of political union was perceived, notably by public opinion, as just another curb on deviation from the convergence discipline warranting the strict observance of the Maastricht criteria. As a result of such utilitarianization of political union, the fundamental objectives have been lost, and the *raison d'être* for the debate – although revived by Jacques Delors, former President of the European Commission, and German Christian Democrats in the 1990s – became entangled in all manner of obstacles relating to both economic developments and national objections – a widely expected outcome against such a confused background.[18]

Political union is indeed not a mere technical prerequisite to the introduction of economic policy instruments. It implies the establishment of a constitutional and judicial architecture promoting guiding economic and social principles, and the democratic involvement of European citizens. In that sense, political union is linked closely to the trust of European citizens in the types of economic and social prospects this will open up.

In this context, the quarrel surrounding France's most insistent request for the creation of the Eurogroup, hailed at that time as the forerunner of the 'euro zone's economic government', illustrates clearly the extreme importance of a venture that extends well beyond mere institutional aspects. The Eurogroup's significance is manifest: it has taken precedence over the Ecofin Council in many fields, even though the latter benefits from a longer history and can claim its legitimacy to be more firmly grounded in European legal instruments. Nevertheless, advances in macroeconomic co-ordination, notably in fiscal policy, remain few to date. Admittedly, in early 1999, the French and German governments jointly criticized ECB monetary policy for being too tight, as France was going through an economic downturn and Germany had been in the doldrums for too long. Yet, after the resignation of Germany's finance minister, Oskar Lafontaine, the French government appeared to be quite isolated when it complained further about the ECB's series of interest rate rises. Since then, successive governments have not been able to soften ECB discourse and decisions, whereas the reverse does not seem to hold true. Indeed, while both European monetary authorities and the European Commission will openly rebuke national governments for their general stance in fiscal policy, and object to the lack of dedication to curbing public deficits, the Eurogroup hardly ever ventures into monetary policy.

By taking a long-term view – since Europeans can now look eagerly to Europe's future – and yet without disregarding short-term constraints, one can suggest different structural models for euro zone development,[19] as well as various scenarios for the interlocking of economic and monetary integration with political union. However, both the study of the possible scenarios and the experience from the euro zone's first few years reveal how deeply the treaties and other current provisions bear the historical mark of their origins, notably the quest for disinflation and 'nominal convergence'. Given the Maastricht Treaty's first priority to public finance consolidation, the strict application of the current legal instruments cannot achieve a long-lasting *modus operandi* or provide the co-ordination mechanisms for a satisfactory European policy mix. In contrast, one may question the validity of the 'emerging prudential European economy scenario' (French Planning Agency, 1999) and its complex structure of rules and procedures. It may become entangled in over-rigidity, as it takes for granted that all Europe's national agents can operate readily within this type of architecture and tailor their own rationality smoothly to match a uniform system of rules and procedures. Accordingly, German Ordo-liberalism – a system of mutually-agreed norms regulating the distribution of responsibilities between social agents and the use of their initiative skills – is an example that could easily be transferred to the rest of Europe. In its own way, this last scenario does take a long-term view, but in that case the

long term would be instantly realized, as agents adapted to the requirements of the geared-down prudential regulation and fully integrated
them into their expectations. Yet this does not allow much time for
getting used to the new process, nor does it make for much room for
diversity. What is at issue here is not so much the need for more rules –
especially if these might be conducive to positive co-ordination – nor a
commitment to abide by the rules, but rather the governance of European
public life by a full set of pre-ordained rules that would departmentalize
and depoliticize public action, then hand over responsibility to pro-
fessionals. Thereafter, would there be any arena left in Europe for public
debate to take place?

Now that Europe can afford to take a long-term view, it must become
proficient in time management in order to take on the projects that meet
its real objectives, and muster a common effort among all Europeans. It
is then tempting to look for the symbiosis scenario coalescing the 'treaties'
pragmatic interpretation', where graded experience in co-ordination
and respect for all European specificities combine to blend political and
economic constraints smoothly together through active co-ordination
and 'interdependent sovereign federalism', in which the constitutional
architecture gives meaning to the common values and objectives of all
Europeans, and becomes the guide. Federalism may appear far-fetched
and yet it remains a utopia only as long as the federalist option is
deemed to be sacred. Historically, federalism has rarely stood as an
untainted principle. It has crossed over into other domains of reference,
where the relationships between participants and the various tiers of
the federal whole are weighed and organized differently with regard to
hierarchy, contracts, the rule of law, mutual solidarity and co-operative
partnerships. The federal principle – the distribution of sovereignty, the
common will and the diverse nationalities – includes a difference principle
with respect to national and regional identities. Since its content will
mature only over time, the federal scenario cannot dispense with a
learning process during which experimentation will select the best
methods for common action.

There are good reasons for monitoring this learning process closely:
no one can say for sure which way the euro area is heading, nor how
the geography of Europe will look in the future. Will there be more
symmetry, or asymmetry? Nor did the introduction of the euro solve
the problems of cyclical synchronization or economic harmonization
among nations or regions. The final answer lies in how well private
strategies and the public decision-making process will interact, but this
remains fairly hard to predict. Nevertheless, EU dynamics will probably

not leave developments in decision-making and co-ordination modes unaffected: but they may bring along the leadership or the apt corrections currently needed. The philosophy of European federalism will have to match EU innovation as the latter is already on course to reform local identities by preserving them.

Part IV
Social Integration

7
European Indicators for Social Cohesion: A Step Forward Along the Lisbon Path

This chapter will describe the state of the art of social cohesion policies in the European Union, by focusing attention on the efforts made to elaborate and identify the correct indicators to better understand the different national situations and compare them at Community level.

This effort is part of an overall strategy aimed at developing the integration process, within which the Lisbon European Council (March 2000) marks a turning point. Indeed, after the creation of the Monetary Union, the member states recognized the need to start an equally-committed new phase. This launched a challenge that should eventually give Europe a new and ambitious role – that is, becoming 'the most competitive and dynamic knowledge-based economy in the world'. To take up this challenge, the European Union should combine – or rather integrate – sustainable economic growth with the creation of more and better jobs, the enforcement of social cohesion policies and the eradication of poverty. The Lisbon objectives drew the attention of the Community to new topics, which to date have never been analysed and tackled systematically. Even though social cohesion and social protection have already been given some coverage in European policies, Lisbon marks the first attempt to define common targets consistently, and to plan a mutually consistent intervention in terms of action, comparison and co-ordination between member states.

Indeed, if on the one hand the way towards European Monetary Union (EMU) – which had begun well before Maastricht and came into force on 1 January 2002 – has stressed the integration process, on the other hand that very process requires a strengthening of the links between member states, which should be obtained through forms of co-ordination in other domains as well as the monetary one. As some authors have observed,[1] the increased integration – hence the greater mobility of the production factors of capital and work – might bring about a kind of 'downward rush' of national welfare systems that might lead states to be more competitive in order to attract firms and workers, by reducing their tax burden to the detriment of social security and social assistance. In this view, the Lisbon method would mark an attempt to impose a minimum threshold – a sort of 'minimum guarantee level' – in each member state in keeping with the principles of the European Union included in the Charter of Fundamental Rights of the European Union, which states (art. 34) that 'the Union recognises and respects the entitlement to social security benefits . . . and the right to social and housing assistance so as to ensure a decent existence for all those who lack sufficient resources'.

The European Social Agenda – approved in December 2000 at the Nice European Council – takes into consideration possible initiatives to ensure 'minimum guaranteed resources' on the part of social protection systems, stresses the need to 'continue co-operation and exchanges between States on strategies designed to guarantee secure and viable pensions in future' and 'analyses, on the basis of each of the Member States' policies, the adjustments made to social protection systems and the progress still to be made in order to make work pay and promote secure incomes and encourage reconciliation between work and family life'. The European Social Agenda sets the priority objectives on which the member states' efforts should concentrate in the implementation of the Lisbon decisions, namely creating more and better jobs, anticipating and capitalizing on changes in the working environment by creating a new balance between flexibility and security; fighting poverty and all forms of exclusion and discrimination in order to promote social integration; modernizing social protection; promoting gender equality; and strengthening the social policy aspects of the enlargement to Central–Eastern Europe.

A fundamental and innovative instrument for the successful implementation of the Lisbon strategy is the so-called Open Method of Co-ordination (hereafter OMC), which focuses on five areas for action – as defined by the Laeken Council of December 2001[2] – namely employment, innovation and research, economic reforms, social cohesion, sustainable development and environment. The implementation mechanisms envisage the identification of specific objectives for the introduction of Community guidelines into national policies, the adoption of a battery of quantitative indicators for the evaluation of the results attained, and a constant action of testing, monitoring and cross-country comparison.

The Council decided[3] to devote a specific Spring meeting to the OMC and to setting up a Social Protection Committee. Regarding social cohesion, member states are expected to draw up National Action Plans against Poverty and Social Exclusion (hereafter NAPs/incl) – similar to what happens for employment – describing their planned or implemented policies and initiatives, along with examples of good practice, to tackle poverty and social exclusion. The NAPs/incl are to be submitted to the Spring Council through a Joint Report on Social Inclusion drawn up by the Commission and the Council.

The approach adopted is based on the principle of subsidiarity: the social, historical and cultural characteristics of each member state are too different from one another, and their social protection and social assistance systems are too far apart to think about an integrated system of social policies, let alone a single European Welfare State. The social policy systems of member states are too diversified to assume a centralized system responding to the needs of citizens who live so for – even geographically – from each other and have to face completely different kinds of problems. It is much better to look for co-ordination, to concentrate on the outputs stemming from the national-level enforcement of commonly-agreed targets, rather than just providing general guidelines on social policies and welfare systems, and then leave single member states the freedom to choose the best formulas to reach those results.

Admittedly, within this framework, indicators play a key role in measuring and understanding the different national situations, allowing policy outcomes to be compared, and enforcing provisions and practices to reach the commonly-agreed objectives. The definitive list approved at Laeken includes thirty-five indicators (seven for each action area), is intended as the first step towards a definition of a whole range of indicators to be organised in a 'tree-like' structure with different levels. Level 2 should provide a further deepening, which may also be used for the assessment of the Guidelines on Economic Policies, while Level 3 concerns elements of interest for individual countries (presented in the NAPs/incl), specific provisions or significant policy aspects. This indicator-based structure is aimed at guaranteeing a fair balance between the need for a synthesis in describing each country's features, and the opposing need to provide a detailed and thorough analysis of national situations.

This chapter is structured as follows: the next section lists the contents of NAPs/incl; the following section describes the fundamental principles for the construction of indicators, plus the single indicators chosen for social cohesion and their features. A brief comment of individual countries' performances follows. The aspects not considered by the Commission's list are outlined subsequently, together with the importance of these omissions. A few critical remarks are made on the working method adopted and, finally, there is a reflection on the fundamental conditions that guarantee the successful enforcement of the part of the Lisbon process that concerns social cohesion.

The first National Action Plans

In keeping with the decisions taken at the European Council meeting in Santa Maria de Feira, the NAPs/incl were presented for the first time by all member states in June 2001. The analyses elaborated follow some common guidelines for an easier comparison of national situations, and contain a thorough analysis of the overall context and of any specific aspect that social exclusion might take up in individual countries. Hence some risk factors are identified and clear priorities established to reduce those factors and eradicate social exclusion. Then mainline policies and specific provisions are identified – best practices – as they play a fundamental role in the cross-country mutual learning process foreseen by the OMC. For some examples of best practices, see Table 7.1.

The 'learning process' defined with a specific timing by the Council and the Commission[4] started in 2002 and foresaw a mutual dialogue across member states – within the Social Protection Committee – and between member states and the Commission, in order to discuss the approach and provisions adopted, their effectiveness and possible feasibility in other situations. In what follows, some fundamental aspects and common trends emerging in all EU countries, as well as some peculiarities, are described and commented upon.

First, the Spring Joint Report outlines that, in most cases, the approach adopted by a member state is neither innovative nor does it point out important projects or provisions. This happens because of the short time available to enforce the NAPs/incl, while, in most cases, attention was paid mainly to the analysis of the situation, and to the description of the ongoing trends and existing measures.

Data on poverty – with the meaning 'lack of income' – show the substantial stability of the phenomenon. The latest available information, referring to 1998, shows a relative poverty rate[5] in the European Union of some 18 per cent. However, the concept of social exclusion goes well beyond the mere monetary dimension; its multidimensional aspect is one of its peculiarities, which emerges clearly from many studies as well as from the empirical data provided by Eurostat. Hence, low income is only one of the risk factors named in the NAPs/incl. All countries report

Table 7.1 Examples of best practices in social security and protection

Member state	Title of measure	Area of intervention	Brief description
Austria	Integration of atypical workers	Social security	Promotion of social coverage to ensure that all economically active people have social security, even if they are part-time or atypical workers
Austria	Supported employment	Disabled persons	Projects to provide aid and support to disabled persons and to offer employers forms of assistance
Belgium	Spring programme	Employment	Intended for long-term unemployed and minimum-income recipients, it envisages subsidies to fixed-term agencies to reduce labour costs and favour professional training of beneficiaries'
Denmark	Facilitation scheme for ethnic minorities	Employment/ethnic integration	Financial support to firms, to pay employees to provide assistance and facilitate integration of non-Danish employees
Denmark	Corporate social responsibility	Corporate ethics	Creation of a national network of business executives; introduction of a Social Index to allow companies to benchmark themselves against other companies on social/health care policies; respect for households' needs and employment of minority categories
France	Universal health coverage	Health care	Reform of the health care system to make it possible for all to join the social security system, and for the poorest, to have all costs paid (in the past some services were provided by privately-funded social protection systems)
France	Loca-pass	Young people/training	Scheme for young persons under 30 seeking accommodation: a financial guarantee and a deposit is provided to beneficiaries, financed by a 1 per cent solidarity contribution paid by employers

Table 7.1 (Continued)

Member state	Title of measure	Area of intervention	Brief description
France	Trace programme	Young people/employment	Personalized ongoing programme for young people in difficulty – maximum length 18 months – tailored to promote early intervention to help job-seekers to find a long-lasting job upto at least 50% of beneficiaries
Germany	Fight against debt	Financial support	Policies to facilitate households in debt (which were more than 2.5 million in 1999); mediation committee, clearance fund after six years, threshold to the seizure of assets to enable survival
Greece	Equal access to education	Education	Equal access to education guaranteed. Free meals to students in need (5,300 beneficiaries), accommodation (4,200 beneficiaries) and transport provided
Italy	Minimum income benefit	Poverty	Monetary allowances to households and measures for the social integration of beneficiaries. Adopted on an experimental basis, it supported 85,000 people in 2000
Italy	Chance programme/Creativity among young people	Young people	Two programmes aimed at helping and supporting young drop-outs. In the Municipality of Naples, the Chance programme brings young drop-outs back into school, even through the help of mobile teaching units working in the advantaged Centres for Social Interaction were set up in 27 municipalities in Northern Italy
Luxembourg	Integration of immigrants' children	Education/ethnic integration	Offering the children immigrant equal access to the education system, first by organizing literacy courses in French and, second by favouring their integration in the country's education system (mainly in German)

Country	Programme	Category	Description
Portugal	Access to state accommodation	Housing	Programme set up to help people living in shanty towns to find better accommodation. Began in 1993 and is aimed at eliminating the problem (helping about 80,000 persons) by 2005
Portugal	Minimum guaranteed income	Poverty	Introduced in 1999, it is aimed at all resident citizens in financial need, at young people with responsibilities and at pregnant teenagers; it also envisages support measures aimed at promoting participation and the inclusion of beneficiaries within society
Spain	Regional action plans against exclusion	Exclusion	Programme set up by Navarra to co-ordinate all regional stakeholders, to provide minimum resources (training, employment, housing, education and health care)
Sweden	Vocational training for adults	Education	Aimed at reducing educational shortcomings as well as unemployment by offering beneficiaries the opportunity to improve their qualifications and working status; about 220,000 persons have benefited from this programme
United Kingdom	Sure Start	Children	Government strategy to tackle child poverty and social exclusion of children under 4 through the development of integrated local programmes

Source: European Council (2001).

other factors, which are by no means less important and which are linked to the complex nature of social exclusion – namely, employment problems (comprising both unemployment and low income), low-quality employment, low qualification levels, family break-ups (connected with the possibility of living in disadvantaged households and then reproducing in adult life the characteristics of the family of origin), disability, poor health, homelessness and problems linked to immigration and racial discrimination. These factors may often overlap and sometimes it is difficult to distinguish the cause from the effect, but the result is a vicious circle causing exclusion.

The core challenges emerging from the NAPs/incl are summarized in the Joint Report in the following eight points:

   (i) developing an inclusive labour market and promoting employment as a right and opportunity for all by favouring policies promoting employability in general, but also policies tailored for people with problems of access to the world of labour;
  (ii) guaranteeing an adequate income and resources to live as dignified human beings;
 (iii) tackling educational disadvantage;
  (iv) preserving family solidarity and protecting the rights of children by supporting vulnerable families and taking into account demographic and sociological changes within families;
   (v) ensuring good accommodation for all, both in terms of access to good quality as well as affordable accommodation;
  (vi) guaranteeing equal access to quality services (health care, transport, social care, cultural, recreational, legal);
 (vii) improving the delivery of services; and
(viii) regenerating areas of multiple deprivation.

Admittedly, the relative weight of each of these objectives is different according to the different state characteristics, as the strategy adopted to pursue them differs according to the specific context and situation of the country at the outset. This is clear when dealing with service delivery and access, but it also emerges when tackling educational disadvantage, which means combating premature school leaving in some areas, developing new forms of life-long learning in another, or eradicating the causes for adult illiteracy elsewhere. Generally speaking, the differences across states may be identified through three fundamental elements, namely the nature and extent of social protection systems, the perceived dimension of social exclusion[6] (it may be pervasive in the society as a whole or be limited to the most vulnerable groups) and the existence of an anti-poverty strategy in addition to the OMC.

While analysing NAPs/incl in detail, the Council and the Commission provided a kind of ranking of the different countries according to three elements that provide the basis for developing national plans – namely, the quality of the analysis; the effectiveness of the initiatives (that is, the consistency between the priorities and targets and the situation of the country); and the involvement of all key stakeholders (that is, the existence of an integrated and multidimensional approach aimed at supporting the whole population and not only vulnerable groups). With reference to the first criterion, the NAPs/incl of Germany, France and the Netherlands must be mentioned, though all countries provide in-depth analyses of their situations. With reference to the second criterion, a difference must be introduced between countries already having well-developed social protection systems – where anti-poverty strategies are simply to be included within its welfare policies – and countries where a radical change is necessary, together with the definition of new objectives. In the former group, it is worth mentioning Germany, Finland and Sweden; while in the latter category, the approaches emerging from the NAPs/incl of Portugal and the United Kingdom stand out. Finally, Belgium, Germany, Spain, Italy and Finland tackle the problem through an integrated approach, which is particularly relevant given that, in these countries welfare state competence is often locally decentralized.

The Laeken indicators

After a long debate[7] between Community institutions, national institutions and experts, the list of indicators for social cohesion (the temporary indicators were presented at the first Spring Council devoted to the OMC progress held in Stockholm in March 2001) was approved in Laeken in December 2002. As was discussed above, this marks an important step forward on the way towards the OMC, because indicators are important for the message they convey, namely that Europe wants to create a common databank on social exclusion and poverty, and this is the first fundamental phase to analyse the problems, understand them and identify policies. The timetable set in Stockholm envisaged that indicators were to be approved by the end of 2001, and this commitment was honoured. Alongside these aspects – which are positive and encouraging – one should notice that the indicators leave some problems unresolved which are, however worth noticing. Before focusing attention on these critical areas, we should analyse the indicators that were approved, and their features.

The 'desirable' characteristics of indicators

The European Union's desire to become a competitive 'knowledge-based' economy requires indicators respecting some basic characteristics. First, each indicator must be significant and have an easily-readable interpretation. So there must be no doubt as to the information it provides or its consistency in relation to the problems analysed. To this end, two remarks are necessary. First, as a consequence of the principle of subsidiarity, attention is focused on measurement of outputs – that is, on the policies' effects, and not on policies themselves, (for example, inputs). That is why parameters such as the share of public finances devoted to education or the percentage of poor people affected by specific support measures are not evaluated: countries may choose their most suitable formulas to pursue their objectives – for example, through specific public transfers or active policies. Second, the importance must be stressed of a common approach involving – both in the identification and the monitoring phases – all institutions and citizens; that is, all stakeholders and even the vulnerable groups themselves, in order to set a battery of commonly-agreed relevant indicators with a clear specification of their meaning.

The second characteristic concerns the purely methodological aspect and requires that indicators be robust and validated statistically. This explains why the indicators are based as much as possible on the information provided by Eurostat and by national Institutes of Statistics. Furthermore, indicators must be computed correctly and must-not be very sensitive to sample variations. Robustness must be ensured, not only for the statistical aspect, but also for the economic one; in other words, indicators must not imply fluctuations linked to cyclical economic changes unless they are caused by social aspects or unforeseeable external events.

The third characteristic concerns the relationship between performance and political framework. Indicators must be responsive to policy interventions, but they should not be vulnerable to manipulation. The data collected should reflect the policies enforced in a country; but at the same time any possible direct intervention of policy-makers should be avoided, to guarantee that data are not altered in the attempt to obtain a better evaluation of the progress a country is making in its way towards the OMC.

Other standards concerning single indicators state that they should be easily comparable across member states, that they are available promptly, and that their collection does not present too heavy a burden for member states. The first requirement stresses the role of indicators as a method of comparison within the OMC. Thus indicators specifically concerning problems typical of one country (which should be tackled at Level 3) should be avoided, as should those implying a computation method or reference data that cause systematic distortions favouring some countries to the detriment of others. The timely availability of data is an obvious requirement, which, however, must not be taken for granted: data on social inclusion at the time of writing (end of 2002) are based on the data of the European Community Household Panel (ECHP) dating back to 1998. In order to improve this aspect, and to ensure the necessary homogeneity without imposing excessive costs on national Institutes of Statistics, a new database has been developed, namely the EU Statistics on Income and Living Conditions (EU-SILC), which in 2003 has become the main point of reference for all statistics on income and social exclusion.

The last three characteristics concern the indicators as a whole. As we have already mentioned, adopting a single overall indicator to describe and analyse social exclusion is by no means the right approach, which is why a basket of data was chosen. In this view the Union strongly discourages the selection of *reductio ad unum* while disseminating data on single member states. Conversely, the European Union recommends the consideration of the whole 'portfolio', which should be easy to read and accessible. However, if the basket is to provide significant and non-contradictory results, the different dimensions considered should be fairly balanced, and indicators must be mutually consistent and have a similar weight in the portfolio; that is, they should be proportionate.

Monetary indicators: poverty rates and income distribution

As we mentioned before, the monetary component alone is not sufficient to describe and summarize all the implications and the ways in which exclusion emerges; however, it is one of the fundamental causes for social exclusion. In the list of indicators approved at Laeken, three out of the seven indicators devoted to social cohesion concern lack of resources. More precisely, the first analyses income inequality and the other two poverty rates and the persistence of poverty, respectively – that is, the 'poverty risk'.[8]

The definitions of these indicators – as for the indicators concerning social cohesion – are underpinned by some fundamental methodological choices. First, the basic unit for counting should be people (and not households), because social inclusion is first of all a problem of individuals.[9]

Besides, the Commission chose income rather than consumption as the variable representing (individuals' and households') resources, and this mainly for pragmatic reasons. This choice is neither obvious nor immediate, as it stems directly from the one concerning the most suitable definition of poverty. For example, if one considers that a person who does not satisfy a series of 'minimum requirements' – appropriately defined and which may be transformed into a monetary value – is poor, then his/her expenditure for consumption would be a better reference variable than would income. However, lacking strong reasons to opt for one of the two variables, the problem was overcome on the basis of practical reasons, as income has been surveyed within the Europanel for a long time.

It is worth mentioning two problems. First, the identification of income as the relevant variable raises questions about the kind of income to adopt; disposable income seems to be the most suitable aggregate, though a rigorous approach would also require the computation of non-monetary components, which is a delicate operation that raises problems of homogeneity across countries (which would undermine the principle of comparability). This choice was criticized harshly by Mediterranean countries.[10] In particular, Spain, Greece, Portugal and Italy observed – also at the institutional level – that rents that were not imputed to house-owner households systematically distorted data, as it brought about an overestimation of poverty rates in those countries where house-ownership is much diffused, even in low-income households. In spite of its harshness, that criticism was not considered at all.

Second, some problems may emerge with reference to the period of income observation. The Europanel reports the previous year's income, and this implies a time lag between the moment to which income is referred and the surveying period to which social-demographic variables refer (age, profession and so on).[11]

As we have already noted, the first indicator measures income distribution inequality: it stems from the ratio between the share of the country's (equivalent disposable) income owned by the highest-earning 20 per cent of the population and the share earned by the lowest-earning 20 per cent. This measure seems to respect the six aforementioned features: in particular, it is an easily read, non-ambiguous indicator. However, it is the first principle that is not fully respected, as that measurement does not respond to variations of the whole distribution, but only to changes of the two ends. For this reason, it is advisable also to adopt (at least in Level 2 indicators) the Gini coefficient,[12] as well as the ratio between deciles (the ratio between the income of the top 10 per cent of the population and the one of the bottom 10 per cent) in order to take also into account situations of more marked inequality and discomfort compared to the basic indicator.

With regard to the poverty risk, a fundamental step (which precedes the definition of indicator) consists of the identification of a correct concept of poverty, namely the threshold below which a person is to be considered poor. The main methods adopted are those of relative poverty, of absolute poverty (standard budget poverty) and of perceived poverty. In the first case, the line of poverty is computed as a percentage of one of the central trend values (mean, median and so on) of resource distribution (in this case, income); the second approach defines a basket of basic goods and services and provides a monetary quantification of them; finally, in the third approach, people are asked which, in their opinion, is the minimum amount of money necessary to live with dignity.[13]

The choice between the different methods is not easy, as none of them fully satisfy the above-listed characteristics. The perceived poverty method is the one that raises most problems, because it poses doubts about its cross-country comparability, its robustness (both statistical and economic), and its responsiveness to economic policies. The comparison between the other methods is even more controversial. Admittedly, the relative poverty approach does not capture the gist of the problems connected with the risk of poverty, but rather depends (as the first indicator) on the degree of inequality in resource distribution. For this reason, the analysis over time of this indicator or its cross-country comparison may provide information that is difficult to interpret, because of its independence of economic cycles and income distribution. Indeed, also its responsiveness to policy actions aimed at reducing poverty is not taken for granted. However, the computation of the absolute poverty threshold is based on an arbitrary basket composition and the definition of a single threshold irrespective of national income distributions – despite being adjusted to the price differentials of individual countries – is no easy task, as it has to pursue the objective of cross-country comparability. To solve this problem, it might be sufficient to set common criteria on minimum standards and then transform those criteria into national baskets on the basis of the countries' behaviour and characteristics.

The problem was underlined again in the Joint Report on Social Inclusion of 2001,[14] which stresses, among other things, that the European Union aims at improving overall quality of life, by ensuring the social integration and participation of all people up to the average well-being obtained in EU member states, and not by safeguarding minimum standards of living. These remarks, together with the timely availability of data, the easy cross-country comparability of outcomes, and its wide adoption in international studies, led the Community to opt for the relative poverty approach. Thus the indicators chosen to measure the poverty risk are the share of people – before and after public transfers – whose equivalent income is below 60 per cent of the nationally equivalized median income, and the percentage of people living in poverty for three consecutive years.

However, though remaining within a relative poverty approach, it would be most helpful to consider the overall income distribution of the European Union, by computing a single poverty line for the whole of Europe,[15] equalling, for example, 60 per cent of the European equivalized median income. This approach – while setting the average level of well-being of the Union as reference parameter – would stress the differences in national poverty levels and would contribute to setting the target of social cohesion at the European level within a framework of ever-growing integration.

Besides, in the absence of a clear answer to the methodological question, it would be better to use both the relative poverty and the absolute poverty approaches to evaluate the poverty risk; all the more so, if one considers that the problem of the availability of a minimum level of resources needed to lead a dignified life is far from being solved in many Union areas. The absolute approach would have enabled, on the one hand, the identification of those population groups living in particularly disadvantaged conditions in all EU countries – even in countries with high standards of living – and on the other, would have highlighted the absolute distance existing between states in the domains of poverty and social exclusion, which is presumably much wider than it appears to be, while adopting the relative poverty indicator, which identifies the poor in each country on the basis of national median incomes.[16] All in all, the adoption of these three indicators (two on the poverty risk and one on income inequality) to estimate the monetary aspects of social exclusion seems not to be an appropriate choice compared to the Lisbon objectives.[17]

With reference to the indicators themselves, the computation of the poverty rate before and after public transfers – even though it provides important information – is by no means a parameter consistent with the objective of estimating the poverty risk, which means that it does not respect the first fundamental characteristic. In the best of cases, if, compared to the *ex post* rate, it measures the effectiveness of social protection policies and is thus an input indicator putting the stress on methods rather than outcomes. It would thus be advisable to include it in Level 3 indicators. Second, as there is a high degree of arbitration in 'tracing the line', an analysis of the sensitivity of results' to the threshold variations – made by including indicators of poverty incidence with alternative lines – would be most helpful also in the relative poverty approach. A country with a high percentage of low- and medium-income recipients – but not of minimum income recipients – might show high poverty rates if one considers 60 per cent of the median income, and smaller rates if one considers a smaller percentage.[18] The countries whose NAPs/incl – through maintaining the relative poverty approach – provide data on monetary poverty computed with different threshold values are many: for further details, see Table 7.2.

Table 7.2 Monetary poverty standards adopted in different countries

Member state	Relative poverty threshold	Other standards
Austria	50% of median income	
Belgium	40%, 50%, 60% and 70% of median income	50% of the mean value
Denmark	50% of median income	
Finland	50% and 60% of median income	
France	50% and (only for international comparison) 60% of median income	
Greece	40%, 50%, 60% and 70% of median income	
Ireland		'Consistent poverty': monetary poverty plus deprivation of basic goods and services
Italy	50% of median income	Absolute poverty
Luxembourg	50%, 60% and 70% of median income	
Netherlands		Financial poverty index as the ratio between the number of beneficiaries with minimum income benefits and the latter's real value (the values referring equal to the basic year set as 100)
Portugal	50% of median income	
United Kingdom	50%, 60% and 70% of median income	40%, 50% and 60% of average income
Spain	40%, 50% and 60% of median income	
Sweden	50% and 60% of median income	

Source: Atkinson *et al*. (2002).

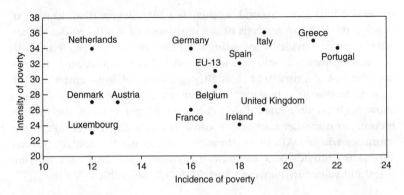

Figure 7.1   Percentages of poverty incidence and intensity rates (poverty gap)
Source: Eurostat (2000a).

Finally, one has to notice that the absence from the list of an indicator measuring the *intensity* of the monetary risk raises many doubts, because it contains important information that is not always correlated with that concerning poverty *diffusion*. In some countries, poverty may hit an large share of the population but not so intensively, while elsewhere poverty may be limited to small groups but may be very intense.

Figure 7.1 below shows the percentages of poverty incidence and intensity rates (poverty gap): this indicator measures the average distance in percentage of the poor from the threshold. By observing the dispersion of the cluster of points, it is evident that the use of poverty incidence rates alone do not provide the overall picture of the phenomenon.[19] Furthermore, the two indicators provide different information according to the different degree of sensitivity to policies aimed at supporting people in need. If those measures were to provide an economic support unable to help even a single person (in extreme cases), the incidence would remain unchanged, while intensity would decrease as all people would be placed on levels closer to the poverty threshold.

With reference to the persistence indicator, there are no doubts as to its usefulness in the analysis of the width and depth of social exclusion. While poverty conditions at any given moment may depend on exceptional events or on a time lag between the surveying period and the one to which the median income refers (for example, for the self-employed), the persistence of poverty over a long period mirrors a situation of deep discomfort and, presumably, the social exclusion process is already ongoing. To this end, it is worth noticing that the use of panel data requires caution because of the emergence of some purely statistical problems that might distort estimates.[20] These factors, together with the consideration that coming out of a situation of poverty – if it is temporary – might be a result of exceptional events or occasional variations in income distribution, led to a change in the indicator proposed by the Social Protection Committee: originally defined as the percentage of the poor for three consecutive years across the total population, it was reformulated to consider the so-called persistently poor; that is, people considered to be poor in the surveying year and in at least two of the previous three years.

Non-monetary indicators: education, employment, regional cohesion

Looking at non-monetary factors, education plays a key role among risk factors leading to social exclusion. A high level of education is undoubtedly a benefit in terms of successful job-seeking, of easier access to more highly qualified and better-paid jobs, and of more opportunities to participate actively in social, cultural and political life, thus exposing one's family to a smaller risk of exclusion. In 1996, the poverty incidence rate[21] in Europe (excluding Sweden and Finland) for people living in families where the head of household or his/her spouse had completed higher secondary education (high school diploma or higher) was 7 per cent. That figure doubled with an average education level, and reached 26 per cent in households where neither parent had completed lower secondary education. In addition, the observation of the level of education among the younger age groups allows for the gathering of information on medium-term monetary poverty rate trends – that is, on the greater or smaller risk for people outside the labour market, or for first-job seekers, to be hit by poverty in their future working life.

The proposed (and approved) indicator covers the percentage of the population between 18 and 24 years of age with a junior school diploma but who did not attend high school course. That standard seems to be significant,[22] and consistent with the above-mentioned characteristics. In particular, it is responsive to policies aimed at prompting education. However, it might be interesting to integrate it (perhaps at Level 2) with an index concerning a larger population share: in particular, the same kinds of measurements, applied to all people of working age, might provide a proxy for the human capital stock of each country. Besides, a relevant factor not considered so far concerns differences in the access to education, hence in education costs and in the education and income levels of the household to which individuals belong. In this case – which is also dealt with by the NAPs/incl of countries such as Belgium, France and the United Kingdom – the main problem is improving availability, reliability and comparability of data. Finally, in the analysis of the education level as a possible variable explaining social exclusion, mention was also made[23] of the role of family links and, in particular, of the importance – and this applies also to poorly educated people – of having contact with more educated people. To this end, the proposal was submitted to add an indicator on the number of people living in households where all components were poorly educated.

With regard to employment, two indicators are present, namely the long-term unemployment rate (twelve months or more) and the percentage of people living in jobless households where nobody (of those elegible to belong to the labour force) is working. The definition of this indicator was modified compared to the 2001 list, which surveyed the percentage of jobless *households* rather than individuals. The Commission accepted some remarks[24] submitted by the ad hoc sub-committee created by the Social Protection Committee for the study and analysis of social indicators, which required more attention to be paid to people, on the basis of the considerations we discussed above for monetary indicators.

Furthermore, employment, which represents one of the specific action areas defined in Lisbon, already appears in the overall list with the other seven indicators. The inclusion of two other parameters in the social cohesion area tends to underline the cause/effect links connecting these phenomena and the importance they have in analysing the mechanisms of poverty emergence. However, it is worth noting that these links are by no means automatic: in many European countries unemployment growth in the 1970s and 1980s caused no poverty rate variation.[25] Indeed, in some cases, the effectiveness of the social protection system is crucial.

Similarly, the employment growth in recent years did not lead automatically to a decrease in poverty. This seems to corroborate the thesis whereby fighting poverty cannot uniquely mean – as sometimes happens – creating new jobs, because other employment-connected aspects[26] may affect the economic conditions and individual resources, such as the presence of discouraged workers (who are not part of the work force and are not counted in unemployment rates) or of the under-employed and, in particular, the possibility of having poor and inadequate wages and, more generally, the emergence of the so-called working poor. Another proposed indicator is defined by the percentage of people having a sufficiently stable job (that is, having a job for two consecutive years) but living in a condition of poverty (that is, with an equivalent household income below 60 per cent of the median income).

One observes that, from the viewpoint of social exclusion, the quality and stability of a person's job has a non-negligible impact in providing people with higher self-esteem, autonomy of assessment and ability to play an active role in society, and a higher degree of freedom in making choices that are relevant in the person's life. The failure to include all these aspects among the indicators seems to be a fundamental short-coming.[27] Indeed, the two indicators of long-term unemployment and of jobless households focus on elements for which the links between poverty and social exclusion seem to be more evident, namely an extreme and long-lasting disadvantaged employment – which may bring about a strong risk of social exclusion – and family difficulties, which may highlight the problem of vicious circles leading to exclusion that are so difficult to break.

Finally, with reference to regional cohesion, the coefficient of variation of the unemployment rate between different regions in each country is evaluated. The definition of that indicator has been modified many times, using the unemployment rate and the per capita GDP alternatively as reference variables to estimate regional differentials.[28] The Commission[29] stresses the extreme sensitivity of that indicator to missing data or to small changes in the regional breakdown caused by the small number of observations.[30] This is a violation of the principle of statistical robustness. Perhaps, rather than considering a specific indicator on this subject, it would be better to propose for some of the indicators on the list – whenever significant – a breakdown aimed at highlighting the degree of convergence of the different areas of each country. In other words, that indicator appears to be redundant, as regional cohesion, rather than being a separate problem, is an aspect or a way through which other phenomena appear.

More generally, a specific breakdown would be useful for all the indicators approved at Laeken, so as to highlight the population brackets, the individual characteristics and the areas where there is the highest concentration of poverty and social exclusion, and in which the risk of exclusion is greater. This kind of analysis would contribute towards identifying strategies aimed at combating specific problems in given areas, thus enhancing their degree of effectiveness. This shortcoming is even more evident if one considers that the areas defined in Lisbon comprise some significant indicator breakdowns, even though they are not enough to highlight the complex nature of the problems ana-lysed. For example, in employment, a breakdown is made for the overall employment rate; for the employment rate for older workers (by gender); for the number of accidents at work (by seriousness of accident); in innovation and research by the level of Internet access (by type of user); and by ICT expenditure (broken down into information techno- logy expenditure and communications) and so on. If one analyses to what extent the three main characteristics of the whole portfolio are not respected, one observes that the least respected is the one con- cerning the fair balancing between the dimensions considered.[31] Indeed, three out of seven indicators refer to monetary exclusion – identifying only resource distribution – and two others refer to employment (which is also dealt with by seven indicators at Level 1), while the last indicator is redundant, as we said before. It is worth noting that, while all NAPs/incl underline the many facets of the phenome- non, ranging from 'family risk' to 'disability' to 'weak health', from 'housing' to 'ethnic-racial' risk, none of these aspects is described adequately in the list of indicators. This lack of fair balance seems to suggest that the multidimensional approach to social exclusion is merely paid lip service. This criticism deserves a more thorough examination, but only after having a brief look at the performance of the indicators officially agreed upon at Laeken.

The approved indicators: data

The examination of indicators provides important information (see Table 7.3), though it confirms some of the criticism levelled at the basket imbalance: the portrait of the country stemming from them is limited and partial.

With reference to the first three (or four, as the poverty rate is computed both *ex ante* and *ex post* of public transfers) indicators, three homogeneous groups may be distinguished. The first consists of the Scandinavian countries plus Austria, where monetary poverty is quite low (10 per cent) and the ratio between the overall income of those who are better-off and that the poor is lower than the European average and equal to 3, thus showing a low degree of inequality in resource distribution. At the other end there is the group of Mediterranean countries (Greece, Italy, Portugal and Spain) which show very high poverty risks (more than 20 per cent) and marked inequalities (the first indicator takes up values between 6 and 7). The third group consists of the remaining countries (namely Central European countries plus the British Isles) which generally have intermedi- ate levels of poverty and income inequality. Obviously, separation is not so rigid: for example, for Italy, the first indicator equals levels similar to those of the continental countries, while with reference to poverty rates, Luxembourg and the Netherlands are close to the minimum European levels and the United Kingdom belongs fully with the group

Table 7.3 The performance of social cohesion indicators

	Incomes of the top quintile/incomes of the bottom quintile[a]		Relative poverty rate before public transfers		Relative poverty rate after public transfers		Poverty persistence	Regional cohesion[b]		Early school leaving		Long-term unemployment rate		People in jobless households
	1995	1998	1995	1998	1995	1998	1998	1995	2000	1995	2001	1995	2001	1998
Austria	4.3	3.8	25	25	13	13	7	26.2	29.0	12.1	10.2	1	0.9	1.8
Belgium	6.4	5.8	29	28	17	16	9	37.7	54.2	15.1	13.6	5.8	3.8f	5.9
Denmark	2.9	2.7	31	26	12	9	3	–	–	6.1	16.8	2.3	0.9	–
Finland	–	3.0c	–	27c	–	8c	–	10.9	30.9	11.1d	10.3	5.7	2.5	–
France	4.8	4.7	28	28	17	18	12	18.0	24.3	15.5	13.5	4.7	3.7f	6.2
Germany	5.7	4.8	24	24	17	16	10	39.1	48.7	13,.3c	12.5 (7)	4	4.0f	4.5
Greece	6.5	6.8	23	23	22	22	10	24.3	17.3	22.4	16.5	4.6	5.4	3.7
Ireland	5.8	5.3	34	33	19	17	11	–	–	21.4	18.9c	7.8	1.3	7.9
Italy	6.1	5.9	23	23	20	20	12	57.9	71.5	32.4	26.4	7.3	5.9	5.4
Luxembourg	4.8	4.6d	25	26d	12	12d	–	–	–	33.4	18.1	0.7	0.5f	1.0
Netherlands	4.7	4.4	25	21	11	12	5	10.6	22.3	17.6d	15.3	3.1	0.8	3.7
Portugal	7.6	7.2	28	27	23	20	16	30.3	32.5	41.4	45.2	3.1	1.5	2.0
United Kingdom	6.0	5.7	33	33	22	21	11	28.7	45.0	5.8	–	3.7	1.3	6.7
Spain	6.2	6.8	27	25	20	19	10	24.1	41.3	33.3	28.3	12.3	5.1	10.0
Sweden	–	3.4	–	30	–	10	–	14.0	28.8	7.5d	7.7g	2.5	1.2	–
EU	5.7	5.4	27	26	18	18	11	56.4	63.8	21.6e	19.3g	5.2	3.2	5.9g

Notes: (a) Absolute values; (b) The indicator is not relevant for Denmark, Ireland and Luxembourg; (c) 1997 data; (d) 1996 data; (e) Temporary 1996 data; (f) 2000 data; (g) Temporary data.
Source: Eurostat (figures updated in 2002).

of Mediterranean countries. It is interesting to note that the groupings themselves also hold true when considering transfer effect-iveness. The three Scandinavian countries succeed in reducing their poverty rates considerably through public aid (between 65 per cent and 70 per cent), while the four Southern countries are less effective: the incidence variation equals 25 per cent in Spain and Portugal, 13 per cent in Italy and even 4 per cent in Greece, while the average European reduction is 30 per cent. Finally, with reference to the persistence of poverty, it is worth mentioning the particularly high figure for France and the limited – compared to the standards of those countries – values of the United Kingdom and Spain, which thus belong to the intermediate group.

Data also confirm that the poor regional cohesion within countries is very serious in Italy, where the phenomenon has been harsher since the end of the last decade, while it is not a problem in Austria, Finland, France, Greece, the Netherlands, Portugal or Sweden. Notice that in some cases the reduced dimensions of a country or the inclusion of sparsely inhabited areas (as in Scandinavian countries, for example) favour, *ceteris paribus*, a higher regional cohesion. In this view, the strong French cohesion takes on a greater importance compared to the data from other countries, while the performance of small countries such as Belgium seems to be all the more serious. With reference to education, the percentage of young people aged between 18 and 24 having no higher secondary school diploma and attending no course is high (though decreasing) in Italy and Spain, very high in Portugal, but very low in Sweden, Austria and Finland, Germany, France and Belgium.

Finally, employment indicators underline some additional points. In particular, data on Ireland and the United Kingdom, where unemployment hits a large number of households (6.7 per cent of people in the United Kingdom and 7.9 per cent in Ireland live in jobless households, compared to an average figure of below 6 per cent), are surprising, though it is not long-term unemployment (the long-term unemployment rate of both countries – 1.3 per cent – is smaller than the average figure for the EU-15, which is 3.2 per cent). Data seem to mirror effectively the high degree of dynamism characterizing the labour markets of Anglo-Saxon countries. Conversely, in Italy and even more so in Greece, one of the characteristics of unemployment is its persistence (they have the highest rates in the Union), while the particular social-demographic structure of these countries – with stronger family links compared to the European average – ensure more often than elsewhere the presence in households of at least one source of working income. Finally, the performances of both employment indicators appear to be very critical in Spain, while

Germany and France show figures above the average on the first and second parameters.

The Laeken shadows

The basket's shortcomings: health care, housing and living conditions

While studying the links between social exclusion and health, it is difficult to establish which the cause and which the effect: admittedly, an ongoing process of exclusion – for example, because of an inadequate income or precarious and unhealthy accommodation may lead to a person not receiving the necessary medical controls and treatment, thus causing his/her overall health to deteriorate. However, it is also true that weak health may cause an individual to abandon his/her job (the so-called selection effect), thus causing a strong growth of the exclusion risk. Hence, it would be most helpful to include indicators considering these aspects in the list of indicators.

There is a problem of lack of comparable data: indeed, attention in identifying social exclusion indicators is paid not so much to collecting data on health-care systems of the member states, but rather on gathering information on the differentials between population brackets and on the access to health-care services of people with different characteristics. One example of these difficulties is provided by recording mortality. There are a lot of data available on mortality levels and life expectation in the various countries, while there are very few comparative studies on mortality rate broken down by socioeconomic characteristics or by income level.[32] The connection between administrative data and information on single people is sometimes uncertain, and that is why the comparison over time or space for indicators based on those data sets is extremely difficult. *Ad hoc* surveys would be necessary: they should be cross-country, consistent and homogeneous for the whole European Union.

Similar problems emerge when dealing with data on morbidity, but in this case a useful solution may be found (that is, making reference to the way people perceive their health status); this variable is surveyed by the Europanel, which also provides information on income and on other individual characteristics. The subjective nature of these data, hence the possible systematic distortion of replies in some countries, may be offset by considering ratios rather than absolute values. For example, an interesting proposal[33] in this view is the one aimed at calculating the ratio between the proportion of those declaring they had 'weak' or 'very weak' health in the lowest 20 per cent of the population (identified through the equivalent households' income) of the total number of people belonging to that income bracket and the same proportion calculated for the top 20 per cent of the population. In 1996, this ratio ranged between 1.4 in Spain and 2.2 in Luxembourg, thus suggesting a possible wider diffusion of the perception of a weak health status in the whole Spanish population compared to Luxembourg. The European average equalled 1.5.

The proposals of the Social Protection Committee of October 2001 were in keeping with this view, as the Council and the Commission proposed to include in the list of indicators the perception of a person's health status by income level and life expectation at birth. As has already been discussed, the latter indicator would have more significance if it were connected to information on income and socioeconomic conditions. However, given the importance of the matter and its connection to social exclusion, the use of the 'raw' indicator was advisable, postponing any further deepening to future surveys and to an improvement in the available data. Also, these observations were not accepted by Community institutions and the approved list does not comprise any indicator on the health status of countries.

With reference to housing, the (already mentioned) Charter of Fundamental Rights of the European Union recognizes the right to live in adequate accommodation to maintain human dignity, and NAPs/incl considers that objective as one of the areas for political action. The main problem consists in finding a definition of 'adequate accommodation', which is homogeneous on the one hand, and takes into account national peculiarities on the other, as the concept of 'adequacy' changes according to environmental and social conditions. One might consider 'inadequate' accommodation without basic services or with intolerable shortcomings (for example, no ventilation, signs of persistent dampness and so on), hence one might include among poverty indicators the percentage of people living in inadequate accommodation. Many indications may be derived from the Europanel, which contains data on accommodation, on the presence of lavatonés and a means of heating, of excessive damp and so on.

Additionally, it is useful to include – perhaps at Level 2 – indicators considering other aspects: the problem of 'overcrowded' accommodation, for example, or the households' capacity to afford home maintenance. Indeed, difficulties in paying for home maintenance may be the first step on the way towards housing discomfort, which may eventually end up in homelessness, a clear signal of social exclusion. The use of an indicator based on 'objective' criteria (a percentage of rent fee on total income, heating costs and so on) may pose problems both for the difficulty of treating in a comparable way house owners and renters, and for the poor data availability. Similarly to what was proposed for health, the solution lies in the construction of parameters based on the respondents' perceived satisfaction of their own needs. In this case, one might, for example, collect data on the punctuality of payment of home maintenance expenses (be they rent fees, bank loan instalments or domestic bills).

It also seems strange that no mention was made of the problem of homelessness. Admittedly, the analysis of homelessness poses problems in the surveying phase, as well as difficulties in identifying homogenous definitions and methods, and in the cross-country comparison of results. For this reason too, data on this topic are difficult to find: no data are provided by the Europanel and only few member states survey and analyse this problem. Indeed, only the NAPs/incl of France, Finland and the Netherlands show indicators on this topic, while Germany and Italy have carried out occasional surveys (Germany has provide annual estimates of the number of homeless between 1994 and 1999, while in Italy the first – and at the time writing, the last – official survey dates back to 2000).[34] However, suitable methodologies[35] are needed and resources should be invested at Community level to develop an indicator on this topic.

In a multidimensional optics, there are many other aspects that would be relevant in identifying the many risk factors of social exclusion: in particular, an indicator measuring access to basic services – be they public or private (banks, pharmacies, police departments, schools, transport and so on) – and one concerning the degree of indebtedness and financial vulnerability of people. Also for those dimensions, given the difficulty of providing homogeneous definitions and comparable data, one might suggest a resort to indicators based on subjective information ('Do you have any difficulties in gaining access to those services?'; 'Do you have difficulty in paying bills and obtaining credit?'). As with to the indications for health, it is advisable to adopt methods of neutralising systematic distortions connected to the subjective nature of replies.

Some critical remarks on method

Alongside the critical aspects and methodological problems concerning indicators and their shortcomings – for which a risk is run of providing a partial a picture of a problem that is multidimensional – it is worth emphasizing some general doubts on the way in which the list of indicators is identified and elaborated.

First, there is little co-ordination between the bodies taking part in the portfolio construction with different capacities. This problem emerged while the phases that led to the list of indicators were being reviewed. The first document, providing a complete list of structural indicators to be used within the Lisbon strategy, was drawn up by the Commission[36] in September 2000. In the area of social cohesion there were six indicators (namely those approved in Laeken which have already been discussed above) apart from the long-term unemployment rate, which was included in employment, with some (already mentioned) changes in the definition of regional cohesion and of jobless households. The document also hinted at some possible developments, while under-lining the importance of the multidimensional aspects of exclusion and suggesting some research guidelines, leaving in-depth analyses to the Social Protection Committee. The first data referring to those parameters[37] were submitted at the Stockholm Council in March 2001.

In the meantime, the Economic Policy Committee drew up a document to comment on and analyse the Commission's indicators,[38] and the so-called 'Sub-Committee on Indicators' was set up within the Social Protection Committee. The final document presented by the Committee contained a series of practical indications analysing the phenomenon much more thoroughly than had been done by the Commission, and proposed a complete list which included many of the criticisms that have been highlighted in this chapter. The incidence of poverty before public transfers was removed from the main list (and included in Level 2), while numerous additional breakdowns were presented (by gender and age, by occupational status, by type of household, by house ownership). An indicator of the intensity of poverty was also included, together with the two indicators concerning health which we discussed above.

In addition, the Social Protection Committee presented for the first time a list of Level 2 indicators, which marked the first attempt to build the 'tree-like' structure with different levels that was mentioned in the Lisbon strategy. The measures proposed in that additional list further investigated the poverty risk: indeed, responsiveness analyses were elaborated by utilizing different lines (either by modifying the income percentage according to which the threshold is computed, or by fixing the threshold at a given moment and updating it only to include price rises).[39] Furthermore, a thorough analysis was carried out of income distribution by computing the Gini coefficient, of unemployment by considering the long-term unemployed (more than 24 months) and of the level of education, by proposing breakdowns by gender and by age brackets not considered in the Level 1 indicator.

The Commission's reactions were contradictory. On the one hand, the Commission included at least some of the Committee's proposals in its Joint Report on Social Inclusion of 12 December 2001, namely the list of parameters of the long-term unemployment rate, the Gini coefficient, many breakdowns of the incidence of poverty, and analyses of the rate of sensitivity to threshold variations. But on the other hand, the Commission insisted on the old list with its Communication[40] on Structural Indicators of October 2001, and with the approval at Laeken and the subsequent submission at the Barcelona Council of a battery of indicators very close to the original list. Thus the contribution of the Social Protection Committee, originally considered important, seems almost to have been ignored in fact, because of the alleged need to maintain a stable list to evaluate the progress made in 2001 and to limit the enlargement of the number of parameters, particularly after the inclusion of environment among the areas of action. The Commission uniquely recognized the need to better develop the multidimensional aspects of exclusion, particularly for those concerning health, and socialeconomic status, housing and living conditions.

Reading the NAPs/incl gives the impression of little co-ordination in this area. The 'tree-like' structure defined that, when deciding upon the OMC, indicators were to cover specific aspects of each member state, which are not very interesting for the Union as a whole. What is less obvious is that the list of parameters shows methodological differences, not only among single member states, but also between them and the Commission's indications: those divergences can only be explained by the lack of a truly common approach. For example, with reference to the risk of poverty, some countries utilize the relative poverty approach, whereas others (the United Kingdom, Italy, Portugal) also adopt that of absolute poverty. Indeed, even the definition of relative poverty thresholds itself is different, as percentages other than the commonly-agreed one are adopted, and not all of them consider the median as the reference value for the central trend.

In official documents, with the exceptions of the proceedings of the Social Protection Committee and of the Economic Policy Committee, there is no trace – not even for the other action areas of Lisbon – of the three levels of parameters that would guarantee a thorough analysis combined with an easy-to-follow scheme of the main results. Indeed, as the Commission itself[41] recognized, 'we are still far from a common approach to social indicators'.

Concluding remarks

Over the past few years, along with the creation of the Monetary Union, a new European sensitivity to the topic of social inclusion has been emerging. Even though, in the area of welfare, the principle of subsidiarity has not been discussed, social cohesion problems have been tackled with an Open Method of Co-ordination which foresees, among other things, the adoption of quantitative indicators aimed at enabling the evaluation and monitoring of the results obtained, and a comparison between member states.

This chapter has described the process of construction of indicators for social inclusion, highlighting positive and negative aspects, both in terms of significance and adequacy of indicators, and in terms of consistency and co-ordination between the institutions committed in the 'basket' definition, and between them and the member states.

Stress was laid on the positive aspects, starting from the identification of new priority targets for the European Union which took place in Lisbon. Thanks to that process, attention was shifted from an economic financial viewpoint to an employment social one, looking for a fair balance between the two. The definition of an overall action strategy involving both European and national institutions marks an important step forward. The intention also to include the performances of EU candidate countries[42] in the Commission's analyses and in its Report starting from 2003 marks a clear signal of the importance attached to those topics at Community level, with the intention to enforce an Open Method of Co-ordination. Indeed, a list of thirty-five indicators was eventually approved, and the member states drew up the first NAPs/incl, which the Commission analysed. Institutions and resources were used to implement what had been planned two years before.

There are, however, doubts about the indicators chosen, the methods adopted, the degree of co-ordination between the partners who took part in the enforcement of the Lisbon method and, finally, about the real effectiveness of a procedure that does not commit states to pursue certain policies, but merely provides guidelines and suggestions regarding the targets. In a word, *open* co-ordination is running the risk of becoming *soft* co-ordination, where the lack of binding commitments and sanctions is undermining the final outcome.

This is even more so if one considers that, with reference to social inclusion, very few objectives were clearly[43] set at the European level indicating values, targets and timing, compared to what has been taking place for a long time in the area of employment. Admittedly, from an OMC view, one might assume that individual member states set their own targets according to their national situation and autonomously-fixed policies; however, NAPs/incl sometimes do not specify real targets. Besides, the risk might emerge that, leaving the responsibility to set targets and their attainment to single member states, national governments tend to privilege action areas where results are easier and more obvious, to the detriment of more far-reaching objectives or structural interventions.

The Commission should have an adequate answer to all of that, thus guaranteeing the credibility of the whole process, and prompting member states not to neglect any of the aspects outlined in Lisbon. The exchange in best practices, the submission of NAPs/incl and their control at Community level, and the analysis and cross-country comparison of indicators should guarantee that peer pressure which – together with the real commitment of all member states – would enable the achieving of objectives.

To this end, it is necessary to act effectively, so that all partners contribute to the overall debate. Indeed, some positive signals emerge in this sense: a Committee for the Community Action Programme to Combat Social Exclusion, consisting of experts from all EU countries, was set up in 2001 with the aim of supporting the Commission in enforcing the Open Method of Co-ordination.[44] That Committee should be the link between member states and European institutions, thus guaranteeing common intentions and methods.

In particular, the Committee's tasks are the following: facilitating the understanding of the phenomenon of social exclusion by further developing co-operation between national Institutes of Statistics and the elaboration of comparable indicators and common methodologies; organizing a cross-country exchange of experiences and best practices by drawing up technical studies and an Annual Report on Social Exclusion; enabling the participation of all partners by creating a European network and organizing an Annual Conference in collaboration with the European presidency and the other institutions. Within this framework, stress is laid on the importance of a close collaboration with the Social Protection Committee.

Thus there are attempts to look for solutions for the aspects that are considered to be critical for the success of the whole Lisbon strategy in social exclusion, and this is a further positive signal that the European Union wants to make progress towards sustainable development, employment growth and greater social cohesion. The degree of effective-ness of these solutions depends on the ability to match words with deeds, and it is up to the community of experts, research institutes and institutions to urge, stimulate and monitor the results obtained in this area.

8
From Tax Competition to Social Race to the Bottom? European Models and the Challenge of Mobility[1]

In all the fields in which the European Union (EU) feels anxious to make progress, the welfare state seems to be the most urgent cause for reform. As the issue runs deep into most European citizens' everyday life, it is only natural that it should become the focal point of the EU's anxieties and hopes, at a time when it is torn between the erosion of national sovereignty and its elusive replacement by that of a federal state.

However, the debate over the 'European social model', as the EU authorities have chosen to call it, seems to have got off to a poor start. Much too often the discussion boils down to the basic argument where antiquated national social policies must give way to would-be-historical irrevocable developments, such as 'globalization' and the advent of the 'knowledge-based economy'. Both vague and biased, this approach fails to convince.

The problems raised by the future of the Welfare State in Europe undoubtedly need attention, but a proper debate would have to remain closer to EU realities, and preferably stay well clear of any 'theology of competition and competitiveness'.[2] If a convincing debate is to take place, it should focus on the truly European forces at work in the economic and social areas, which the launch of the single currency and the completion of the common market have delimited.

According to Wildasin (2000), 'increasing mobility of labour and capital is a fact of life in modern Europe'. Then what is the future for European social models, when productive factors keep integrating ever more closely, when a new entity is progressively coming into being and thus opening the way for the eventual rule of the free movement of goods, services, capital and people?

Tax competition and social competition highlight how this 'mobility challenge' is bound to influence the redistribution impact of the member states' fiscal policies. Distinct and yet closely related, both types of competition raise the issue of the real meaning of a 'social Europe'. In doing so, they do not so much raise the issue of the 'European social model' as question the future of the various existing European welfare states: the rise of tax and social competition will not necessarily challenge their existence, but it will ultimately influence their purpose. The general outlook of a 'competitive Europe' in the making must therefore be considered. To begin, one should ponder over the ideological discourses that have accompanied these developments.

The debate over the 'European social model'

From de facto product to productive factor

The EU conception of social protection, before being given its 'modern' translation in Lisbon in the year 2000, can be found in the Rome Treaty and characterized, in two related meanings, as the outcome of a 'model of separation': first, an institutional separation, the Treaty recognizing a form of 'social sovereignty' of member states by leaving the definition and conduct of social policy in their hands, while at the same time taking aim at the unification of their economic structure and policies. Thus, accordingly, there is an analytical separation: social protection being conceived as a by-product of economic integration. In the words of Scharpf (2002), a 'political de-coupling of economic integration and social protection issues... has characterized the real process of European integration from Rome to Maastricht'. The 'new social Europe' under construction in the EU institutions can be seen as an attempt to revise the plans of this divided construction and start to build a new, integrated one, relying on the 'open method of co-ordination' and the idea that 'social protection is a productive factor' as means of institutional and analytical reconciliation.

Two parallel developments must be distinguished with regard to the gradual evolution of the community law of social protection. The first development can be described as 'institutional'. It goes back to the Treaty of Rome, and only its broad outlines will be recalled here. In the Commission's own official words (see Quintin and Favarel-Dapas, 1999), social progress was then seen as simply stemming from economic progress. Accordingly, the original European Community Treaty clearly states that member states should not feel constrained in their social choices.

The only restrictions imposed by the Treaty concerned migrant workers' social security matters, the achievement of equal pay opportunities for men and women, and the setting up of a European Social Fund.

While the 1986 Single European Act reaffirmed that social policies fell within the competence of member states, it extended the European Community's competence by introducing a clause that aimed at initiating qualified majority voting for directives dealing with workers' health and security in the workplace. The Charter of Fundamental Social Rights, adopted in 1989, marked the limit to the Community's institutional competence in the field of social protection: while the Charter lists the criteria of a possible 'European social model',[3] it clearly abstains from granting them any overriding status.

These provisions were reinforced by the Protocol on social policy annexed to the Maastricht Treaty in 1992. While the agreement extends the areas in which the Council is empowered to resort to qualified majority voting (information, workers' consultation, equal treatment of men and women, and integration of the people excluded from the labour market), it also acknowledges 'an essential role' for social partners. The Treaty of Amsterdam (1997), which reflected the new priority given in the EU to employment, went beyond these dispositions: at last, the Protocol on social policy became an integral part of the Treaty, and thus Europe was given the social coherence it had been lacking ever since the United Kingdom opted out of the process.

This overall historical background has become common knowledge and it pervades all the literature on European social policy (see, for example, Meyer, 1998). Yet it can be misleading, because it plays down the developments specific to social protection, which are in fact more faithful to the spirit of European integration. Indeed, as the impossibility of direct harmonization became more evident, the European institutions have shifted from 'hard' to 'soft' law in order to influence the member states in the definition of their social policies, and thus indirectly to curb their sovereignty. Hence the Union's 'soft law' presents a fairer picture through its comments, recommendations, opinions and other news releases. De La Porte (2000) reviewed this branch of law as it was upto 1999. Thanks to her work and to the other official documents the European authorities have published since then, it is possible to form a more detailed opinion of the developments and more recent shifts in the Union's position on social protection. It seems indeed that, as early as 1974, the European authorities worked out a well-thought-out strategy intended to by-pass the problems of 'social sovereignty': they introduced a host of legally non-binding instruments which none the less constrained the national governments' power, as they became hallmarks on the way to a common social policy.

Two different periods in the European authorities' 'social activism' can be distinguished. The first has now disappeared from view. Initiated in 1974, when the Council adopted its first social action programme, it reasserted the principle of equal treatment of men and women, and urged member states to establish basic rules in employment and social dialogue. For De La Porte (2000), however modest the programme's content and scope, it initiated the European governments' opposition to the 'monolithic harmonization' of social systems over the 1980s, and the change in the European authorities' methods from 1992.

The second period, though less active, was thus marked by a proliferation in the number of published EU instruments. The texts still remained non-binding, but they were phrased in increasingly precise terms. In 1992, the Council adopted two recommendations (92/442 and 92/441) which described the convergence of the member states' social protection objectives in scrupulous detail. A White Paper followed in 1993, then a Green Paper in 1994: both were entirely devoted to the definition of common social criteria. This new strategy culminated in Lisbon in 2000 with the definition of the 'new open method of co-ordination'.

As this soft approach was starting to bear fruit, the objective of the harmonization of social systems was gradually displaced from 1995 (Commission communication 95/466 on 'The future of social protection, a framework for a European debate') by the insistent call for the modernization of European systems. Logically, the attempt to reconcile the member states and the EU in the institutional field was combined with an effort to reconcile the economic and social policies on theoretical grounds.

Based on the approach advocated by the OECD (1996) and following the Dutch Presidency Conference on 'Social Policy and Economic Performance', the 'Modernizing and improving social protection' communication (European Commission, 1997) marks the launch of the new theoretical integrated strategy. The overall new objective is to 'optimize' social policy in order to respond to the challenge of 'economic competitiveness'. To do so, European Welfare States must be 'activated', following Schumpeter rather than Keynes: the renewed, most dynamic institutions must no longer rely on 'passive' social spending but promote 'active' social investment. In the process, social policy, employment policy and economic policy are supposed to form a virtuous triangle fostering social cohesion, full employment and economic dynamism. This new doctrine

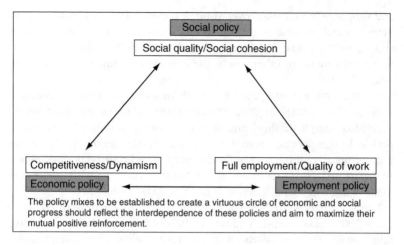

Figure 8.1 The virtuous European triangle
Source: European Commission (2000a).

was first expressed explicitly in a speech delivered by Anna Diamantopoulou, the Commissioner for Employment and Social Affairs before the European Parliament on 31 August 1999. European success takes on the shape of a 'virtuous triangle' whose respective sides represent social policy, economic policy and employment policy. The three sides are supposed to interact to promote general progress (see Figure 8.1).

The Conclusions of the Lisbon summit (European Council, 2000a) fully embraced this new strategy by coining the new EU motto, 'to become the most competitive and dynamic knowledge-based economy in the world capable of sustainable economic growth with more and better jobs and greater social cohesion'. It is to be noted that, in these conclusions, the 'new strategic goal' is related directly to the need of 'modernising the European social model', by 'building' an 'Active Welfare State'.

The Social Policy Agenda (European Commission, 2000a) accordingly recommended: 'In order to confront successfully technological and societal changes ... the modernisation and improvement of the European social model ... required to underpin economic dynamism and pursue employment-generating reforms' and advocates 'quality of social policy' to 'invest in people to increase their employability'.

As explained above, the conceptual redefinition of 'social protection as a productive factor' is an attempt to end the separation between social and economic policy. Moreover, it often presents itself as a an attempt to 'rescue' social protection from 'economic victimisation': social protection should no longer be considered a 'dead body' pulling down European 'competitiveness'. In other words, the intention behind activation seems 'social-friendly'.

But the new EU integrated approach to social protection advocates a reconciliation by absorption: the absorption of social responsibility by individual 'employability', and absorption of social policy by economic policy. In this process, from Rome to Lisbon, the line of separation has not disappeared: it has moved from departing social and economic policy to departing labour market and the rest of the economy, with unemployment being considered solely as a labour market problem.

The speech delivered by the Commissioner at the time of the new 2000–2005 social agenda's adoption did confirm the change of course taken by the European authorities. From being a mere by-product, social protection was promoted to the level of competitiveness tool status. Social protection was no longer a residue; it became an appendix.[4]

As a summary of its recommendations, the European Commission (2000b) addressed a warning to the Union's member states: 'Europe must make sure its social model is flexible and robust enough so it can effectively face up to the new challenges, while still making progress towards its objectives of increased competitiveness and cohesion.' Nevertheless, the fundamental objective of the new policy, the 'modernization' of the 'European social model', is highly contestable. This unique model does not exist in reality: the common characteristic of existing welfare states, if any, is precisely to be very different from one another.

Social Europes

The pertinence of the European Commission's strongly advocated 'concerted strategy' is based mainly on the notion that national social protection systems are currently facing common challenges. How does this approach confront reality? The 1999 Report on social protection, published by the European Commission (2000c), noted clearly the existence of common trends in the different member states' attitudes to social protection. In 1996,[5] total social protection expenditure made up 28.5 per cent of EU GDP. Even though the figures were increasing in most EU countries, their real growth slowed down (over 1990–3, social spending posted an average 25.5 per cent–28.5 per cent GDP increase because of the economic recession). With the exceptions of Portugal,

Greece, Germany, Austria, Belgium and Luxembourg, social spending has indeed come down compared to 1993–6 GDP figures.

Breakdowns of the various social protection components show that old-age payments take up the largest amount, close to 43 per cent of the overall total. Health care adds up to 21.5 per cent, disablement and unemployment payments are 8 per cent, and family and child allowances take up 7.5 per cent of total EU social spending. Social contributions financed an average 63 per cent of total expenditure in 1996. Between 1990 and 1996, the social contributions to total spending ratio remained almost stable, from 65.5 per cent to 63 per cent of total spending. However, a tentative shift from social contributions to direct taxation can be noted for several member states. This holds true especially for countries with the highest contribution rates, such as France, Belgium, Germany and, more recently, Italy.

In addition to these data, 'Social trends: prospects and challenges' (European Commission, 2000b) lists the member states' major common trends in social evolution. From the member states' common features (that is, the rising number of working women, low participation and high unemployment rates), the Commission (European Commission, 2000c) set up five objectives for social policy: it required governments to make work more rewarding, basic wages more secure, to set up viable pension schemes, promote social integration, and finally provide for high and long-lasting health protection. The new agenda presented in June 2000 and adopted in Nice that same year simply took up the same objectives, albeit with the addition of references to gender equality and the fight against all types of discrimination.

In a second stage, one may wish to take another look at this apparent convergence of member states and see whether they lead to a convincing single model. The above-mentioned aggregate data need to be broken down further according to their national characteristics. The result is then somewhat different. First of all, social protection spending levels vary greatly from one country to another. The range goes from over 30 per cent of GDP for Nordic countries to 18.5 per cent for Ireland. France, Belgium and Germany, and social spending in the Netherlands is 30 per cent. It reduces to a 22–23 per cent range for Greece, Spain and Portugal. On 30 October 1998, Eurostat stated that there was a 'marked' difference between member states with regard to social expenditure. It underlined that, in 1995, the difference between the member states' highest and lowest levels was a ratio of 3.4 to 1. The financing of social spending also shows great variations: social contributions vary from a minimum of 33 per cent for France, Belgium, the Netherlands, Germany,

Italy and Spain, to 25 per cent in Denmark. The total is under 50 per cent for Luxembourg, Sweden and Finland, while for Portugal, the UK and Ireland it is under 40%.

How can these discrepancies be justified when the European authorities have tried hard to achieve harmonization since the 1970s? According to a Eurostat news release of 3 March 1998, 'The differences between Member States reflect the differences in their social protection systems, demographic evolution, unemployment rates and other social, institutional and economic factors'. Indeed, it is necessary to go beyond the data to shed light on the differences, or even the 'institutional' divergence between the different European social models. By attempting such a description one should acknowledge that the 'European social model' is nowhere to be found, apart from in the European literature. Some European social models do exist.[6] They are most distinct, and in some ways, contradictory. Along with the Commissariat Général du Plan (1999), it is possible to present a tentative draft of these different types (see Box 8.1).

Box 8.1   The four European models

It must be noted that two aspects most distinct in reality have been put together below: labour conditions and work relations on the one hand, social protection systems on the other. The two elements are presented together only to make it possible to draw up a list of the major features of the four European 'social families'. The French system cannot be listed as it belongs to more than one category.

The liberal model (UK and the Republic of Ireland)
Social bargaining is most decentralized. Co-operation between social partners is weak. Employment legislation is flexible. The National Health Service is the only universal protection system available in the UK. Privately-funded social insurance plays an important part. Firms finance supplementary protection schemes. Tax-payers finance the social protection system.

The social democratic model (Sweden, Finland, Denmark)
Social partners play a key role in the labour market, contractual policy rules (notably in the fields of pay, work conditions and redundancy procedures). Collective bargaining is centralized. Universal social protection underpins the system. Pension schemes allow for supplementary benefits.

The Christian-Democratic model (Germany, The Netherlands, Belgium, Luxembourg, Austria)
Collective bargaining and contractual policy play an essential part. Unions have become secondary, the law is paramount. Social insurance follows the lines of the Bismarck model.[7] Social contributions are paid by both employers and employees. The most needy benefit from a 'safety net'.

The state/family-based mixed model (Spain, Greece, Italy, Portugal)
Trade unions play an important role, along with law and contractual policy. The state and social partners hold joint power. Social insurance follows the lines of the Bismarck model. Social services are little developed and the family network remains essential.

Source: Commissariat Général du Plan (1999).

This fourfold approach to 'social Europe' can be tuned further by disregarding the elements specific to the labour market.[8] Drawing again on the Commissariat Général du Plan study, the supposed existence of overall unity, as claimed by the European Commission, is called into question even more (see Box 8.2).

Box 8.2 The three 'social Europes'

The conservative model (Continental Europe)
This follows the Bismarck tradition. Based on social insurance contributions. Payments depend on the type of job held. System financed by social insurance contributions and run by the social partners.

The social democratic model (Sweden, Finland, Denmark)
This follows the Beveridge tradition. Universal payment through redistribution is the norm, and depends on citizenship and residence. Tax-payers finance the system, which is run by the state on a decentralized basis.

The liberal model (UK and the Republic of Ireland)
This follows the Beveridge tradition. Payments are restricted to the target population of the poor and the needy. Tax-payers finance the system, which is run by the state on a centralized basis.

Sources: Commissariat Général du Plan (1999); Esping-Andersen (1990).

Given this context in which the different European models have survived the economic integration process,[9] the debate over the future of Europe's social protection may need refocusing on the current trends in EU development. Even though the diversity briefly mentioned is certainly an asset, it is also important to gauge the potential dangers they present in the context of the free movement of production factors.

Four freedoms and a currency

The European economic and monetary environment of the first decade of the twenty-first century is marked by the launch of the single currency and the partly completed integrated area 'in which goods, people, services and capital move freely', as set out in the Commission's 1985 White Paper (see Box 8.3).

Box 8.3   The European Union's four freedoms

The free movement of goods (article 28 of the EC Treaty)
The free movement of goods between member states requires both the harmonization of taxes and customs duties, and common regulations on the protection of health, consumers and the environment, along with the removal of all other trade barriers. With the establishment of the single market in 1993, the Community's goal has been achieved to a large extent.

The freedom of establishment (article 43) and the free provision of services (article 49)
Freedom of establishment is the right for EU citizens and firms to set up and freely pursue industrial, commercial, professional or farming activities in another member state (articles 52 to 58 of the EC Treaty). Although all limits to the freedom of establishment were lifted from 1 January 1970, some remain in place de facto because of differing national work regulations and job requirements. Further harmonization and the mutual recognition of diplomas have put an end to some of these restrictions.

The free movement of capital (article 56)
In 1988, the Council of Ministers decided all capital flow between EC member states would be free from 1 July 1990. It is undeniable that since that date, at least since 1 January 1993, capital has flowed freely within the Union.

The free movement of persons (article 42)
In principle, EU member states' workers, both salaried and self-employed, have the right to live and work in any EU member state, and to receive all the social allowances available in their place of residence, on equal terms with local nationals, which excludes any discrimination based on nationality (article 42 of the EC Treaty). With the establishment of the single market, all EU citizens have the choice to live, work or retire to any EU country.

Source: europa. eu. int.

But these achievement are not without their drawbacks. In the words of the OFCE (1998) survey on tax competition:

> With the introduction of the single currency national governments can no longer make use of monetary policy or the exchange rate, two supposedly major economic control instruments of competitiveness. In this context, taxation remains governments' last readily available tool when they wish to make their national economy less sluggish and more competitive.

As a result, tax and social competition could become a serious threat to Europe's social protection. It is therefore important to assess the risks involved.

Capital flows and tax competition

To avoid any confusion about terms, a distinction must be made between two types of tax competition. 'Tax dumping' or 'unfair tax competition' bring into play standard taxation schemes and the special schemes that apply only to non-residents – for example, tax havens. It is this type of competition that the OECD, for example, intends to combat. This commitment goes back to its 1998 Report entitled 'Harmful Tax Competition: An Emerging global issue'. The fight was resumed in June 2000 with a new report on unfair competition practices. This listed forty-seven potentially unfair tax systems and thirty-five jurisdictions that can be described as tax havens. The European authorities also support this global fight. Such an approach to tax competition, also referred to as 'harmful' in some other reports, leads logically to another definition.

In fact, the existence of some 'harmful' tax competition implies the existence of beneficial competition as its counterpart. The European

Parliament's resolution of 18 June 1998 spoke of a 'beneficial tax competition among Member States as a tool to increase the competitiveness of the
European economy confronted with the challenges of globalisation'. It
could not have been couched in clearer terms. For its stalwart supporters,
this competition leads to more effective use of public spending by the
competing authorities. The overall argumentation is undoubtedly
convincing from a standard economic viewpoint. Nevertheless, it must be
added that such competition is by no means akin to unfair tax competition.
It is not the kind of distortion that needs correcting because it is standing
in the way of the economic integration process in Europe, or elsewhere:
it is desired and accepted as an integration process in itself. In sum, tax
competition is not viewed as a mere phenomenon but as a paradigm. It
is far from obvious that such integration would be the best way forward
for the Union, given its repercussions on social protection systems.

Even though the free flow of capital has now virtually become a fact
within the EU (see Wildasin, 2000), the damaging consequences of
financial liberalization can be modelized into a strategy of taxation
downplaying between uncooperative member states, since tax is being
levied on a mobile base. This results in 'a lower reallocation factor of
overall tax and social security contributions, weaker social protection
and increasingly poor national public sectors' (Hugounenq *et al.*, 1999).
Sinn (1998) recalls that one of the arguments put forward by the advocates
of unfettered tax competition for Europe rests on the very fact that this
could curb state budgetary activism. Indeed, the serious threats to the
social protection systems' financing, and thus redistribution, capacity
may be set against the virtuous circle of tax competition.

Further to the discussions[10] on the current situation and future developments, and despite the difficulty in producing irrefutable empirical
evidence, it seems tax competition has increased in recent years in the
European Union – see, for example, Le Cacheux (2000) and Genschel
(2001). Since the late 1980s, member states have thus embarked on tax
competition on savings and, to a certain extent, corporate taxation.

With savings, the competition-boosting device is fairly straightforward.
The savings invested by non-residents is tax-free in most countries, and
most often non-residents take advantage of inefficient information
systems and fail to declare their income from foreign sources to their
national tax authorities. This works as an incentive to invest abroad.
Large capital transfers have thus been witnessed on several occasions,
which tends to confirm that taxation plays a significant part in savings
location. For example, the flight of capital to Luxembourg prompted
the German authorities to phase out the 10 per cent withheld at source

Table 8.1 The evolution of nominal corporate tax rates, 1990–8

	1990	1991	1993	1994	1998
Germany[a]	50/36	50/36	50/36	45/30	45/30[b]
Belgium	43	39	39	39	39[c]
Denmark	40	38	38	34	34
Spain	35	35	35	35	35
France[a]	37/42	34/42	34	33.3	36[b, c, d]
Ireland	43	43	40	40	32
Italy[a]	36	36	36	36	37
Luxembourg	34	33.33	33.33	33.33	30
Netherlands	35	35	35	35	35
Portugal	36.5	36	36	36	34
UK	35	34	33	33	31

Notes: (a) The first rate shows the taxation rate on ploughed-back investment (retained earnings); the second rate is that of distributed profits; (b) An extra 5.5% is applied to this rate; (c) An extra 3% is applied to this rate; (d) Standard rate is 33.3%, but an extra 10% or 20% can be applied in some cases.
Sources: A Tax Guide to Europe, 1994, Arthur Anderson; *Les impôts en Europe* 1997, Eura Audit; *European Tax Handbook*, 1998.

tax on interest that it had introduced in January 1989. There was a similar situation in Belgium, which dropped a 25 per cent tax.[11]

In the case of corporate tax (CT), the decrease in apparent rates between 1990 and 1997 in the majority of countries (see Table 8.1), together with the introduction of special taxation schemes for head-quarters and co-ordination centres,[12] shows that the states embraced competition. Yet the wish for competition and the subsequent impact are separate matters. CT indeed depends on the rate levels, but also on how the taxable base is calculated. A rate decrease is not sufficient in itself to translate into a lower tax burden for firms, and cannot on its own cause delocalization.[13] Numerous studies[14] have reviewed the various ways firms can reduce their tax bills (for example, they can delocalize subsidiaries, set up umbrella companies, or take advantage of transfer prices). However, there is scant evidence to show whether these devices are ever being used). Nevertheless, it would seem that the creation of co-ordination centres might have influenced profit transfers[15] between member states, notably in the case of large international groups.

In contrast, value added tax (VAT) does not seem to encourage competition. Between 1990 and 1996, it can be noted that rates tended to rise along with revenue levels (see Table 8.2). As they had to sort out their public finances, member states had no option but to raise VAT

Table 8.2   The evolution of basic VAT rates, 1990–8

	1990	*1991*	*1992*	*1993*	*1994*	*1995*	*1996*	*1998*
Germany	14	14	14	15	15	15	15	16
Austria	20	20	20	20	20	20	20	20
Belgium	19	19	19.5	19.5	20.5	20.5	21	21
Denmark	22	22	25	25	25	25	25	25
Spain	12	12	13[a]/15[b]	15	15	16	16	16
France	18.6	18.6	18.6	18.6	18.6	20.6	20.6	20.6
Finland	–	–	–	–	22	22	22	22
Greece	18	18	18	18	18	18	18	18
Ireland	23	21	21	21	21	21	21	21
Italy	19	19	19	19	19	19	19	20
Luxembourg	12	12	15	15	15	15	15	15
Netherlands	18.5	18.5	17.5	17.5	17.5	17.5	17.5	17.5
Portugal	17	16	16	16	16	17	17	17
UK	15	17.5	17.5	17.5	17.5	17.5	17.5	17.5
Sweden	23.46	23.46	25	25	25	25	25	25

Notes: (a) From 1 January 1992; (b) From 8 August 1992.
Sources: European Commission; *European Tax Handbook*, 1998.

rates, as work was already heavily taxed and capital seemingly offered the most mobile base.[16] Also, but contrary to what happened with CT, rising rates did not mean that differentials in VAT rates had no effect on behavioural patterns. At the time of writing cross-border trade makes up only 5 per cent of total intra-European trade, but there is no evidence to show that European citizens are aware of all the trade-off possibilities. Finally, the suspicion that tax evasion tricks are being used – for example, setting up of fictitious export networks to claim VAT exemption in the national market, remains unfounded.

How did the European authorities react to tax competition? The debate over tax harmonization that began in the late 1980s/early 1990s prior to the opening of national borders in 1993, signalled three possible routes:

(i) national tax systems would be unified by the introduction of similar bases and rates, which implied a common approach to public finance within a single economic and political whole as well as a centralized decision-making process;

(ii) tax competition (namely no harmonization), would bring about a policy of ever-lower taxes that would encourage each country to try to attract firms, customers and financial inflows; and

(iii) harmonization would undergo a consultation process, the aim of which being to limit the distortions caused by competition, and thus curb tax competition. This demanded that states come to an agreement with regard to taxes with the most mobile bases.

Note that the tax harmonization process made real progress only on VAT and excise duties (see Box 8.4). The way the two sets of taxes work are fairly similar in all member states, with the essential differences concerning the level of rates applied. By contrast, the implementation of the finalized tax system, which was to introduce the principle of taxation in the country of origin for European cross-border trade, was postponed to a later date.

Box 8.4 The evolution of VAT harmonization[17]

The following objective underpinned the Commission's proposals on indirect tax reform: all restrictions to free trade of goods and services had to be lifted, so both each member state's national trade and European cross-border trade receive equal treatment.

With this objective in mind, the 1967 first Directive imposed the value added tax (VAT) tax system on all member states and all other tax systems were phased out (e.g. sales taxes). The 1977 Sixth Directive paved the way for common rules on the VAT tax base (tax liability, assessment rules and exemptions), whom and what to tax, and how to calculate and pay the tax. The Directive did not, however, include common rules on setting tax rate levels.

The tax system applicable to cross-border trade between firms since the First Directive's adoption is based on the principle of taxation on arrival. Goods are exported free of tax until they reach their destination. Tax is then levied at the country of arrival's current tax rate. For example, a French company purchasing goods in Italy is not liable to Italy's VAT. However, when bought in France, the goods become liable to VAT at France's current rate. In other words, tax is levied in the country where the goods are consumed, and the tax rate applied within a country's national border is the same, regardless of the goods' country of origin. With that system, competitive distortion caused by differentials in VAT rates is avoided. Nevertheless, administrative control procedures – that is, when a company claims a zero-tax rate for export purposes, it must prove that the goods have in fact been exported – still get in the way of free trade.

Box 8.4 (Continued)

To make sure that each member state's national trade and European cross-border trade receive equal treatment, the European Commission suggested as early as 1987 that the taxation at source principle be applied to all cross-border trade. According to this principle, the rate applied to goods depends on where the goods were produced and no longer on where they are consumed. To go back to the example mentioned previously, the French company would then have to pay Italian VAT to the Italian authorities. For the same goods, the French consumer would then become liable to France's VAT. Since the company can reclaim back the VAT paid on purchases, competition remains unaffected. However, this principle changes the distribution of tax revenues among member states, and it may consequently require the support of a budgetary compensation mechanism of some sort. By the same token, as rate differentials are likely to prompt those not liable to VAT in their country of residence to turn to countries with the lowest VAT rates for their supplies, VAT rate harmonization was put on the agenda.

Confronted by the member states' reluctance to act, the Commission (Directive, 16 December 1991) introduced a 'transitional' system in 1993, at the same time as national borders were phased out. For those liable to VAT, cross-border trade is still tax free, but VAT is now due, not when going through customs, but when goods are received in the destination country. Control procedures have not been phased out but amended. Yet this is no solution to the problem of equal treatment between national trade and cross-border trade.

For those not liable to pay VAT – private individuals, administrations and so on – prior to 1993 purchases were monitored at border checkpoints. Since border controls have now gone, consumers are free to purchase goods in the country of their choice. They pay VAT at the rate current in the country where the goods are bought, and can therefore take full advantage of the VAT differentials between member states. However, safeguards have been put into place regarding, for example, the purchase of new means of transportation, mail-order and sales to some categories of persons not liable for VAT, such as charities and medical practitioners.

Furthermore, in its Directive of 19 October 1992, the Commission set minimum VAT rates of 15% for the basic rate, and 5% for the reduced rate. Member states may still apply two reduced rates on goods from a selected list of agreed items. The reduced 12% rate may still be applied to some unlisted goods, if they already belonged to the reduced category prior to 1991. Finally, for goods with a VAT rate of below 5% before 1991, this rate can still apply.

Since 1993, the year when the current 'transitional' VAT tax system was introduced, the Community's situation has changed only slightly. Initially, the plan was that on 1 January 1997, the 'transitional' system would be replaced by the final system, as set out in the original principle, but this shift has not yet taken place. Nevertheless, the Commission has not given up on the project. In June 1996, it suggested a new work schedule whose objective was to promote the Union's progress towards a common VAT system. The idea was to discuss at set intervals the principles on which a common system could be set up (1997), who would be liable to VAT, what were the possible exemptions and on what conditions, the taxation point of origin, compensation schemes (1998) and tax harmonization (1999). In 1998, the talks on the VAT common system were not resumed.

As for CT and savings, the Commission's proposals went unheeded to a large extent. In anticipation of the impending impact of the liberalization of capital transfers in 1990, the Commission, as early as 1989, prepared a directive paving the way for the introduction of a minimum 15 per cent tax to be withheld at source. It also recommended further co-operation between national tax authorities. Member states turned the plan down. In order to avoid double taxation on CT dividends, a 1990 directive proposed the phasing out of all withheld at source taxes on the dividends paid by subsidiaries to their parent company. A similar proposal on interest payments and other payments made between companies was not accepted, nor were any of the Ruding Committee's proposals. Finally, there has been no proposal on the harmonization of personal income tax or social contributions, which both fall into the member states' exclusive competence.

Moreover, recent EU viewpoints on tax matters tend to confirm that competition could have positive consequences. After the period of intense consultation over tax harmonization guided by Mario Monti, the European Commission, under the aegis of Commissioner Bolkenstein, seems clearly to have embarked upon a practical approach to tax issues. The idea that harmonization should start from existing national legislation seems to have been abandoned. Closer co-operation between member states has replaced it: codes of conduct must be issued, and the sharing of tax information developed. National authorities must get together and sign bilateral agreements. Cleaning up VAT tax systems appears to have become the very first item on this technical agenda. Is regulating rather than curbing tax competition the answer? As it cannot be avoided, should it be encouraged as long as it is not 'harmful'? The beginnings of a positive answer can be found in the Commission's Communication of 23 May 2001 – 'Tax Policy in the European Union, Priorities for the Years Ahead': 'It is important to recognise that, while harmful competition must be addressed both at EU and broader international levels...some degree of tax competition within the EU may contribute to lower tax pressure.'

Labour mobility and social competition

It may at first appear difficult, if not far-fetched, to distinguish tax competition from social competition. It is a fact that the above-mentioned trends tend to look at social security and welfare systems in terms of taxation, so much so that the two types have started to merge and could thus eventually lead to a social-tax competition approach.[18] In addition to previous developments, it nevertheless seems important to keep both separate, since the production factor's real or potential mobility that instigate the one or the other is not the same. As Europe's social competition is increasingly being referred to,[19] the notion must first be clearly delineated, as has been the case with tax competition, so it is not confused with 'social dumping', which goes back at least to the start of the twentieth century, when German lawyers coined the phrase 'Schmutzkonkurrenz' or 'dirty competition', an allusion to the comparative advantage gained from poor working conditions. The supposed threat posed by low-wage developing countries to Western economies has become the updated international version of the same discourse. Since the introduction of the single currency, the threat of social competition has changed: it now comes from the inside. Drawing on Alber and Standing (2000), one can define it as a race to the bottom between social protection systems whose characteristics are being eroded under budgetary constraints. What types of social competition must then be considered?

The canon of social competition is to be found in Tiebout's seminal work (1956). In a federation of public communities characterized by a strong integration of goods, money and production factors, labour mobility urges communities to produce different public goods (for example, tax burdens and welfare benefits) depending on the collective preferences of their members, who can vote with their feet when they have decided where they belong. Labour mobility can thus be seen as a prerequisite to social competition.

As shown previously, because of the heterogeneous nature of national social systems in the EU – notably their different requirements for access to social benefits – the analysis has to focus on the concept of 'social migration'. Le Cacheux's intuitions (2000) can serve as a starting point for further discussion:

> First, the people deprived of financial resources may be tempted to take up residence in the countries offering the most generous social benefits – whereas those on high incomes would choose countries where income tax is the lowest. Then, because social-tax and public finance systems redistribute resources not only between the persons belonging to different income brackets, but also on an individual basis over people's entire life cycle, the most mobile citizens may be tempted to opt for social-tax nomadism, and thus change their country of residence at different stages of their life cycle, according to the result of their cost/benefit analysis of the different national systems.[20]

Such migration flows cannot avoid putting the member states' social protection systems at risk. So what broad outlines could be suggested for this type of competition in the European Union? Drawing on Keiser (1996), one can imagine a sketch of social migration flows according to the characteristics of the European Union's three social protection models (see Figure 8.2).

The idea underlying the fairly basic diagram in Figure 8.2 raises an issue that lies at the heart of our concern here. When it comes to social migration flows, overall labour mobility is much less important than certain categories of workers' 'marginal mobility'. Sinn (1998) shows that labour marginal mobility in itself sets the conditions for social competition because it serves as a signal to governments, in the same way as competition is stimulated by the marginal demands sent to firms in the private sector.[21] In other words, even if labour is at the time of writing virtually immobile in the EU[22] – possibly for some time[23] – it is also true that some categories of workers *are* mobile,[24] or may become so in the future.[25] In fact, even marginal labour mobility has a knock-on effect on all social protection systems. Young working people and unskilled workers represent two types of

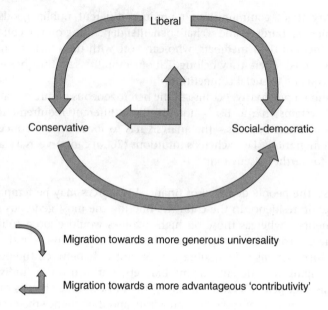

Figure 8.2 European social models and 'social migration'
Source: Adapted from Keizer (1996).

marginal mobility which are most interesting illustrations of the issue under discussion.

Luring the 'contributors'

The first type of social competition is essential in the European Union, given the current demographic problems caused by the ageing population. The comparison between young-worker marginal mobility and pensioner immobility is a key issue. This ideal-type model's overall principle can also be found in the annexes to the Commissariat Général du Plan (1999) study on social Europe, cited above. As a starting point, the report considers two countries with similar demographic patterns, similar living standards and similar basic pension contributions levels. It then goes on to assume that one of the countries is hit by a demographic asymmetrical shock, such as an increase in life expectancy. If the shock is absorbed through a cut in pensioners' living standards or the postponement of the retirement age, there will be no impact on migration flows. Conversely, if all or part of the adjustment implies higher worker social contributions, then the mobile workers will emigrate and the initial shock will be amplified. Worker migration will simply add to the immobility of the pensioners, who have no choice but to remain in the country where they can draw their pension.

This model rests on the principle of people's decreasing mobility over their life cycle.[30] Wildasin (1999) demonstrates that young workers are more footloose (with regard to their jobs/and family commitments) than pensioners. The removal costs incurred by young workers are therefore lower. Since social security systems depend to a large extent on financial transfers between generations, the ageing of the European population combined with the high mobility rate of young workers puts pension schemes at some risk. Young workers are indeed net contributors to the systems in place at the time of writing. In a situation of labour immobility, young workers cannot avoid contributing to the social system. The immediate result of perfect labour mobility is that governments can no longer force young workers to pay social contributions.

Von Hagen and Walz (1994) have established a direct link between the situation described above and the future of Europe's pension schemes. They note that the social-tax burden carried by the working population has increased significantly in most industrialized countries. Germany's example is the most striking, as the tax level required to finance German pension schemes rose twentyfold over the twentieth century. If Europe's social security systems are not harmonized more closely, the younger generation will find it more profitable to emigrate to a country with lower pension contributions if they do not wish to pay their debt to the older generation. This viewpoint is somewhat alarmist as it implies that adjustment will cause mass migration. As long as migration has not become a burning issue, national governments will tend to wait until the pressure of events forces them to reform their respective social systems. This is obviously of particular importance, as once workers have decided to migrate, they will be leaving in large numbers and it will be too late for reform.

To substantiate this assumption, it may be interesting to consider not so much the overall ageing of Europe's population, but also its differentiated time structure. It then becomes obvious that European countries' populations not only do not become older at the same rate, but also that the future trend seems to point to increasingly divergent patterns: the European spread ranged over 10 points in 1999, and it is forecast to reach 14 points in 2010 (see Table 8.3).

Table 8.3 Dependence ratios for the EU-15

	1999	Projected 2010
Ireland	17	17
Netherlands	20	22
Luxembourg	21	24
Denmark	22	25
Finland	22	25
Portugal	22	24
Austria	23	26
Germany	23	30
UK	24	24
France	24	25
Spain	24	27
Belgium	25	27
Greece	25	29
Italy	26	31
Sweden	27	28

Source: Eurostat.

Turning away the 'unwanted'

In his presentation of the second type of social competition, Sinn (1998) pursues a theoretical approach akin to that adopted in the first. This time, skilled workers are perfectly mobile and unskilled workers perfectly immobile. Because of its competition drive to attract workers with the highest income, the state finds it harder to redistribute resources. Redistribution implies that wealthier skilled workers contribute more than poorer unskilled workers to the financing of the national social-tax system. In a context of social competition, any effort at making social protection systems more redistributive immediately causes the emigration of the 'rich' and the immigration of the 'poor'. This problem is compounded by decreasing payments by the 'rich' and increasing social payments to the 'poor', and therefore the immobile factor (unskilled work) incurs a heavy net loss. The whole situation becomes paradoxical when social competition produces negative effects for those who initially were meant to benefit from the national economy's income redistribution policy.

Heuristically, even though no survey is currently available for Europe, several studies of the situation in the USA highlighted the existence of such competition for social aid through the example of Aid to Families with Dependent Children (AFDC). The relative autonomy left to states in deciding their aid level makes the study even more interesting for the EU.[31] The situation is seen here from the opposite view point compared to the previous model: instead of considering that states compete among themselves in order to attract the highest-skilled workers, it examines the case when states compete among themselves to turn away the people most in need of social aid. In this context, states strive to keep the highest possible number of high-wage earners. Brueckner (1998) and Saavedra (1999), among others, produced results confirming the suggestion that, because they do not wish to become 'welfare magnets', US States have embarked on a 'race to the bottom' when setting their AFDC levels. Each State's decision depends on those of close or neighbouring States.

The EU's enlargement will undoubtedly involve migration issues. This will offer a welcome opportunity to put the various problems presented here to the test. Given all the social competition models, it is only natural to try to consider how a unified greater Europe should respond to the labour mobility challenge and arbitrate between its positive aspects – for example, more easily financed pensions – and its potential drawbacks – for example, heavier welfare payments. Because of a fear of massive migration inflows from the new member states, some authors have called for protectionist measures, but the question must be raised whether this is an appropriate answer. Sinn (1999), drawing on the experience of German reunification, suggests the European Union should subsidize East and Central European countries (ECEC) to avoid the westward migration of a large number of Eastern workers who may feel tempted by their new partners' generous social protection systems. Suggesting a way of preserving Western systems' sustainability, Sinn even goes as far as to propose that newcomers should only be entitled to the welfare benefits of their country of origin. Although it is a debatable point, Germany's Federal Ministry of Finance's Scientific Committee took up the idea in a study published on 15 February 2001 accessed at http://www.bundes finanzministerium.de/fach/abteilungen/beivat/gutfreizueg.pdl. It is suggested that 'delayed social integration' should apply to ECEC workers so that the free westward circulation of Eastern workers would have only a limited impact.

The last prickly issue is whether European governments are not already feeling the pressure of competition in the field of social protection. In the light of the European economies' previous gradual integration, Boeri (2000) states that the current risks set by social competition are largely overestimated. The Italian economist's article shows that over the period 1986–1997 there was no sign that competition was causing any levelling in EU social protection systems. He comes to the conclusion that 'past experience refutes the idea that the deeper integration induced by Economic and Monetary Union should put social protection systems at greater risk of dismantling'. The author's claim is substantiated by Fondazione Rodolfo de Beneditti's data on the social reforms carried out by EU countries between 1986 and 1997. Paradoxically, Boeri's data can be used to amend his own optimistic view. It must indeed be noted that from 1992, the year when European integration markedly intensified, the member states' reforms of their unemployment benefits and basic pension schemes, with the aim of making the systems 'less generous', gathered speed. Out of the series of thirteen structural reforms carried out since that date (seven on pensions and six on unemployment benefits), twelve (six and six, respectively) aimed at making the system 'less generous'.

Conclusion: how to cope with the mobility challenge?

Given that the Nice treaty of 2000 did not allow any progress on qualified majority voting in the fields of social and tax matters, the numerous rather worrying issues raised in this chapter still remain unresolved.

Moreover, although actively supported by the Commission since the late 1980s in the aftermath of the European Single Act, the tax harmonization process has virtually become unstuck. Vainly presented since the 1980s as the way to solve the problems caused by the full exemption of this type of undeclared income, the proposal that each member state should be free to decide what type of tax withheld at source (either set or variable) it should levy on income paid to European non-residents was finally agreed in principle by the European Council in November 2000, under the French presidency. Yet implementation has suffered long delays, notably because of pressure from the British and Luxembourg governments, which set so many restrictive preconditions that the directive may well never come into effect.

With regard to corporation tax, only the most obviously discriminating aspects of tax competition have been banned explicitly by the 'code of conduct'. Yet here again, implementation has been spread over several years and 'harmful' practices given a restricted definition. However little inclined to tax harmonization and much opposed to limits to tax competition in that area it may be, the Commission proposed, in its November 2001 Communication, the EU should proceed towards a closer co-ordination and transparency. The Commission advocated the harmonization of the basis of the tax on corporate profits and the adoption of the principle of consolidated profits. The sole avowed aim was to prevent taxation from hindering the functioning of the internal market. Such co-ordination did not mean the end of tax competition, but it tended to make it more transparent to firms and more conspicuous to EU citizens.

So what real solutions are there to face up to these challenges? A first answer would be to internalize competition issues and consider social protection only as a productive factor. Viewed from this standpoint, close enough to the policy chosen and supported by the European authorities, social policy merges into the mould of economic policy. As explained above, it would in fact mean that little progress has been made since 1957.

A second possibility would be to seek to take the social protection systems' harmonization process well beyond what exists at the time of writing. This option is certainly both debatable and hard to implement. Yet, if tax and social competition were to make their presence felt over the next few years, it would be fair if the European states made the pledge to their respective societies not only to allow their hands to be tied, but also to lash themselves to the ship's mast when the sirens eventually start singing. Why should the EU nations deprive themselves of a solution that could outdo the unabated competition of market forces, if it was only to bring the sort of social protection level that none of them had ever wished for?

Notes

1 Democratic Legitimacy and Political Representation in the EU Institutions

1 For a radical interpretation of the problem, see the article by Luciani (2001).
2 It is worth recalling that the Treaty of Nice has modified the weighting system of voting within the Council as from 1 January 2005. On the basis of this weighting formula, each of the four major countries (namely France, Germany, Italy, United Kingdom) has 29 votes (they used to have 10); Spain has 27 (8); the Netherlands, 13 (5); Belgium, Greece, Portugal, 12 (5) per capita; Austria and Sweden, 10 (4); Denmark, Finland and Ireland, 7 (3); and Luxembourg, 4 (2). The qualified majority is reached with 169 (62) out of the 237 (87) total votes. The Treaty of Nice, with the annexed Declaration on the Enlargement of the European Union (n. 20), defined the vote weighting in the European Council as being enlarged to twelve candidate countries from 2005. Further details were introduced in Nice with the Declaration on the qualified majority threshold and the number of votes for a blocking minority in an Enlarged Union (n. 21).
3 This is known as the 'irreconcilable triad': for a thorough and detailed examination of which, with particular reference to the European Union, see Beretta *et al.* (2001) and, more generally, Rodrik (2000).
4 The 'Eurobarometer' was established by the Commission in 1973 and publishes the weekly reports of the face-to-face interviews showing European citizens approaches to the social and political topics that are at the heart of the European debate.
5 Greece became a full member in January 1981; Portugal and Spain in January 1986; and Austria, Finland and Sweden in January 1995.
6 The comparison between the priorities perceived by citizens and by European MPs is particularly complex because of the varying survey methods adopted for the two groups. Citizens were asked to express their opinions on a list of priorities defined by a questionnaire included in the 'Eurobarometer'. Members of the European Parliament, always with reference to the priority objectives, received an 'open' questionnaire. Hence the opinions they expressed were more diverse. Furthermore, EMPS data refer to a survey carried out in 1996, which is less penalising than what initially seems if one considers that they reflect the assessments of MPs whose mandates fell due in 1996. In a word, the 'delay' of replies amounts to one legislature.

2 Overruled Europa: Market versus Democracy in the EU

1 Fitoussi (1999).
2 European Council (2001a).
3 See Fitoussi (2002).
4 The 'exit' and 'voice' theories are both taken from Hirschman (1970).

5 This typology, proposed by Balassa (1961) intends to identify the successive steps of regional economic integration from a basic free trade area to the eventual introduction of a single currency.

6 See, for example, European Commission (2000a).

7 Parts of this section are drawn from Fitoussi (2002).

8 Resolution of the European Council on the Stability and Growth Pact, Amsterdam, 17 June 1997 (Official Journal C 236 of 2/08/1997).

9 See Fitoussi (1999).

10 The problem of both was to find out how to make a collective decision matching a multitude of different individual preferences. Arrow showed that no social choice procedure can lead to a rational decision when starting from individual preference. See Kenneth J. Arrow, *Social Choices and Individual Values*, Cowles Foundation for Research in Economics at Yale University, 1951.

11 Robert J. Barro, *Determinants of Economic Growth: A Cross-Country Empirical Study* (Cambridge Mass.: MIT Press), 1997.

12 In *Le libéralisme économique* (Paris: Le Seuil) (1979, 1989), p. 3

13 One can well imagine how mere complexity will act as a perfect foil to any constitutional amendment procedure after the EU's enlargement to twenty-five members.

14 At the time of writing, there was still hope that the delegates to the Convention would ultimately make further progress on this before handing in the final version of their work by July 2003.

15 Parts of this section are drawn from Laurent and Le Cacheux (2003b).

16 The text has given rise to much hesitation, many reservations and even open hostility on the part of both the member states and the Commission.

17 Could.

18 See 'Eurobarometer' (2003).

19 See Le Cacheux (2000) and Laurent (2002) for in depth details on this.

20 Dan Usher, *The Economic Prerequisites of Democracy*, Columbia University Press, 1981.

21 See Laurent and Le Cacheux (2003a).

22 See Kagan (2002).

3 The Mirages of Nominal Illusion: Variations on Convergence

1 This chapter is a re-edited version of chapter 3 of the 1999 OFCE *Report on the state of the European Union* (Fitoussi, 1999).

2 Robert A. Mundell's (1961) classic example shows a shift in final demand from one country to the next. A fall in demand brings about a drop in output and employment in the country hit by recession, and overheating in the other country's economy. Devaluation then allows the country hit by recession to restore its competitiveness by increasing its own final demand while reducing that of the other country.

3 With Mundell's example, if no devaluation occurs, workers will move from the recession-hit economy to the one that is expanding, and full employment will ensue without any change in prices or real wages. A fall in prices causes a real depreciation that will balance demand between the two regions.

4 Because of a lack of compatible data, it was impossible to consider all countries for all the indicators concerned. The countries reviewed include:

Inflation rate: Canada, the USA, Japan, Austria, Denmark, Finland, France, Germany, Italy, the Netherlands, Norway, Sweden, Switzerland and the United Kingdom.

Nominal interest rates: Canada, the USA, Austria, France, Germany, Norway, Sweden and Switzerland.

Growth in the nominal monetary supply: Canada, the USA, Japan, Austria, Denmark, Germany, the Netherlands, Norway, Sweden and Switzerland.

Nominal salary growth: Canada, the USA, Japan, Denmark, Finland, Germany, Ireland, Italy, the Netherlands, Norway, Sweden, and the United Kingdom.

5 It must be noted that the shock eventually spread to Germany's European partner economies, and thus became a common European shock.

6 See Bayoumi and Eichengreen (1992, 1996) and Boone (1997).

7 See Helg *et al.* (1995).

8 See Artis and Zhang (1995), Beine *et al.* (1998).

9 See e. g. Barro and Sala-I-Martin (1991) and Beine *et al.* (1998).

10 For example, regions that specialize in similar industries are likely to have a similar reaction when those industries are hit by a shock, whether it be a demand shock, an input price shock or even a technological shock affecting this particular branch of activity.

11 Antonelli (1994).

12 See Fatãs (1997) and Forni and Reichlin (1997).

13 As is the case for national asymmetry analyses, different indicators such as per capita GDP, GDP and employment, and different definition criteria for the European heart were considered.

14 See Fuss (1998b).

15 See Bayoumi and Eichengreen (1996).

16 See Fatãs (1997).

17 See Helg *et al.* (1995).

18 See De Nardis *et al.* (1996) and Fatãs (1997).

19 Once they become EU members, CEEC countries will still not be allowed to be part of the Schengen area agreements.

20 Unlike the United Kingdom and Sweden, new EU entrants will have to take part in ERM 2, a system with fixed parities against the euro and a standard fluctuation band to within 15 per cent of the central rates. When these countries meet the Maastricht criteria, they will have to adopt the euro.

4 Regional Differentials and Policies for Territorial Cohesion in the European Union

1 The asymmetric distribution of the population (and of productive activities) in the European territory is well described by the example of the 'hot banana' – that is, the strong concentration of light through the centre of Europe, namely in the area from north of London to northern Italy, which is shown by satellite photos at night. From a theoretical point of view, the idea whereby integration prompts economic agglomeration has developed

in the literature as the 'new economic geography' (see Fujita *et al.*, 1999). The possibility of a lack of convergence in per capita income levels of richer and poorer regions was outlined by the 'new growth theory' (Lucas, 1988; Grossman and Helpman, 1991). Recent contributions attempt to merge localization with convergence themes (see, for example, Martin and Ottaviano, 2001).

2 Regional policies are not based on an undoubtedly grounded assumption, as there are opposing forces pushing towards an excessive agglomeration, on the one side, and dispersion, on the other. In particular, firms and workers tend to migrate from peripheral areas to the core regions, on the basis of purely personal convenience, not considering the 'external' effects of their choices on other agents. This implies that the concentration produced by the market may result excessive if firms and workers, while moving towards the core, do not consider the welfare loss of those remaining in periphery, or insufficient, if firms and workers moving towards the core only consider their private benefits and not of those deriving from their choices for other firms and for the growth process of the European area (see Puga, 2002).

3 In the text, the words per capita GDP, income and value added are used as synonyms to evaluate the regional development levels.

4 Over the past few years, many contributions to the analysis of convergence process between European regions were published. Among these, Barro and Sala i Martin (1991 and 1995), Armstrong (1995), Fageberg and Verspagen (1995), Neven and Gouyette (1995), Quah (1996), Paci and Pigliaru (1999), Acconcia (2002), Terrasi (2002) and Boldrin and Canova (2001).

5 The evaluations of regional gaps are based on Cambridge Econometrics dataset concerning 119 regions NUTS-2 and NUTS-1.

6 The evaluations reported in the text look at the real convergence and are therefore based on data on the per capita income expressed in constant PPP of the base year (1990). Hence they differ from those based on current PPP to which the European Commission normally refers in its official documents.

7 A recent work made at ISAE has shown how the stock of infrastructure positively and significantly influences FDI in the Italian provinces (Basile, 2001).

8 The data on the infrastructural stock are drawn from Di Palma (1990).

9 Recent theoretical and empirical works have surveyed the impact of social capital on growth and development in the economy. With regard to empirical works, see Aschauer (1989); Easterly and Rebelo (1993); Holtz-Eakin and Schwartz (1995); Khan and Kumar (1997); Acconcia and Del Monte (2000); Acconcia (2000) and Demetriades and Mamuneas (2000).

10 See Boldrin and Canova (2001).

11 The larger European contribution (co-financing) in favour of regions under Objective 1 meets a general need for equity, as these regions are the poorest. In the programme for 1994–9, the EU co-financing in favour of Objective 1 regions ranged from a minimum of 50 per cent to a maximum of 75 per cent of the total project value. It could reach 80–85 per cent for regions of countries that also benefited from the cohesion fund, and for extremely peripheral regions. For the regions involved in Objectives other than Objective 1, the co-financing ranged from a minimum of 25 per cent to a maximum of 50 per cent of the total cost. For financing to firms, the EU resources were not to exceed 50 per cent of the overall value in the case of firms operating within Objective 1 regions, and 30 per cent for other regions. In the programme

for 2000–06, the co-financing legislation remained approximately the same with regard to investment projects (except for the introduction of some maximum ceilings for investments in profit-generating infrastructure). Indeed, the EU's participation in the form of direct contributions to firms was reduced: it no longer amounted to 35 per cent for those localised in the Objective 1 regions, and no longer equalled 15 per cent for Objective 2 regions.

12   Among the most significant works published recently, see European Commission (1999, 2001a), and the papers by Fayolle and Lecuyer (2000), Boldrin and Canova (2001) and Puga (2001).

13   A further confirmation of the small impact of structural policies on the development of backward regions comes from the results (not reported here) of the correlation analysis between the growth rates of income, productivity and employment, on the one hand, and the variables measuring the allocations of structural funds and total projects co-financed by the EU, on the other. The correlations were computed for the whole sample of regions considered, for each member state, for the four geographical clubs (southern periphery, northern periphery, intermediate regions and centre) and for the two groups of Objective 1 and Objective 2 regions. In synthesis, a positive and significant correlation emerges between the employment rates and the resources committed (both with structural funds and national contributions) for the subgroup of intermediate regions, for that of northern periphery and for the French regions. For the whole sample, and for all other subgroups, there is no significant positive relationship, or a negative significant relationship is registered. This is the case in Italy and the United Kingdom (for per capita income), and of the group of Objective 2 regions (for productivity).

14   The improvement of the connection between two regions with different development levels may favour one or the other of the two extremes of the connection line. This provides firms in the poorer regions with a better access to the input supply and to the market of the least developed regions. However, a better connection enables firms of the richer area to supply the backward (but thickly populated because of the low migration level) region with more favourable transport costs, thus increasing the centre/periphery gap (see Martin and Rogers, 1995). With reference to this point, Faini (1983) showed how the reduction of transport costs between the north and south of Italy – obtained in the 1960s through the construction of the major Italian highways – eliminated the 'protection' of high transport costs that was granted previously to southern firms, thus accelerating the deindustrialization process of the *Mezzogiorno* of Italy.

15   This point was dealt with thoroughly in Chapter 2. Notice that many causes were outlined to explain the net reduction in the interregional labour mobility experienced in Europe compared to the 1950s and 1960s. The lower differences in the regional per capita incomes occurring up to the 1970s, may have increased the degree of attraction exerted on 'potential' emigrants by their places of origin (de la Fuente, 1999). The reduction in the migration propensity, particularly among the young, may have been influenced by the larger support ensured by the households' incomes and by public transfers that fuelled that income (Attanasio and Padoa Schioppa, 1991). Finally, in some countries (particularly Spain), the distortions of unemployment schemes may have acted as a disincentive to the geographical labour mobility (Antolin and Bover, 1997).

16 See Faini (1999) on this point as well.
17 See Barca and Pellegrini (2000).
18 See Presidenza del Consiglio (2001).

5 The Conduct of Macroeconomic Policies in the Euro Area

1 See ECB (1999a).
2 The reference value for the M3 growth was fixed in 1999 at an annual amount of 4.5 per cent, which was confirmed for the years 2000, 2001 and 2002. On the basis of the monetary quantitative equation $DM = DQ + DP - DV$ (where DM = monetary variation rate, DQ = real GDP growth rate, DP = price variation rate, DV = variation rate of the monetary circulation velocity), the reference value for the monetary growth rate is the figure compatible with potential growth and with price stability, given the velocity trend of monetary circulation. Setting for the euro area, an annual GDP potential growth equalling 2–2.5 per cent, price stability meant as an annual price growth below 2 per cent and assuming a velocity reduction trend of monetary circulation equal to 0.5 per cent–1 per cent per annum, the formula leads to a an annual reference value for monetary growth equalling 4.5 per cent.
3 See Svensson (1999).
4 See Clarida *et al.* (1999).
5 In the presence of a demand shock, income and inflation move in the same direction, but if the oil price rises, income and inflation are affected by opposing thrusts. In the latter case, an action aimed at reducing inflation would first of all cause an income dynamics contraction and then a fall in inflation, with ample output variations.
6 See Taylor (1993).
7 The rule represents the reduced form of a simple model consisting of a Phillips curve (the ratio between the inflation variation and the output gap), an IS ratio (between income and interest rate) and a 'loss function' of the monetary authorities to minimize whatever (squared) inflation deviations from the objective figure, or income deviations from the potential level, emerge. Taylor developed the rule after examining and comparing the results obtained from the major models.
8 For an analysis of the different methods of computing the potential output, see Brandimarte *et al.* (1998).
9 On the basis of the consumer price index net of energy products, foodstuffs, alcohol and tobacco.
10 Note that, in the last quarter of 2001, a dummy was included to take into account the uncertainty effects and the risks deriving from the terrorist attacks of September 11.
11 See ECB (1999b).
12 See Rogers (2001), who used a price database created by *The Economist* in twenty-six towns in eighteen countries.
13 The validity of the law of one price was also questioned within individual countries by Engel and Rogers (2001), and for absolutely homogeneous goods, such as concrete, by Abbott (1994).
14 See, for example, Sinn and Reuter (2001).

15   In what follows, reference is made to the version of the Treaty that includes the amendments made in the Amsterdam Treaty (June 1997).

16   The Council decides to address the necessary recommendations and make them public by voting with a qualified majority (two-thirds of the votes) upon proposal by the European Commission.

17   To this end, see European Council (2000c), sect. 41.

18   The deficit is not considered to be 'excessive' whenever the excess has an exceptional or temporary nature, or when it is close to the reference value. It is considered to be exceptional or temporary when it results from an unusual event outside the control of the member state concerned, and has a major impact on the financial position of the general government, or when it results from a severe economic downturn (if there is an annual fall of real GDP of at least 2 per cent). The member state may prove the exceptional nature of its deficit by providing adequate evidence in support, namely the sudden and unexpected nature of the fall of economic activity, or the amount of the production fall compared to the past. However, the decision is up to the Ecofin Council.

19   If, for example, a country has a deficit equalling 3.5 per cent of GDP, the sanction foresees a non-interest-bearing deposit equalling 0.25 per cent of GDP; that is, $0.2\% + (3.5 - 3) \times 0.1\% = 0.25\%$.

20   The coefficients of sensitivity indicate the cyclical components of the budget balance; that is, they measure the effects of economic fluctuations (for example, the impact of the smaller fiscal revenues obtained in low-growth periods). The dimensions and volatility of the cyclical components depend both on the dimensions and volatility of the economic fluctuations and on the budget sensitivity to the cycle; that is, on the intensity of the automatic fiscal stabilizers' functioning. The sensitivity coefficients are used to compute the budget balance which enables the cyclical variations to be tolerated without exceeding the threshold of 3 per cent of GDP. Admittedly, the higher is the budget sensitivity to cyclical fluctuations, the greater the volatility of the economic activity, and the stricter the required budget constraint.

21   Using similar procedures, the OECD (1997) and the IMF (1998) provide consistent estimates, namely structural deficits equalling 1.5 per cent and comprising between 0.5 per cent and 1.5 per cent, respectively, which respect the threshold of 3 per cent of GDP. The European Commission (2000d) provides evidence of further studies leading to results consistent with the indications shown in Table 5.3.

22   The figure is the one indicated by the European Commission to define the 'closeness to budget balance' (European Commission, 2000d). See the following section.

23   The values of the debt-to-GDP ratio for Germany might equal 60.8 per cent and 60.1 per cent in 2002 and 2003, respectively (European Commission, 2002d).

24   The most effective measures to sustain demand in the short term (for example, an employment expansion in the public sector) seem also to be the most dangerous provisions for medium-term growth (European Commission, 2001c).

25   For a detailed discussion of this point, see 'The Operation of Automatic Fiscal Stabilisers in the Euro Area' ECB (2002).

26   There are those who feel that it is the public sector dimension, and not the deficit size, that produces the greatest effects on the cycle stabilization; in

particular, the main source of stabilization lies in direct taxation. For an empirical analysis, see Fatás and Mihov (2001); for a discussion of the literature see Ardy *et al.* (2002).

27 For a critical evaluation of the cyclically adjusted budget objectives, see Mills and Quinet (2001).

28 In the next few years, the European Commission wants to replace the method based on the HP filter with the production function method.

29 For a thorough list of the difficulties met in computing the NAIRU, as well as of the OECD computation method, see Richardson *et al.* (2000).

30 Hemming and Kell (2001) state that the objectives in terms of public expenditure growth rates are compatible with automatic fiscal stabilizers also on the expenditure side, if the objectives take into account suitable margins or exclude from the objectives that part of public expenditure sensitive to cyclical fluctuations.

31 See ISAE (2004).

32 See Laurent and Le Cacheux (2004).

6 The European Policy Mix: Law and Order

1 The conservatives' primary, if not only, objective is reasonably expected to be the fight against inflation.

2 The game refers to street contests where two cars charge straight at each other. The winner is the driver who manages to force the oncoming vehicle to swerve off course and avoid a crash. The driver who 'chickens out' is the loser. See, among others, *Rebel Without a Cause*, the film starring James Dean as the 'winner'.

3 See *Lettre de l'OFCE*, no. 224, 11 October 2002.

4 See Creel and Fayolle (2002).

5 See Bénassy-Quéré and Cœuré (2002).

6 See Dornbusch (1976) for the underlying theory.

7 Barro and Gordon have developed the analyses as a follow-up to their 1983 paper. For a summary of the discussions in terms of 'rules versus discretion', credibility, commitment and so on, the reader can refer to Walsh (1998), ch. 8.

8 See Solans (2000), p. 4: 'Being unaware of the limited use of the forecasts made by ECB staff in [Europe's] monetary policy decision-making process would paradoxically reduce rather than enhance the level of ECB policy transparency, and yet, such transparency should be the Bank's main objective.'

9 Estimates drawn from the Eurodollar and Euribor 3-month option prices.

10 After the financial turbulence of late 1999, the French relaunched the idea of international monetary co-operation whereby some sort of target levels would be set up between the US dollar, the yen and the euro.

11 Prime Minister Lionel Jospin's May 2000 speech before the French National Assembly caused a commotion in Frankfurt because it hinted that 'the euro zone economic policy and the necessarily political nature of the authority in charge of it require better visibility'. '*I* am Mr Euro', Duisenberg retorted at once. He added that 'cooperation between the Finance Ministers in charge of the euro-11 zone and their continuous dialogue with the ECB constituted a most acceptable, and even pleasant framework which should not head

towards the institutional and political developments that would run against the current progress at work.'

12 See, for example, Demertzis *et al.* (2000).

13 See Creel *et al.* (2002a).

14 See Creel *et al.* (2002b).

15 See Chapter 3 of this volume.

16 The recent numerous financial crises – Argentina, Brazil and Turkey, but also Vivendi Universal or France Télécom – confirm the point. The poor efficiency of market mechanisms in imposing financial discipline is also evident from a historical viewpoint, as shown by Flandreau *et al.* (1998).

17 This is not the same as imposing a strict limit such as the 60 per cent-of-GDP ceiling derived from the 'Maastricht criteria'. The limit was eventually dropped after the introduction of the euro, since some EU countries' public debt ratios – like those of Italy, Belgium or Greece, for example – were far above the limit.

18 In a speech delivered at the 3–4 November 1999 Institute Français de Relations Internationals conference, Germany's federal president, Johannes Rau, raised the issue strongly. He emphasized the need for a common effort at determining the fundamental objectives of European unification, a concern the Maastricht Treaty talks had left undiscussed.

19 See Chapter 1 of this volume.

7 European Indicators for Social Cohesion: A Step Forward Along the Lisbon Path

1 See Giammusso and Tangorra (2002).

2 Sustainable development was not included originally among the areas of interest of the European Council and was inserted for the first time on the occasion of the Council meeting at Laeken. Besides, in the area of employment, common objectives and a convergence process already existed, in what was known as the 'European Employment Strategy', and defined at the European Councils of Luxembourg (November 1997), Cardiff (June 1998) and Cologne (June 1999). The difference between the Employment Strategy and the OMC lies in two main elements – that is, the former contains policy indicators alongside performance indicators, and more attention is paid to the definition of concrete objectives at the Community level. We shall deal with these aspects later.

3 The decision was taken at the European Council meeting of Santa Maria de Feira in June 2000.

4 In the first Joint Report submitted to the Laeken Council; see Council of the European Union (2001) and European Commission (2001b).

5 This rate is computed as the percentage of persons living in households whose income is below 60 per cent of the national equivalized median income.

6 Many authors have studied the multidimensional characteristics of social exclusion, from Townsend (1962, 1979) to Sen (1976, 1999), from Atkinson and Bourguignon (1982, 1987), to Maasoumi (1986), and to Nolan and Whelan (1996). It was also analysed deeply by the United Nations in the UNPD Reports (1999, 2000). ISAE has often tackled these problems, particularly in

2000 (ISAE, 2000, 2001). For data on Europe, the main reference is Eurostat (2000a).

7 Significant steps forward in the debate devoted to the creation of a list of indicators for social inclusion may be found in the works of both the Economic Policy Committee (2000) and of the Social Protection Committee (2001), and in some documents of Eurostat (2000b) and of the European Commission (2000a, 2000b, 2000c, 2002b). The Commission's contribution to the Stockholm Council provides a temporary list of indicators with early data (European Commission, 2001b). Besides, in September 2001, under the auspices of the Belgian presidency, the European Union organized an International Conference on the subject of 'Indicators for Social Inclusion: Making Common EU Objectives Work', held in Antwerp. Finally, some interesting contributions on the matter were submitted by Atkinson *et al.* (2002) and Giammusso and Tangorra (2002).

8 The term 'poverty risk' underlines that a lack of resources does not necessarily and automatically determine a situation of poverty and exclusion, which may be the outcome of many risk situations, though the lack of income remains one of the main causes for poverty.

9 Note that the computation unit may differ from the analysis unit, which may vary according to the most appropriate definition for the phenomenon that is being measured. For example, in the case of poverty, there is a point to analysing households, as this is in general the social unit where individuals share resources. Thus, for example, the poverty rate indicator (or rather the poverty risk indicator) is defined as the ratio between the number of individuals living in (suitably defined) poor households and the total number of individuals. That approach inevitably implies the need to face the problem of making equivalent the resources of households differing in dimension and composition. The problem is solved through the adoption of a so-called 'OECD modified' equivalence scale, which is commonly used in international comparison. It attaches weights according to the number of household components and their age. More precisely, the weight equals 1 for the head of family, 0.5 for each further component over 18, and 0.3 for each further component under 18. See Hagenaars *et al.* (1994) and World Bank (2000).

10 See Social Protection Committee (2001) and Tsakloglou (2002).

11 To overcome this problem, a proposal was submitted (Atkinson *et al.*, 2002) aimed at estimating income by using the most recent available data. This proposal defines the so-called *current modified income* computed by adding the monthly perceived components referring to the latest available month, which are weighted with annual data, and the most recent data of annual items. Although this proposal seems to respond to the criticism of the time lag between surveying period and the period to which the income refers, it is also true that such a modification would enlarge the fluctuations of this variable and would imply a review of the methods adopted by member states with a consequent 'statistical burden'. This would be out of keeping with two of the six features of indicators. This is why a review of the income adopted is not being studied at present.

12 The Gini coefficient measures the degree of inequality in income distribution. It is expressed as:

$$G = 1/2n\overline{X}_i \sum_{J=1}^{n} |X_i - X_J|$$

where x_j is the income perceived by the individual j; x is the mean value of distribution; and n is the number of individuals. This index is widely adopted in the literature, but it has an important limitation given its different sensitivity to income transfers from one person to another in the distribution according to the personal ranking. Indeed, the index is the summation of incomes with decreasing weights as their ranking increases, and a transfer from a rich person to a poor person has a greater impact, the wider the distance between the rankings of the two people. Hence, 'heavier' transfers are those around the mode (see also Toso, 2000). For this reason, other inequality indexes were proposed – for example, the Atkinson index – although the Gini index remains by far the most utilized.

13 The are also other criteria; for example, the normative method, whereby the threshold is the one foreseen by rules and regulations on some social security instruments, or the indirect method, whereby one computes the mean share of resources allocated to buy some 'necessary' goods, thus defining as poor whoever spends a higher income share to obtain those goods. The former method is clearly unsuitable because the threshold – hence data on poverty – would be influenced easily by policy-makers, while the latter raises the problem (as does the absolute poverty approach) of which goods are considered necessary.

14 Council of the European Union (2001).

15 The method is described in Padoa Schioppa (2001); see also Eurostat (2000a).

16 It is all too evident that the adoption of a single European threshold would highlight the differences between states compared to national thresholds (see, on this point, Padoa Schioppa (2001) and Jäntti, 2002). In conceptual terms, the absolute poverty method considered here is equivalent to tracing a single threshold, as the definition of minimum standards would take place at the European level. The difference with the national threshold would only be in the scientific definition of the basket (which would take into account the consumption habits of single states) and in the monetary computation (which would consider the different costs of living).

17 Similar conclusions were reached by the Economic Policy Committee, which proposed the inclusion of an absolute poverty rate in the list of indicators; also in Atkinson et al. (2002) the need is stressed to investigate, in the medium term, other approaches to the measurement of the poverty risk. See also Padoa Schioppa (2001) and Tsakloglou (2002).

18 Please note that the higher the percentage (even 100 per cent), the more the relative poverty threshold tends to coincide with the median and the smaller are differences between countries; by definition, the percentage of poor people would be close to 50 per cent everywhere (Jänntti, 2002).

19 Eurostat (2000a) observes that the poverty gap may be very responsive to data quality: in particular, very low incomes, null incomes or even negative

incomes – as they are very far from the poverty threshold – have a considerable influence on the indicator. For this reason, different alternative methods were proposed (Atkinson *et al.*, 2002), namely computing the average gap after making a bottom-coding – that is, recoding the low income values (for example, below 10 per cent of the median income) with a threshold value, or utilising the median gap rather than the mean gap. The latter method was adopted by the Social Protection Committee (2001), which proposed the inclusion of the median gap in the list of indicators.

20 Errors may emerge (namely under- or overestimates varying from one measurement to another or from one country to another) as well as the phenomenon of 'worn out' data (loss of panel units).

21 See Eurostat (2000a).

22 There are, however comparability problems between the different schooling systems in identifying the junior school level precisely (Atkinson *et al.*, 2002).

23 See Brandolini (2002).

24 Also reported in Giammusso and Tangorra (2002).

25 See Förster (2000).

26 See Atkinson (2000), Conseil d'Analyse Économique (2001) and Atkinson *et al.* (2002).

27 Some considerations on indicators including these aspects are proposed in Brandolini (2002).

28 The GDP was used in the first formula (European Commission, 2000b), then, at the Stockholm European Council, reference was made to unemployment rates. In 2001, per capita GDP was adopted again (European Commission, 2001b) and eventually unemployment was adopted.

29 European Commission (2002g).

30 This problem is linked to the adoption of a low level of regional breakdown: the coefficient of variation is computed with reference to the NUTS (Nomenclature of Territorial Units for Statistics) Level 2 rather than Level 3.

31 See also Abrahamson (2002).

32 See, for example, Eurostat (2001) and OECD (2001a, 2001b). Many analyses on the mortality differential by status concern single countries: among the few comparative studies it is worth mentioning Kunst *et al.* (1998), Cavelaars *et al.* (1998), Fox (1989), Mackenbach *et al.* (1997), Van Doorslaer *et al.* (1997).

33 See Atkinson *et al.* (2002).

34 For Germany, reference is made to the survey of the Ministry of Labour and Social Affairs on living conditions, while for Italy it is the last Report of the Italian Commission on Social Exclusion – *Commissione d'Indagine sull'Esclusione Sociale* (2001) – which contains the results of a survey carried out by the Fondazione Zancan.

35 For example, the Italian survey is based on a method whereby cities are sampled by demographic dimension and the number of homeless counted simultaneously on the same night (the so-called 's-night' approach). The figure obtained is then weighted with values derived from other sources of information.

36 European Commission (2000b).

37 With the only exceptions of regional cohesion (the definition of which changed more than once) and of the long-term unemployment rate, which was included among social cohesion indicators.

38 Economic Policy Committee (2000).
39 In this way, an attempt is made to cancel the effect of income distribution variations on poverty rates.
40 European Commission (2001b).
41 European Commission (2001a).
42 This intention, solemnly stated in the European Social Agenda, was reiterated in 2001 (European Commission, 2001b).
43 Just before the Barcelona Council, the Commission invited the European Council to decide on the practical objective of halving the number of people in need by 2010 (European Commission, 2001b).
44 The official act of the Council and of the European Parliament setting up the Committee dates back to 22 November 2001; see European Commission (2002b).

8   From Tax Competition to Social Race to the Bottom? European Models and the Challenge of Mobility

1 This chapter is an extended version of chapter 3 of the 2002 *Report on the State of the European Union* of the OFCE. This new edited version also includes excerpts from the 1999 Report's second chapter.
2 Fitoussi (2000a).
3 The 1989 Charter of Fundamental Social Rights includes the following headings: Freedom of movement; Employment and remuneration; Improvement of living and working conditions; Social protection; Freedom of association and collective bargaining; Vocational training; Equal treatment for men and women; Information, consultation and participation of workers; Health protection and safety at the workplace; Protection of children and adolescents; Elderly persons; Disabled persons.
4 On 28 June 2000, Anna Diamantopoulou said: 'The agenda aims at taking up the new social challenges derived from both the radical transformation of the economy and European society, and more especially those entailed by the new knowledge-based economy. We do not seek to harmonise social policy, but to reach the common European goals that will lead us to the strategic target decided on in Lisbon: making Europe the most competitive and dynamic knowledge-based economy in the world.'
5 The annual social report published in March 2002 by Eurostat produces rather similar figures on the basis of the 1998 data.
6 Scharpf (2002) rightly evokes the EU's social 'legitimate diversity'.
7 Social payments depend on social contributions, and payments are made according to the position held regarding the labour market. Conversely, following the Beveridge model, social protection rests on solidarity, and actual work is no prerequisite.
8 For a convincing analysis specific to the diversity of Europe's labour markets, see Fitoussi and Passet (2000) and Cadiou *et al.* (1999).
9 For a comprehensive survey of all member states' social specificities, see 'The Organisation of Social Protection in the EU Member States', and the documentation supplied by the Commission's Directorate for Employment and Social Affairs at http://europa.eu.int/comm/employment_social/.

10 For more on this point, see Salmon (2000).

11 See Julie Etienne 'L'harmonisation fiscale européenne', mémoire de fin d'études (Université Libre de Bruxelles, 1998).

12 Headquarters (France, Luxembourg and so on) or co-ordination centres (Belgium) are centres comprising only the main departments (general management, administration and so on) used jointly by all the companies within the same group. The payments made by the subsidiaries for the services provided by the centre constitute a transfer of profits. The group can therefore reduce its tax payments in countries with a special tax scheme for the centre.

13 V. Tanzi's argumentation (1996) rests on the calculations of the firms' effective taxation rate and their return on assets to prove the part played by taxation on US firms' out sourcing in Ireland. Statistics on the frequency of out sourcing cannot be disproved, nor can any conclusion be drawn about the firms' real motives from the above-mentioned calculations only. Other factors can interfere, such as the economic environment or the quality of the labour force. Each motive must be apportioned its due part in the decision to establish a company abroad. Another example is F. Gara's 'Les entreprises industrielles françaises face aux enjeux de la globalisation, in 'Les mutations de l'économie française c. de Boissieu (ed.) (Paris: Economica, 1998). In this article, the author identifies breaking into the market as the single most important factor that pushes French firms to move their business to a foreign country.

14 V. Tanzi (1996); OECD (1998).

15 A. Weichenrieder (1996) 'Fighting International Tax Avoidance: The Case of Germany', *Fiscal Studies*, vol. 17, no. 1 pp. 56–82.

16 D. Janssen (1997) 'Analyse dynamique et stochastique de l'intégration fiscale en Europe' Thèse de doctorat, Universite Paris I.

17 For the harmonization process of excise duties (that is, tobacco, alcohol and 'mineral oil' products), see H. Sterdyniak, M. H. Blonde, G. Cornilleau, J. Le Cacheux and J. Le Dem (1991). *Vers une fiscalité européenne, Economica*. Since then, the 25 February 1992 Directive has set the rules on holding, transporting and controlling the items on which excise duties apply. The rates have been harmonized on the basis of minimum rates and came into effect on 1 January 1993.

18 See Fitoussi (2000b).

19 See Bean (1998), Commissariat Général du Plan (1999) or Gorce (2000).

20 When resorting to 'social-tax nomadism', consumers react to time constraints along the same rational patterns as multinational firms which turn to 'social shopping' when forced to adapt to geographical ones.

21 In *Capitalism, Socialism and Democracy* (New York: Harper & Row, 1942), Schumpeter showed strikingly how 'virtual' and 'perfect' competition were very much alike.

22 EU mobile wage earners are evaluated by the European Commission at 0.4 per cent of the overall labour force.

23 See Krueger (2000).

24 For a review of the work mobility of young French graduates, see Ferrand (2001).

25 The Spanish Presidency (January–June 2002), for example, made labour mobility one of its priorities.

26 It must be noted that Pestineau and Jousten (2001) come to similar conclusions by considering worker mobility before, during and after the working life cycle.

27 As part of the 'Personal Responsibilities and Work Reconciliation Act', 'Temporary Assistance for Needy Families' (TANF) replaced AFDC in 1996.

Bibliography

Abbott, T. A. (1994) 'Price Dispersion: Product Heterogeneity, Regional Markets or Local Market Power?', *Journal of Economics and Business*, vol. 46, no. 1, pp. 21–37.

Abrahamson, P. (2002) 'Indicators for Social Inclusion: Making a Distinction Between Poverty and Social Exclusion', *Politica Economica*, vol. 18, no. 1.

Acconcia, A. (2002) 'Convergenza: un'utopia per le regione europee?' Studi Economici, 76 (1), pp. 129–46.

Acconcia, A. and A. Del Monte (2000) 'Regional Development and Public Spending: The Case of Italy', Studi Economici, 72(3), pp. 5–24.

Alber, J. and G. Standing (2000) 'Social Dumping, Catch-up or Convergence? Europe in a Comparative Global Context', *Journal of European Social Policy*, vol. 10, No. 2, pp. 99–119.

Alesina, A. and R. Perotti (1995) 'Fiscal Expansions and Adjustment in OECD Countries', *Economic Policy*, vol. 21, pp. 205–48.

Alesina, A. and R. Wacziarg (1999) 'Is Europe Going Too Far?', NBER Working Paper No. 6883.

Alesina, A., A. Angeloni and L. Schuknecht (2001) 'What Does the European Union Do?', NBER Working Paper No. 8647.

Antolin, P. and O. Bover (1997) 'Regional Migration in Spain: The Effect of Personal Characteristics and of Unemployment, Wage and House Price Differentials Using Pooled Cross-Sections', *Oxford Bulletin of Economics and Statistics*, vol. 59, no. 2, pp. 215–235.

Antonelli, C. (1994) 'Technological Districts Localized Spillovers and Productivity Growth. The Italian Evidence on Technological Externalities in the Core Regions', *International Review of Applied Economics*, vol. 8.

Ardy, B., I. Begg, W. Schelkle and F. Torres (2002) 'EMU and Its Impact on Cohesion: Policy Challenges', Paper prepared for the Workshop on 'EMU and Cohesion', Burssels, 19 April.

Armstrong, H. W. (1995) 'Convergence Among Regions of the European Union, 1950–95', *Papers in Regional Science*, vol. 74, no. 2, pp. 143–152.

Artis, M. and W. Zhang (1995) 'International Business Cycles and the ERM: Is There a European Business Cycle?', CEPR Discussion paper No. 1191.

Aschauer, D. A. (1989) 'Is Public Expenditure Productive?', *Journal of Monetary Economics*, vol. 23, no. 2, pp. 127–200.

Atkinson, A. B. (2000) 'Agenda social européen: comparison des Pauvretés et transferts sociaux', in Conseil d'Analyse Économique (ed.), *Questions europennes, Rapport du Conseil d'Analyse économique*, No. 27 (Paris: La Documentation Française).

Atkinson, A. B. and F. Bourguignon (1982) 'The Comparison of Multidimensioned Distribution of Economic Status', *Review of Economic Studies*, No. 12.

Atkinson, A. B. and F. Bourguignon (1987) 'Income Distribution and Differences in Need', in G. R. Feiwel (ed.), *Arrow and the Foundation of the Theory of Economic Policy* (London: Macmillan).

Atkinson, A. B., B. Cantillon, E. Marlier and B. Nolan (2002) *Social Indicators: The EU and Social Inclusion* (Oxford University Press).

Attanasio, O. and F. Padoa Schioppa (1991) 'Regional Inequalities, Migration and Mismatch in Italy, 1960–86', in F. Padoa Schioppa (ed.), *Mismatch and Labour Mobility* (Cambridge University Press).

Bénassy-Quéré, A. and B. Cœuré (2002) *Economie de l'euro* (Economy of the Euro), Repères (Paris: La Découverte).

Balassa, B. (1961) *The Theory of Economic Integration* (Homewood, Ill.: Richard D. Irwin).

Balassone, F. and D. Monacelli (2000) 'EMU, Fiscal Rules: Is There A Gap?', Banca d'Italia Discussion paper No. 375, July.

Ball, L. (1997) 'Efficient Rules for Monetary Policy', NBER Working paper No. 5982.

Barca, F. and G. Pellegrini (2000) 'Politiche per la competitività territoriale in Europa: note sul programma 2000–2006 per il Mezzogiorno d'Italia', presented at the First Annual Workshop of the University of Bologna Centre in Buenos Aires, 26–27 April.

Bardi, L. (1989) 'Rappresentanza e Parlamento Europeo', *Rivista Italiana di Scienza Politica*, vol. XIX, no. 2, August, pp. 267–300.

Bardi, L. and P. Ignazi (1999) *Il Parlamento Europeo* (Bologna: Il Mulino).

Barro, R. J. and D. B. Gordon (1983b) 'Rules, Discretion and Reputation in a Model of Monetary Policy', *Journal of Monetary Economics*, 12, July.

Barro, R. J. and X. Sala-I-Martin (1991) 'Convergence Across States and Regions', *Brookings Papers on Economic Activity*, 1.

Barro, R. and X. X. Sala-I-Martin (1991), 'Convergence Across States and Regions, *Brookings Papers on Economic Activity*, no. 1, pp. 107–182.

Barro, R. and X. X. Sala-I-Martin (1995) *Economic Growth*, (New York: McGraw-Hill).

Basile, R. (2001) 'The Locational Determinants of Foreign-owned Manufacturing Plants in Italy: The Role of the South', Riviste. R. Politics Economics, July–August.

Bayoumi, T. and B. Eichengreen (1992) 'Shocking Aspects of EMU', *CEPR Discussion Paper*, No. 646.

Bayoumi, T. and B. Eichengreen (1996) 'Operationalizing the Theory of Optimum Currency Area', CEPR Discussion paper No. 1484.

Bean *et al.* Bentobla, S. and Bestda, G. (1998) 'Social Europe: One for All', *CEPR Monitoring European Integration*, No. 8.

Beine, M., F. Docquier and A. Hecq (1998) 'Convergence des groupes en Europe: une analyse sur données régionales', ministère de la région wallonne, services des études et de la statistique, Discussion paper No. 9801.

Beretta, C., S. Beretta and G. Merzoni (2001) 'Integrazione dei mercati e mobilità dei fattori: le interazioni tra soggetti complessi e problemi del disegno di una organizzazione federale', in A. Quadrio Curzio (ed.), *Profili della Costituzione Economica Europea* (Bologna: Il Mulino).

Bifulco, R., M. Cartaria and A. Celotto (2001) *L'Europa dei diritti* (Bologna: Il Mulino).

Boeri, T. (2000) 'Social Europe: Dramatic Visions and Real Complexity', CEPR Discussion papers No. 2371.

Boldrin, M. and F. Canova (2001) 'Europe's Regions: Income Disparities and Regional Policies', *Economic Policy*, no. 32 pp. 207–253.

Boone, L. (1997) 'Symmetry and Asymmetry of Supply and Demand Shocks in the EU: A Dynamic Analysis', CEPII Working paper No. 97–03.

Brandimarte, C., S. Leproux and F. Sartori (1998) 'Il Patto di Stabilità e Crescita: politiche fiscali e spese per lo sviluppo', *Studi e Note di Economia*, No. 2, pp. 117–64.

Brandolini, A. (2002) 'Education and Employment Indicators for the EU Social Agenda', *Politica Economica*, vol. 18, no. 1.

Brière, M. (2001) 'Politique de communication des banques centrales et réaction des marchés: une comparaison de la Fed et de la B.C.E.', Paper preserved at a conference organized by G.D.R. Monnaie et Financement and Université of Pau-Pays de l'Adour, France, June.

Brueckner, J. (1998) *Welfare Reform and Interstate Welfare Competition: Theory and Evidence*, Report of the Urban Institute (Washington, DC).

CEPR (Centre for Economic Policy Research) (1995) *La distribuzione dei poteri nell'Unione Europea* (Bologna: Il Mulino).

Cadiou, L., G. Guichard and M. Maurel (1999) 'La diversité des marchés du travail en Europe: quelles conséquences pour l'Union monétaire?', Documents de travail du CEPII, Nos 10 and 11.

Cartabia, M. and J. H. H. Weiler (2000) *L'Italia in Europa. Profili istituzionale e costituzionali* (Bologna: Il Mulino).

Cassese, S. (2000) *La nuova costituzione economica. Lezioni* (Bari: La Terza).

Cassese, S. (2001) 'Is There Really A Democratic Deficit?', in EuropEos (ed.), *Institutional Reforms in the European Union. Memorandum for the Convention* (Rome: EropEos).

Cavelaaes, A. E. J. M., A. E. Kunst, J. J. M. Geurts, U. Helmert, O. Lundberg and J. Matheson (1998) 'Morbidity Differences by Occupational Class Among Men in Seven European Countries', *International Journal of Epidemiology*, vol. 27.

Cecchetti, S. G. *et al.* (2000) 'Price Level Convergence Among United States Cities: Lessons for the European Central Bank', NBER Working paper No. 7681.

Clarida, R., J. Gali and M. Gertler (1999) 'The Science of Monetary Policy. A New Keynsian Perspective', *Journal of Economic Literature*, no. 37, pp. 1661–707.

Club di Firenze (1996) *Europa: l'impossibile status quo* (Bologna: Il Mulino).

Commissariat Général du Plan (1999) *Emploi, négociations collectives, protection sociale: vers quelle Europe Sociale?*, Report of the 'Social Europe' group (Paris: La Documentation française).

Commissione d'Indagine sull'Esclusione Sociale (2001) *Rapporto annuale sulle politiche contro la povertà e l'esclusione sociale* (Rome: Presidenza del Consiglio).

Conseil d'Analyse Économique (2001) *Les inégalités économiques, Rapport du Conseil d'Analyse économique*, No. 33 (Paris: La Documentation Française).

Creel, J. and J. Fayolle (2002) 'La banque centrale et l'union monétaire européennes: les tribulations de la crédibilité', *Revue de l'OFCE* (Special issue), March.

Creel, J. and H. Sterdyniak (2000) 'May the Euro Increase Exchange Rate Volatility?', in T. Moser and B. Schips (eds) *EMU, Financial Markets and the World Economy* (Boston: Kluwer), October.

Creel, J., T. Latreille and J. Le Cacheux (2002a) 'Le Pacte de stabilité et de croissance et les politiques budgétaires dans l'Union européenne', *Revue de l'OFCE*, Special issue, March.

Creel, J., G. Dupont, J. Le Cacheux, H. Sterdyniak and X. Timbeau (2002b) 'Le budget 2003: le pécheur non repenti', *Lettre de l'OFCE* No. 224, 11 October.

Daniel, B. C. (1992) 'Price Setting, Imperfect Information and the Law of One Price', *Journal of Macroeconomics*, vol. 14, no. 3, pp. 383–415.

De La Porte, C. (2000) 'Is There an Emerging European Consensus on Social Protection?', *Yearbook of the Institut syndical européen* (ISE/ETUI).

De Nardis, S., A. Goglio and A. Malgarini (1996) 'Regional Labour Market Dynamics in Europe', *European Economic Review*, 39.

De Winter, L. and M. Swyngedouw (1999) 'The Scope of EU Government', in H. Schmitt and J. Thomassen (eds), *Political Representation and Legitimacy in the European Union* (Oxford University Press).

De la Fuente, Á. (1999) 'La dinámica territorial de la población Española: Un Panorama y Algunos Resultados Provisionales', *Revista de Economia Aplicada*, vol. 7, no. 20, pp. 53–108.

Deardoff, A. V. (1994) 'The Possibility of Factor Price Equalization Revisited', *Journal of International Economics*, vol. 36, no. 1–2, pp. 167–75.

Deardoff, A. V. (2001) 'Rich and Poor Countries in Neoclassical Trade and Growth', *Economic Journal*, vol. 111, no. 470, pp. 277–94.

Debrun, X. and C. Wyplosz (1999) 'Onze gouvernements et une Banque centrale' (Eleven Governments and one Central Bank), *Revue d'Economie Politique*, vol. 3, May–June.

Demeriades, P. O. and T. P. Mamuneas (2000) 'Intertemporal Output and Employment Effects of Public Infrastructure Capital: Evidence from 12 OECD Economies', *Economic Journal*, No. 110, pp. 687–712.

Demertzis, M., A. Hughes Hallett and N. Viegi (1999) 'Can the ECB Be Truly Independent? Should It Be?', *Empirica*, no. 26, pp. 217–40.

Demertzis, M., A. Hughes Hallett and O. Rummel (2000) 'Is the European Union a Natural Currency Area, or Is It Held Together by Policy Makers?', *Weltwirtschaftliches Archiv*, vol. 136 (no. 4).

Di Palma, M. (ed.) (1990) *Le infrastrutture a rete. Dotazioni e linee di intervento* (Rome: Sipi).

Dornbusch, R. (1976) 'Expectations and Exchange Rate Dynamics', *Journal of Political Economy*, vol. 84 (no. 6).

'Eurobarometer' (2003), Eurobarometer 59 – public opinion on the European Union (June), Accessed at http://europa.eu.int/futurum/documents/other/oth170603_fr.pdf.

ECB (European Central Bank) (1999a) 'Monthly Bulletin', January. Accessed at http://www.bancaditalia.it.

ECB (European Central Bank) (1999b) 'Inflation Differentials in a Monetary Union', Monthly Bulletin, October. Accessed at http://www.bancaditalia.it.

ECB (European Central Bank) (2001) 'Monthly Bulletin', November. Accessed at http://www.bancaditalia.it.

ECB (European Central Bank) (2002) 'Monthly Bulletin', April. Accessed at http://www.bancaditalia.it.

ECB (European Central Bank) (2003) 'Monthly Bulletin', June 2003, Frankfurt.

Easterly, W. and S. Rebelo (1993) 'Fiscal Policy and Economic Growth', *Journal of Monetary Economics*, vol. 32 (3): p. 417–58.

Economic Policy Committee (2000) *Report by the Economic Policy Committee to ECOFIN on Structural Indicators: An Instrument for Better Structural Policies*, EPC/ECFIN/608/00-final.

Engel, C. and J. H. Rogers (2001) 'Violating the Law of One Price: Should We Make a Federal Case Out of It?', *Journal of Money Credit and Banking*, vol. 33, no. 1, pp. 1–15.

Esping-Andersen, G. (1990) *The Three Worlds of Welfare Capitalism* (Cambridge: Polity Press).

European Commission (1999) 'Budgetary Surveillance in EMU', *European Economy Supplement A*, no. 3, Directorate General for Economic and Financial Affairs.

European Commission (2000a) *Social Policy Agenda*, COM(2000) 379 final, Brussels.

European Commission (2000b) *Les Tendances Sociales: Perspectives et Défis: Communication du 1er mars 2000*, Brussels.

European Commission (2000c) *Rapport sur la Protection sociale en Europe 1999*, Brussels.

European Commission (2000d) 'Public Finances in EMU – 2000', *European Economy*, Reports and Studies No. 3.

European Commission (2001a) *Second Report on the Social and Economic Situation and Development of the Regions of the Community*, Brussels.

European Commission (2001b) *Draft Joint Report on Social Inclusion*, COM(2001) 565.

European Commission (2001c) *Realising the European Union's Potential: Consolidating and Extending the Lisbon Strategy*, COM(2001) 79 final.

European Commission (2002a) *Communication from the Commission. A Project for the European Union*, CO (2002) 247 def.

European Commission (2002b) *Community Action Programme to Combat Social Exclusion 2002–2006 – Annual Work Programme – 2002*, REF SEP 3/01 EN.

European Commission (2002c) 'Public Finances in EMU – 2002', *European Economy* No. 3.

European Commission (2002d) 'Economic Forecasts – Spring 2002', *European Economy* No. 2.

European Commission (2002e) *Community Action Programme to Combat Social Exclusion 2002–2006 – General Guidelines for the Implementation of the Programme*, REF SEP 2/01 EN rev.

European Commission (2002f) *The Lisbon Strategy: Making Change Happen*, COM(2002) 14 final.

European Commission (2002g) *The Lisbon Strategy: Making Change Happen – Commission Staff Working Paper in Support of the Report from the Commission to the Spring European Council in Barcelona* (COM(2002) 14 final), SEC(2002) 29.

European Commission (various years) 'Eurobarometer', DG Press and Communication, accessed at http://europa.eu.int/comm/public_opinion.

European Council (2000a) 'Presidency Conclusions', Lisbon, 24 March 2000. Accessed at http://ue.eu.int/newsroom/newmain.asp?lang=1.

European Council (2000b) 'Presidency Counclusions', Santa Maria de Feira, 19 June 2000. Accessed at http://ue.eu.int/newsroom/newmain.asp?lang=1.

European Council (2000c) *Presidency Conclusions*, Nice, 8 December.

European Council (2000d) *Presidency Conclusions*, Santa Maria de Feira, 19 June.

European Council (2001a) *Presidency Conclusions*, Laeken, 15 December.

European Council (2001b) *Presidency Conclusions*, Stockholm, 24 March.

European Union Council (2001) *Joint Report on Social Inclusion*, 15223/01.

Eurostat (2000a) *European Social Statistics – Income, Poverty and Social Exclusion*, Luxembourg.

Eurostat (2000b) *European Social Statistics – Definitions, Data Sources, Data Availability*, Eurostat/D2/SBS/IPS/DEC00/EN.

Eurostat (2001) *Key Data on Health 2000*, Luxembourg.

Förster M. F. (2000) 'Trends and Driving Factors in Income Distribution and Poverty in the OECD Area', *Labour Market and Social Policy Occasional Papers* No. 42, OECD.

Fagerberg, J. and B. Verspagen (1995) 'Heading for Divergence? Regional Growth in Europe Reconsidered', *MERIT Research Memoranda*, no. 14.

Faini, R. (1983) 'Cumulative Process of De-industrialisation in an Open Region: The Case of Southern Italy, 1951–73', *Journal of Development Economics*, vol. 12, no. 3, pp. 277–301.

Faini, R. (1999) 'Trade Unions and Regional Development', *European Economic Review*, vol. 43, no. 2, pp. 457–474.

Fatás, A. and I. Mihov (2001) 'Government Size and Automatic Stabilizers: International and Intranational Evidence', *Journal of International Economics*, vol. 55, pp. 3–28.

Fatãs, A. (1997) 'Countries or Regions? Lessons from the EMS Experience', *European Economic Review*, no. 41.

Fayolle, J. and A. Lecuyer (2000) 'Croissance régional, appartenance nationale et fonds structurels européens. Un bilan d'étape', *Revue de l'OFCE*, No. 73, pp. 166–185.

Ferrand, A. (2001) *'Mondialisation: Réagir ou subir? – La France face à l'expatriation des compétences, des capitaux et des entreprises'*, *Les Rapport du Sénat* No. 386, Paris.

Fidrmuc, J. and I. Korhonen (2001) 'Similarity of Supply and Demand Shocks Between the Euro Area and the CEECs', BOFIT Discussion Paper No.14, Bank of Finland, November.

Fitoussi, J.-P. (1995) *Le débat interdit* (Paris: Arléa).

Fitoussi, J.-P. (1999) 'L'économie politique de l'après-euro', in J.-P. Fitoussi, *Rapport sur l'état de l'Union européenne* (Report on the European union), OFCE, Fayard-Presses de Sciences Po.

Fitoussi, J.-P. (ed.) (1999) *Rapport sur l'état de l'Union Européenne* (Paris: Fayard and Presses de Sciences-Po).

Fitoussi, J.-P. (2000a) 'L'avenir de l'Europe: l'ambition d'un autre contrat social', Revue de l'OFCE No. 75, October, pp. 165–82.

Fitoussi, J.-P. (ed.) (2000b) *Rapport sur l'état de l'Union Européenne* (Paris: Fayard and Presses de Sciences-Po).

Fitoussi, J.-P. (2002) *La règle et le choix*, La République des idées, Seuil.

Fitoussi, J.-P. and O. Passet (2000) 'Réformes structurelles et politiques macro-économiques: les enseignements des modèles de pays', in J.-P. Fitoussi, O. Passet and Freyssinet 'Réduction du chômage: les réussites en Europe', *Les Rapports du CAE* No. 23.

Flandreau, M., J. Le Cacheux and F. Zumer (1998) 'Stability Without a Pact? Lessons from the European Gold Standard, 1880–1914', *Economic Policy*, no. 28.

Forni, M. and L. Reichlin (1997) 'National Policies and Local Economies: Europe and the US', CEPR Discussion paper No. 1632.

Fox, A. J. (1989) *Health Inequalities in European Countries* (Aldershot: Gower).

French Planning Agency (1999) 'Le gouvernement économique de la zone euro', Report by R. Boyer (co-ordinator) (Paris: La Documentation française).

Fujita, M., P. R. Krugman and A. J. Venables (1999) *The Spatial Economy: Cities, Regions and International Trade* (Cambridge, Mass.: MIT Press).

Fuss, C. (1998a) 'Convergence Among Industrialised Countries: A Time-series Investigation', *Cahiers économiques de Bruxelles*, second quarter.

Fuss, C. (1998b) 'Contributions to the Empirical Analysis of Convergence in the EU', Ph.D. dissertation, Free University of Brussels, Belgium.

Genschel, P. (2001) 'Globalization, tax competition, and the fiscal viability of the Welfare State', MPIfG Working papers No. 01/1, May.

Giammusso, F. and R. Tangorra (2002) 'Indicators on Poverty and Social Exclusion: Moving Towards a Social Europe', *Politica Economica*, vol. 18, no. 1, April.

Giavazzi, F., T. Jappelli and M. Pagano (2000) 'Searching for Non-Keynesian Effects of Fiscal Policy: Evidence from Industrial and Developing Countries', *European Economic Review*, no. 44, pp. 1259–89.

Gorce, G. (2000) '*L'Union européenne face aux risques de dumping social, Rapport de la Délégation à l'Union européenne', Les documents d'information de l'Assemblée Nationale*, Paris.

Gozi, S. (2001) *Il governo dell'Europa* (Bologna: Il Mulino).

Grossman, G. M. and E. Helpman (1991) *Innovation and Growth in the Global Economy* (Cambridge, Mass.: MIT Press).

Habermas, J. (2001) 'Perché l'Europa ha bisogno di una costituzione?', in G. Bonacchi (ed.), *Una Costituzione senza Stato* (Bologna: Il Mulino).

Hagemann, R. P. (2001) 'Comments on Sesssion II: European Fiscal Rules', *Fiscal Rules*, Public Finance Workshp, Bank of Italy, February.

Hagenaars, A., K. de Vos and A. Zaidi (1994) *Poverty Statistics in the late-1980s* (Luxembourg: Eurostat).

Helg, R., P. Manasse, T. Monacelli and R. Rovelli (1995) 'How Much (A)symmetry in Europe? Evidence from Industrial Sectors', *European Economic Review*, 39.

Hemming, R. and M. Kell (2001) 'Promoting Fiscal Responsibility: Transparency, Rules and Independent Fiscal Authorities', *Fiscal Rules*, Public Finance Workshop, Bank of Italy, February.

Hirschman, A. O. (1970) *Exit, Voice and Loyalty, Responses to Decline in Firms, Organisations and States* (Cambridge, Mass.: Harvard University Press).

Holtz-Eakin, D. and A. E. Schwartz (1995) 'Infrastructure in a Structural Model of Economic Growth', *Regional Science and Urban Economics*, vol. 25, pp. 131–151.

Hugounenq, R., J. Le Cacheux and T. Madies (1999) 'Risques de concurrence fiscale en Europe', *La Lettre de l'OFCE* No. 189.

IMF (1998) *World Economic Outlook* (Washington, DC: IMF), October.

ISAE (2000) *Rapporto Trimestrale*, Rome, April.

ISAE (2001) 'La progettazione di nun nuovo indicatore di benessere della collettività romana', in OPER (ed.), *III Rapporto sull'economia romana* (Rome: Municipality of Rome).

ISAE (2004) Le Previsioni per l'Economie Itolioma, Rome, July.

Jäntti, M. (2002) 'Interventions on Indicators for Social Inclusion. Poverty and Income Distribution', *Politica Economica*, vol. 18, no. 1.

Kagan, R. (2002) 'Power and Weakness', *Policy Review*, no. 113, June–July.

Keiser, R. (1996) 'European Welfare States in Competition', Miméo, Carletan College, Northfied, Minnesota.

Khan, M. S. and M. S. Kumar (1997) 'Public and Private Investment and the Growth Process in Developing Countries', *Oxford Bulletin of Economic Growth Papers*, no. 59, pp. 69–87.

Krueger, A. B. (2000) 'From Bismarck to Maastricht: The March to European Union and the Labor compact', NBER Working paper series No. 7456.

Kunst, A. E., F. Groenhof, J. P. Mackenbach and the EU Working Group on Socioeconomic Inequalities in Health (1998) 'Occupational Class and Cause of Specific Mortality in Middle-Aged Men in 11 European Countries: A Comparison of Population-Based Studies', *British Medical Journal*, no. 316, May.

Laurent, É and J. Le Cacheux (2004) 'Large hence vicious, small thus virtuous? The criterion of size in the macroeconomic making of the euro zone "XVI Villa Mondragone International Economic Seminar on" Rules, International Economy and Growth', Rome, 23–24 June.

Laurent, E. (2002) 'De la concurrence fiscale à la concurrence sociale: les modèles européens au défi de la mobilité', in J.-P. Fitoussi and J. Le Cacheux (eds), *Rapport sur l'état de l'Union européenne* (Report on the state of the European Union), OFCE, Fayard-Presses de Sciences Po.

Laurent, E. and J. Le Cacheux (2003a) 'Constitution européenne: l'Union politique dans les limbes', *Lettre de l'OFCE*, no. 238, July.

Laurent, E. and J. Le Cacheux (2003b) 'La Convention et la réforme des institutions européennes', in OFCE, *L'économie française 2003* (The French Economy 2003), Collection Repères, (Paris: La Découverte).

Le Cacheux, J. (2000) 'Les dangers de la concurrence fiscale et sociale en Europe' in *Questions européennes: Les Rapports du CAE*, No. 27, Paris: La Documentation française.

Le Cacheux, J. (2000) 'Les dangers de la concurrence fiscale et sociale en Europe', '*Questions européennes in Les Rapports du CAE*, No. 27.

Lucas, R. E., Jr. (1988) 'On the Mechanics of Economic Development', *Journal of Monetary Economics*, vol. 22, pp. 3–42.

Luciani, M. (2001) 'Legalità e legittimità nel processo di itnegrazione europea', in G. Bonacchi (ed.), *Una Costituzione senza Stato* (Bologna: Il Mulino).

Maasoumi, E. (1986) 'The Measurement and Decomposition of Multi-Dimensional Inequality', *Econometrica*, No. 54.

Mackenbach, J. *et al.* (1997) 'Socioeconomic Inequalities in Morbidity and Mortality in Western Europe', *The Lancet*, no. 349.

Manzella, A. (2001) 'Le cooperazioni rafforzate nell'Unione plurale', in S. Guerrieri, A. Manzella and F. Sdogati (eds), *Dall'Europa a Quindici alla Grande Europa. La sfida istituzionale* (Bologna: Il Mulino).

Manzella, A. (2002) 'The Convention: A New Model for Constitution Making', in EuropEos (ed.), *Institutional Reform in the European Union. Memorandum for the Convention*, Rome EuropEos.

Marsh, M. (1999) 'Policy Performance', in H. Schimdt and J. Thomassen (eds), *Political Representation and Legitimacy in the European Union* (Oxford University Press).

Martin, P. and C. A. Rogers (1995) 'Industrial Location and Public Infrastructure', *Journal of International Economics*, vol. 39, pp. 335–351.

Martin, P. and G. I. P. Ottaviano (2001) 'Growth and Agglomeration', International Economic Review, 42, pp. 947–968.

Melitz, J. and S. Vori (1993) 'National Insurance Against Unevenly Distributed Shocks in a European Monetary Union', *Recherches Economiques de Louvain*, vol. 59, no. 1–2.

Meyer, A. (ed.) (1998) 'L'Europe sociale', *Problèmes politiques et sociaux* (Paris: La Documentation Française).

Mills, P. and A. Quinet (2001) 'The Case for Spending Rules', *Fiscal Rules*, Public Finance Workshop, Bank of Italy, February.

Mundell, R.A. (1961) 'A Theory of Optimum Currency Areas', *American Economic Review*, 51.

Neven, D. and C. Gouyette (1995) 'Regional Convergence in the European Community', *Journal of Common Market Studies*, vol. 33, no. 1, pp. 47–65.

Nolan, B. and C. Whelan (1996) *Resources, Deprivation and the Measurement of Poverty* (Oxford: Clarendon Press).

OECD (1996) *Réconcilier l'économique et le social. Vers une économie plurielle* (Paris: OECD).

OECD (1997) *OECD Economic Outlook*, Paris, December.

OECD (1998) Harmful Tax Competition: An Emerging Global Issue. Paris, France: OECD.

OECD (2001a) *OECD Economic Outlook*, Paris, December.

OECD (2001b) *OECD Health Data 2001: A Comparative Analysis of 30 OECD Countries*, Paris.

OECD (2002a) *Economic Survey: The Netherlands*, Paris.

OECD (2002b) *A Complete and Persistent Macroeconomic Data Set of the Euro Area, Methodological Issues and Results*, February. Accessed from http://www.oecd.org/EN/statistics/0,, EN-statistics-notheme-8-no-no-no-0.00.html.

OFCE (Observatoire français des conjonctures économiques) (1998) 'Etude sur la concurrence fiscale en Europe' in Marini, P. (ed.) *'La concurrence fiscale en Europe: une contribution au débat'*, Les Rapport du Sénat, No. 483 (Paris: OFCE).

Observatoire Social Européen (1999) 'Bilan social de l'Union européenne – 1999', Miméo.

Paci, R. and F. Pigliaru (1999) 'European Regional Growth: Do Sectors Matter?', in Adams, S. and Pigliaru, F. (eds.) *Growth and Change*, Elgar.

Padoa Schioppa, F. Kostoris (ed.) (2001) *Rapporto Annuale sullo Stato dell'Unione Europea* (Bologna: Il Mulino).

Padoa Schioppa, F. Kostoris (ed.) (2001) *Rapporto sullo Stato dell'Unione Europea* (Bologna: Il Mulino).

Parisi, N. (2001) 'L'attuale organizzazione dei pubblici poteri nell'Unione Europea', in A. Quadrio Curzio (ed.), *Profili della Costituzione Economica Europea* (Bologna: Il Mulino).

Pestieau, P. and A. Jousten (2001) 'Labour Mobility Redistribution and Pensions Reform in Europe', CEPR Discussion Papers No. 2792.

Popper, K. (1963) *Conjectives and Refutations: The Growth of Scientific Knowledge*, London: Routledge.

Praesidium de la Convention européenne (2003a) Texte de la Partie I et de la Partie II de la Constitution Brussels, 12 June, CONV 797/1/03. Accessed at http://european-convention.eu.int/docs/Treaty/cv00797-re01.fr03.pdf.

Praesidium de la Convention européenne (2003b) 'Projet de Constitution, Volume II – Projet de texte révisé des Parties II, III et IV', CONV 802/03. Accessed at http://european-convention.eu.int/docs/Treaty/cv00802.fr03.pdf.

Presidenza del Consiglio, Departimento per gli Affari Economici (ed.) (2001) *Allargamento a Est dell'Unione Europea: sfide e opportunità per l'Italia*, Rome, February.

Puga, D. (2002) 'European Regional Policies in Light of Recent Location Theories', Journal of Economic Geography, 2(4), pp. 372–406.

Quah, D. T. (1996) 'Regional Convergence Clusters Across Europe', *European Economic Review*, vol. 40 pp. 351–358.

Quintin, O. and B. Favarel-Dapas (1999) *L'Europe sociale: enjeux et réalités*, Collection Réflexes Europe (Paris: La Documentation française).

Rodrik, D. (2000) 'How Far Will International Economic Integration Go?', *Journal of Economic Perspectives*, vol. 14, no. 1, pp. 177–86.

Rogers, J. H. (2001) 'Price Level Convergence, Relative Prices and Inflation in Europe', Board of Governors of the Federal Reserve System, International Discussion papers, No. 699, March.

Saavedra, A. (1999) 'A Model of Welfare Competition with Evidence from AFDC', Working Paper, Center for European Economic Research.

Salmon, P. (2000) *Decentralization and Supranationality: The Case of the European Union*, Paper presented at the Conférence on 'Fiscal Decentralization', FMI, Washington, DC, 20–21 November.

Scharpf, F. (2002) 'The European Social Model: Coping with the Challenges of Diversity', *Journal of Common Market Studies*, vol. 40, no. 4, pp. 645–70.

Schmitt, H. and J. Thomassen (eds) (1999) *Political Representation and Legitimacy in the European Union* (Oxford University Press).

Sdogati, F. (2001) 'Crescita, competitività, occupazione in un allargamento inevitabile', in S. Guerrieri, A. Manzella and F. Sdogati (eds), *Dall'Europa a Quindici alla Grande Europa. La sfida istituzionale* (Bologna: Il Mulino).

Sen, A. K. (1976) 'Poverty: An Ordinal Approach to Measurement', *Econometrica*, No. 46.

Sen, A. K. (1999) *Development as Freedom* (Oxford University Press).

Sinn, H. W. and M. Reutter (2001) 'The Minimum Inflation Rate for Euroland', NBER Working paper No. 8085.

Sinn, H.-W. (1998) 'European Integration and the Future of the Welfare State', CEPR Discussion Papers No. 1871.

Sinn, H.-W. (1999) 'EU Enlargement, Migration and Lessons from German Unification', CESifo Working Paper Series No. 182.

Sinnott, R. (1995) 'Policy, Subsidiarity and Legitimacy', in O. Niedermayer and R. Sinnott (eds), *Public Opinion and Internationalised Government* (Oxford University Press).

Social Protection Committee (2001) *Report on Indicators in the Field of Poverty and Social Exclusion*, 13509/01.

Solans, E. D. (2000) 'Monetary Policy under Inflation Targeting', Contribution to a Conference held at the Central Bank of Chile, Santiago, December.

Strauch, R. and J. Von Hagen (2001) 'Formal Fiscal Restraints and Budget Processes as Solutions to a Deficit and Spending Bias in Public Finances: US Experience and Possible Lessons for EMU', *Fiscal Rules*, Public Finance Workshop, Bank of Italy, February.

Svensson, L. E. O. (1997) 'Inflation Forecast Targeting: Implementing and Monitoring Inflation Targets', *European Economic Review*, no. 41.

Svensson, L. E. O. (1999) 'Inflation Targeting as a Monetary Policy Rule', *Journal of Monetary Economics*, no. 43, pp. 607–54.

Tabellini, G. (2002) 'The Allocation of Tasks', in EuropEos (ed.), *Institutional Reforms in the European Union. Memorandum for the Convention*, mimeo, Rome.

Tanzi, V. (1996) 'Globalization, Tax Competition and the Future of Tax Systems', IMF Working Paper, 96/141.

Taylor, J. (1993) 'Discretion Versus Policy Rules in Practice', *Carnegie–Rochester Conference Series on Public Policy*, No. 39.

Terrasi, M. (2002) 'National and Spatial Factors in EU Regional Convergence', In Cuadrado-Roure J. R., Parelleda, M. (eds), *Regional Convergence in The European Union: Facts, Prospects and Policies*, Berlin: Springer-Verlag.

Thomassen, J. and H. Schmitt (1999) 'Issue Congruence', in H. Schmitt and J. Thomassen (eds), *Political Representation and Legitimacy in the European Union* (Oxford University Press).

Tiebout, H. (1956) 'A Pure Theory of Local Expenditure', *Journal of Political Economy*, vol. 64 (pp. 416–24).

Tizzano, A. (1998) *Il Trattato di Amsterdam* (Padua: Cedam).

Toso, S. (2000) 'Distribuzione personale del reddito e tassazione progrsssiva', in P. Bosi (ed.) *Corso di scienza delle finanze* (Bologna: Il Mulino).

Townsend, P. (1962) 'The Meaning of Poverty', *British Journal of Sociology*, No. 8.

Townsend, P. (1979) *Poverty in the United Kingdom* (London: Allen Lane & Penguin).

Tsakloglou, P. (2002) 'Indicators of Social Cohesion in the European Union: Thoughts and Suggestions', *Politica Economica*, vol. 18, no. 1.

UNDP (1999) *Human Development Report 1999* (New York: Oxford University Press).

UNPD (2000) *Human Development Report 2000* (New York: Oxford University Press).

Van Doorslaer, E. *et al.* (1997) 'Income-Related Inequalities in Health: Some International Comparisons', *Journal of Health Economics*, vol. 16.

Van Els, J., A. Locarno, J. Morgan and J. P. Villetelle (2001) 'Monetary Policy Transmission in the Euro Area: What Do Aggregate and National Structural Models Tell Us?', ECB Working Paper No. 94.

Von Hagen, J. and U. Walz (1994) 'Social Security and Migration in an Ageing Europe', CEPR Discussion Papers No. 1022.

Walsh, C. (1998) *Monetary Theory and Policy* (Cambridge MA: MIT Press).

Weiler, J. H. H., U. R. Haltern and F. C. Mayer (1995) 'European Democracy and Its Critique', in I. E. S. Hayward (ed.), *The Crisis of Representation in Europe* (London: Frank Cass).

Wildasin, D. E. (2000) 'Factor Mobility and Fiscal Policy in the EU: Policy Issues and Analytical Approaches', CESifo Working Paper No. 344, October.

Winkler, B. (2000) 'Which Kind of Transparency? On the Need for Clarity in Monetary Policy-Making', ECB Working Paper No. 26, August.

World Bank (2000) *Making Transition Work for Everyone – Poverty and Inequality in Europe and Central Asia* (Washington, DC: World Bank).

Index